*Fred Hut…
and the …
Cincinnati Reds*

Fred Hutchinson and the 1964 Cincinnati Reds

DOUG WILSON

McFarland & Company, Inc., Publishers
Jefferson, North Carolina, and London

LIBRARY OF CONGRESS CATALOGUING-IN-PUBLICATION DATA

Wilson, Doug, 1961–
    Fred Hutchinson and the 1964 Cincinnati Reds / Doug Wilson.
        p.   cm.
    Includes bibliographical references and index.

    ISBN 978-0-7864-5942-1
    softcover : 50# alkaline paper ∞

    1. Hutchinson, Fred, 1919–1964.   2. Baseball managers—
United States— Biography.   3. Cincinnati Reds (Baseball team)—
History — 20th century.   I. Title.
GV865.H87W45   2010
796.357092 — dc22 [B]   2010038424

British Library cataloguing data are available

Front cover: Cincinnati Reds manager Fred Hutchinson (National
Baseball Hall of Fame Library, Cooperstown, New York)

Manufactured in the United States of America

McFarland & Company, Inc., Publishers
  Box 611, Jefferson, North Carolina 28640
  www.mcfarlandpub.com

Acknowledgments

THE CONTRIBUTIONS of many people were invaluable in helping bring this book to print. The players who freely gave their time and thoughts were extremely gracious. I enjoyed talking to them and reliving baseball of the past. I would like to thank the following for their interviews and correspondence: Dave Bristol, Jim Brosnan, Al Dark, Ryne Duren, John Edwards, Sam Ellis, Mike Holzinger, Jay Hook, Jack Hutchinson, Patsy Hutchinson, Rick Hutchinson, Eddie Kasco, Bobby Klaus, Jerry Lynch, Bill McCool, Dan Neville, Jim O'Toole, Don Pavletich, Mel Queen, Charlotte Hutchinson Reed, Bernie Stowe and Al Worthington.

I would like to especially thank the Hutchinson family for their support and memories. As intended by the "old doctor," it is truly a great family of high achievers.

I would like to thank Joe Garagiola for being Joe Garagiola — one of the all-time nice guys of baseball.

I would like to thank the staff of the Bartholomew County Public Library and the Cincinnati Public Library for their help with books (interlibrary loan is a great invention) and assistance with the microfilm machines.

The following provided assistance with photographs for which I am truly grateful: Gordon Calhoun of the Hampton Roads Naval Museum, Karolee Gillman of the Grand Rapids Public Library, Mark Blau of Tacoma, Muriel Jackson of the Washington Memorial Library in Macon, Georgia, Nick Peyton at the Pacific Northwest Diabetes Research Institute, Jarrod Rollins of the Cincinnati Reds, Clay Luraschi and Rakiat Gdadamosi of the Topps baseball card company, and Patricia Kelly at the National Baseball Hall of Fame.

Carol Insalaco, Linda Gainer and Christi Loso at the Fred Hutchinson Cancer Research Center were extremely helpful with finding pictures and getting in touch with Hutchinson family members.

A number of books were especially helpful. Cincinnati Reds fans were lucky to have the team covered by some of the all-time greats, particularly

Earl Lawson and Ritter Collett who were kind enough to write down their memories of their years covering the team in two fine books, *All My Cincinnati Seasons: My 34 Years With the Reds* and *The Cincinnati Reds: A Pictorial History of Professional Baseball's Oldest Team*, respectively. Frank Robinson wrote very detailed information about his Cincinnati years in his first autobiography, *Baseball is My Life*, published in 1968. Pete Rose wrote, as Pete Rose often said, more books than he read. Some of them are better than others, all are entertaining. A remarkable resource was *We Played the Game: Memories of Baseball's Greatest Era*, a collection of interviews of over 60 former players from the years 1946 to 1964, edited by Danny Peary. This priceless work of historical art should sit on every baseball fan's shelf.

I would like to thank my mother for her encouragement and my brother for his encouragement, ideas and advice.

Nothing good can occur without strong backing at home. I would like to thank my wife for her support and for not laughing at me when I suggested that I could write a book.

Finally, I would like to acknowledge the memory of my father who first told me stories about Crosley Field, Jerry Lynch, Gus Bell and Wally Post. He would have liked this book.

Table of Contents

Preface

THE YEAR was 1964 and baseball was still the national pastime. The nation watched as one man waged a battle to keep time from passing...

A visitor to The Great American Ballpark in Cincinnati will find nine numbers displayed on the façade of the upper deck facing the field. These numbers honor the immortals of Reds history. Some of the numbers and the feats which placed them here are well known to all baseball fans. Others, unfortunately, have faded with time.

During a recent game, my teenage son pointed to the façade and asked, "Who was number one and why is his number up there?" I gave him the standard abbreviated explanation: "That was Fred Hutchinson. He was manager when the Reds won the pennant in 1961. He died of cancer a few years later. His number was the first one retired by the Reds." As my son, seemingly satisfied, turned back to watch batting practice, I was struck by the thought that this explanation was sadly inadequate. There is much more to the story.

It's the story of a popular, hard-charging manager who suddenly finds himself in a battle he can't win, against an unseen opponent no amount of determination can defeat. It's the story of a talented group of players, with names like Robinson, Rose, Nuxhall and Perez who must watch, helplessly, as their leader's health slowly declines throughout the season; a season which turns out to have one of the epic pennant races of all time. It is a team which suddenly catches fire at the end of the season and puts itself into position to win the pennant for that leader on the last day of the season. It's also the story of a remarkable older brother who years earlier had chosen medicine over baseball; an innovator who had worked for years to build a world class cancer research center and the cruel twist of fate which accompanied the fulfillment of his dream.

The major league baseball season is unique for its length and number of games. Successful teams must manage their emotions—the highs and lows

1

encountered over eight months and 162 games—as well as their ability. Both the slump and the winning streak can inexplicably come and go at any time. The baseball clubhouse is a high-testosterone environment in which the ability to express one's feelings is not a particularly valued trait. Players of different backgrounds, races and even languages are brought together and united by a common purpose. Each clubhouse has its jokers and brooders; natural leaders, clubhouse lawyers and agitators; veterans and rookies; gifted athletes and grinders. They are not always friends—sometimes they don't even like each other—but they still must work together on the field to try to win. The Reds' clubhouse of the preceding season, 1963, admittedly had its share of strife and bad chemistry. How would these players react when the subject of death was thrust upon them—not suddenly as in an accident, but with excruciating slowness and inevitability over months?

Courage is the one word which has been used more than any other to describe Fred Hutchinson's 1964 season by those who witnessed it. Ernest Hemingway defined courage as grace under pressure. Fred Hutchinson would have compared favorably with the classic Hemingway hero—a stoic man's man who is placed in a situation in which he must confront death and, in doing so, his actions reveal his true character. What is it about a man that inspires tributes and memorials after his death? What qualities cause friends and relatives to feel that they need to "do something" to honor the departed?

The material for this book was pieced together from written accounts in newspapers, magazines and books along with personal interviews with the people who were there. Nothing has been invented, no literary liberties taken. The game accounts were derived from newspapers of the day and statistics were verified from readily available sources on the internet. I attempted to interview every surviving member of the Reds of the early 1960s. The players who agreed to be interviewed were extremely helpful and honest in their discussions, as were the family members of Fred Hutchinson. For the most part, their memories were amazing for the accuracy of details stored over such a long period of time. Two players asked specifically that I take care not to include anything negative about teammates or the Reds from their comments and I complied with their wishes. The language of the clubhouse is sometimes sprinkled with certain phrases not often used in everyday polite speech. I have included most of these in the players' own words. Just in case my mother or minister decides to read this book, I have left one word partially deleted. It is important to the context of the story, however. If you can't figure it out, please write me and I will explain it to you.

This book is not meant to be a comprehensive biography of Fred Hutchinson. Nor is it meant to be a play-by-play commentary of the 1964 season. It is intended to illustrate the importance and significance of Fred

Hutchinson, the reaction of his family and players to his illness and his behavior during his final season in an attempt to explain how he created his legacy. Baseball fans have a responsibility to preserve the history of the game for future generations—not just the statistics, but the stories of the men who played the game. This book is meant to do just that.

1

"He was the John Wayne of baseball"

FRED HUTCHINSON always looked forward to Anna Maria Island in the off-season. He and his wife Patsy, tired of the constant moving of professional baseball, had built a home on the island in 1949. Located on a narrow strip of land at the southern part of the entrance to Tampa Bay, it had been a tropical paradise back then. The pristine white beaches were unspoiled by crowds. There were palm trees, herons, sea gulls, and gorgeous sunsets across the emerald Gulf waters. The off-season was a time for golf, cookouts, fishing and relaxation. Fred always looked forward to returning there to unwind and reconnect with the family.

Just 44 years old, Fred Hutchinson was already a veteran of eleven seasons of managing major league baseball, the last five with the Cincinnati Reds. Known to everyone in baseball as Hutch, he had spent his entire adult life in professional baseball. He had pitched for the Detroit Tigers in the 1940s and early 1950s, and then had been named player-manager in 1952 at the age of 32. He was well known, well respected and well liked by virtually all of baseball — players and executives alike.

The baseball season of 1963 had been particularly trying for Fred Hutchinson and his Cincinnati Reds. Just two years removed from their pennant-winning season of 1961, the team possessed plenty of talent but had struggled, finishing in fifth place. Several stars had played well, such as pitcher Jim Maloney who had won 23 games and centerfielder Vada Pinson who had hit .313 with 22 home runs and 106 RBIs. They also had Pete Rose who Fred was certain would be a star in the future. The confident, hustling second baseman had unexpectedly won a starting job in spring training and ended up capturing the Rookie of the Year Award. In Fred's mind, losing was an abomination and fifth place was a disgrace for a team such as this.

The Reds had experienced problems on the field, with injuries limiting the effectiveness of the previous season's best hitter, Frank Robinson, and best pitcher, Bob Purkey. Off the field, there had also been problems. One player had described the Reds as "a team of strangers."[1] There were whispers of a Robinson-Pinson "clique" on the team which affected team morale. The rookie Rose had been shunned by his veteran teammates. Late in the season, the normally reserved Pinson had decked *Cincinnati Post* reporter Earl Lawson in the clubhouse after an argument about critical columns. Lawson had responded with an ugly lawsuit.

So the 1963 off-season was especially welcome. Fred spent time with his children: Rick, 19, Jack, 18, Patty Jo, 15, and Joseph, 10. Enjoying the off-season, recharging the batteries, Fred was soon looking forward to the 1964 season and doing what he truly loved: manage a major league baseball team.

A large man with immense physical strength and energy, Fred had very much earned the nickname "The Bear." He could be intimidating to people who did not know him. The first thing one noticed about Fred Hutchinson was his stature. Standing 6 feet, 2 inches tall and weighing more than 220 solid pounds, Fred was more imposing than most of the men he managed. His large powerful shoulders made him appear even bigger than he was. "At first, no one wanted to be in the room alone with him," says pitcher Jim O'Toole. "We were afraid he would kick our butts."[2]

"When I first met him," said first-baseman Gordy Coleman, "I remember saying to myself, 'Man, if you put this guy in a cage with a bear, you'd have to bet on him.'"[3]

While his physical appearance was impressive, it was his face which was so characteristic and moved many a sportswriter to hunt a thesaurus. Over the years, descriptions had ranged from ruggedly handsome to having "a face that might have been hacked out by an angry sculptor with a dull chisel."[4] He was described as stone face, basset hound face and always looking like he had just lost an argument with an umpire.[5] In 1963, *Sports Illustrated* described it like this: "The face of Fred Hutchinson is probably the most interesting in all of baseball, but everyone knows it isn't a real face. No sir, not that face. Hutch's face was made from the baseball

Fred Hutchinson (Cincinnati Reds).

novels and dime pulps; it looks the way a baseball manager's face is supposed to look—craggy and mean and knowing ... and when he has good days he sometimes smiles two or three times."[6] Joe Garagiola had famously said that Fred was really a happy guy inside but his face didn't know it.[7]

Fred's passion for winning was the one thing that separated him from his contemporaries. In an era in which competitiveness was regarded as a virtue, he was singularly competitive. How bad did Fred Hutchinson want to win? How bad did Ahab want to catch that damn fish? It was an unrelenting, consuming obsession. A pitcher of modest talent with a below-average fastball, Fred had used his brains, drive and an utter, absolute hatred of losing to make himself a success. Hall of Famer Hank Greenberg, a teammate on the Tigers, once said, "Hutch is the greatest competitor baseball has ever known — greater than Cobb ... greater than any of them."[8]

Fred's explosive temper had been legendary since his early playing days. He had left a trail of broken clubhouse furniture, equipment and light bulbs across the league as testimony to his frustration over losing. Rival manager Gene Mauch once said, "Hutch doesn't throw furniture, he throws whole rooms."[9] Fred had been appreciated by fans for his obvious devotion and effort. He wore his emotions on his sleeve while on the playing field, for all to see. People understood how much winning meant to him. Though his temper was known throughout baseball, it was said that the only one he was ever really mad at was himself (and an occasional myopic man in blue). He never started a fight or threw a punch on the baseball field.

There was nothing contrived or fake about Fred Hutchinson. He was respected for his honesty, even when that honesty was not what people wanted to hear. "He was so principled," says his oldest son Rick Hutchinson. "He truly felt that his word was a bond and meant something. He didn't go back on his word. That's the way he lived his life. And he did not believe in wasting words by beating around the bush."[10]

"If he said something," says pitcher and author Jim Brosnan, "you could guarantee it was true and useful and you better pay attention. People respected that."[11]

Fred was loved and respected by his players. He was definitely old school in his attitude but at the same time, strangely, he was considered a player's manager. He treated the players as adults and did not overmanage. He did not take credit when they did well, but readily deflected guilt to himself when they did poorly. "He was very supportive of his players," says pitcher Jay Hook, "and they appreciated that."[12] Fred's ability to handle men was another attribute which made him stand out as a manager. He was capable of inspiring individuals to play better than they thought they could and he was able to convince players to do what was best for the team. He could keep players happy even while reducing their playing time or changing their roles.

More than anything, Fred's players strived to gain his approval. "The smile of Fred Hutchinson is a treasured one. His ballplayers vie hopefully for it. By playing well and winning they earn it," wrote Jim Brosnan in *The Long Season*.[13] Once a player gained that approval, received that rare pat on the back of appreciation, earned that brief smile, the player felt like he could conquer the world and it inspired an incredible desire to do it again.

Fred Hutchinson had earned wide acclaim nationally and eternal adoration locally in the baseball-mad city of Cincinnati with the 1961 season. He had taken a team which no one expected to finish higher than sixth place, and inspired and drove it to a surprising National League pennant. Several players who had been picked off other teams where they had been labeled as failures had turned in brilliant efforts. Fred had been rewarded with his second Manager of the Year award after the season. Writer Al Hirshberg wrote the next year that the 1961 team shared a common bond: "Everyone was scared to death of Hutch — and everyone was devoted to him."[14]

Writers adored Fred Hutchinson. He never ducked a question, never played games and never performed for them. He met every issue with the same straight-ahead honesty he was known for on the playing field. His never-wavering characteristics were easy to lampoon and he could accept a joke at his own expense. His lifelong love of the game of baseball was plainly evident. Though not boisterous in personality, there was something about Fred Hutchinson that drew people to him and made them like him. He had a quiet manly quality which, coupled with his honesty and straightforwardness, gave people confidence. "Hutch was out of the John Wayne mold," Reds beat writer Earl Lawson said. "Women were attracted by his rugged good looks and masculinity. Men admired and respected him."[15]

"He's every guy's ideal guy," Reds reserve outfielder Pete Whisenant told a reporter in 1962. "Playing for him is like playing for your father — not a father who intimidates you, but one you like and love."[16]

"You had to be around the man," said the Cubs' Ron Santo, who is from the same hometown. "He exuded energy, charisma. You felt good being around him. He was just a winner."[17]

"He really liked people," says oldest son Rick, "but he wasn't outgoing. He was very much like John Wayne. Even now, when I watch John Wayne in *The Quiet Man* or *The Searchers*, I think of my father."[18]

"He was the John Wayne of baseball," says Jim O'Toole,[19] unaware of Rick Hutchinson's comment. That name, John Wayne, keeps popping up when people discuss Fred Hutchinson. To a certain generation, there can be no greater compliment for a model of masculinity and respect.

Fred Hutchinson was not accustomed to periods of illness or weakness. He had never been one to complain. Injuries and physical discomfort were to be borne silently and not allowed to interfere with the task at hand. So he was not overly concerned when he began having trouble swallowing in the winter of 1963. Having recently passed his annual physical with the Reds, he felt there was nothing to worry about. When he developed pain on the right side of his neck and discovered a lump, he finally mentioned it to his wife who was very concerned. Patsy talked him into seeing a local doctor who also seemed very concerned and suggested that he see a surgeon. Fred's brother Bill was a prominent surgeon in Seattle and Fred had always trusted him with medical matters. Fred called Bill who told him that he wanted to have a look at the lump. So Fred boarded a plane for Seattle in late December of 1963, leaving Patsy and the children at their home. He would only be gone a short time — just long enough to see Bill and get this thing cleared up.[20] It was natural that Fred would be going to Seattle; he had seemingly always returned to Seattle when there was a problem. They had always loved him in Seattle.

2

Seattle

"To understand the importance of (Fred) Hutchinson, you have to understand the early history of Seattle baseball in the '30s."[1]

THE CITY OF SEATTLE was relatively new when Fred Hutchinson was growing up there. Although the area had been inhabited for at least 4,000 years, European settlement did not begin until the middle of the nineteenth century. In 1792, a British ship captained by George Vancouver dropped anchor just inside the harbor and Lt. Peter Puget was dispatched to conduct a survey of the area. This was the first penetration of white men into what would later be known as Puget's Sound. It was not until 1851 that a settlement was established. It was officially named Seattle in 1853 when the first plats for the village were filed. The name was taken from Chief Seattle, the leader of the Duwamish Indians who inhabited the region.[2]

Early Seattle was marked by periods of booms and busts. The first boom was provided by the lumber industry. The abundant lumber in the area and ample port for shipping were put to good use. The city grew rapidly with the influx of financial institutions for the West Coast, such as Washington Mutual which was founded in 1889. However, the financial panic of 1893 hit the area hard.

Seattle fortunes rebounded with the Klondike Gold Rush of 1897 as the city became the main transport and supply point for miners in Alaska and the Yukon. Seattle's business of clothing miners and feeding them salmon created much more lasting riches than the mining fields did for most prospectors. Seattle business boomed well into the early twentieth century. The first street cars appeared in 1889 and their rails were thoughtfully laid out to help create a well-defined downtown and strong neighborhoods at the end of their lines. Seattle's population rose from just 3,533 in the 1880 census to over 80,000 by 1900. It would be more than 300,000 by 1920.[3]

It was into this growing new city that Dr. Joseph L. Hutchinson moved with his wife, Nona, in 1907 from Wisconsin. The young couple settled in a southeast section of Seattle bordering Lake Washington called Rainier Beach and Dr. Hutchinson opened a store-front medical practice. The first doctor in that part of Seattle, Joseph was a horse and buggy doctor, taking care of the entire area, performing surgery, delivering babies on kitchen tables and making house calls.

The Hutchinson's first child, William (Bill), was born in 1909. He was followed by John three years later and finally Fred on August 12, 1919. The family lived comfortably in a large, three-story hillside house. A large man, sporting a distinguished looking goatee, Joseph was soon well known throughout Seattle as a dedicated professional and a prominent citizen.[4]

Stern and principled, Joseph preached the value of hard work and academic achievement to his children. Education was not only highly encouraged, it was expected. The children of Joseph Hutchinson were instilled with a high regard for honesty and a strong work ethic. They were taught that their word was their bond. "My grandfather set the stage for achievement for the whole family," says Charlotte Hutchinson Reed, Bill's oldest daughter. "When you do something, try to do it as well as you can. Be the best. And you work hard. That's the formula for success. Other people may do a crappy job, but you'd better not."[5]

An often told story illustrates the determination and, perhaps, stubbornness of Dr. Joseph Hutchinson. When the city of Seattle decided to raise the rates on the trolley cars, Dr. Hutchinson felt that the new rates were too high. In a protest, he walked the entire way from downtown Seattle to Rainier Beach on the rails, in front of the car, forcing it to follow him at a snail's pace.[6]

Dr. Hutchinson, later known to all as "the old doctor," was famous for his hard work and for his benevolence. "He was the greatest man I've ever known," says Patsy Hutchinson, Fred's wife. "The only trouble he ever had with his wife was that he would never send any bills. People would just pay him as they could or as he felt they could. She'd get kind of upset about that sometimes."[7]

"If people couldn't pay him, they would bring him eggs or chickens or whatever they could," says Charlotte. "He would always accept that."[8]

Joseph would continue to work hard until felled by a stroke in his seventies. "During World War II, he had been retired but came back to work," says Patsy Hutchinson. "They gave him an area to care for. Of course, by then they had to give him a driver because he was a wild man behind the wheel."[9]

Small and very ladylike, Nona kept her children well fed and ran a strict but loving household. "She was a great cook," says Charlotte. "Cookies, cakes, there was always something good to eat at Grandma's house. She made sure there was lots of laughter and things that make really strong families."[10]

A Presbyterian Church was across the street from their house and Mrs. Hutchinson "saw to it that the kids got over there every Sunday," says Patsy.[11] But it was sports that would occupy most of the Hutchinson kids' lives. The old doctor loved sports. He had reportedly played semi-pro baseball at the turn of the century before becoming a doctor.[12] He was later the team doctor for the local high school and the Seattle professional baseball team. He passed this love on to his children. Fred later told a writer that he couldn't remember the day when he wasn't crazy about baseball.[13]

One does not have to search far to find the origin of Fred's famous drive and competitiveness. He was definitely a product of his environment. In a 1962 profile, Al Hirshberg stated that Fred's mother constantly reminded him that any game worth playing was worth winning, and that if he couldn't win he shouldn't play. In later years, when he got home after a game, her first question would be, "Did you win?" If the answer was "no" she had nothing more to say. If the answer was "yes" she would want to hear all about it.

His father reacted just the opposite. He would say nothing if Fred won, but if he lost, would demand to know why. Fred had to explain and was not allowed to blame anyone else or make excuses. "Just remember," his father told him, "there's always something that you must have done wrong. If you had done it right, you might have won."[14]

Fred would grow up obedient to his parents. Hirshberg stated that Fred dearly loved his father. In later years, his children all remembered the reverent, respectful manner in which Fred treated his parents.[15]

As Joseph kept busy with his medical practice, the two older boys assumed the role of teacher and coach for young Fred and they took their training seriously. At the time, baseball and boxing were the national sports and, in Seattle, baseball was by far the favorite. "Fred was always tagging along with his older brothers and they would let him play with them," says Charlotte. "They would get him to shag balls for them to keep him busy. They just had a lot of fun together growing up."[16] Often the older brothers would stand Fred in front of the barn and pitch to him by the hour.

But it wasn't always fun and games for Fred. Like any big brothers, Bill and John enjoyed tormenting their younger sibling. "When I was a small kid they'd pitch me the tennis ball in the backyard," Fred told a reporter in 1963. "They'd let me hit, let me hit, and I felt good. Then they'd whiz it past and I couldn't get another piece of it. They'd pitch it and sting me, hit me, too. I'd get so mad...."[17]

Although Fred was a natural righthander, his brothers decided he should hit lefthanded to give him the advantage of being a couple of steps closer to first base. Speaking of Fred, Bill once proudly told Emmett Watson, a family friend and journalist for the *Seattle Times*, "I raised the kid." Watson wrote that Bill nurtured in Fred a "combative thrust toward excellence."[18]

Intensely competitive even as a child, young Fred learned his older brothers' lessons well. He was bigger, stronger and more naturally athletic than other kids his age. He also is remembered as more mature and a natural leader even in elementary school. Judith Hjertstedt Crist wrote to the *Seattle Times* in 1999 of a story from her father's youth which had been passed down. Hugo Hjertstedt was a friend of Fred's at Emerson Elementary in the 1920s. Hugo was from a poor Swedish immigrant family with 12 children and his father was a part-time gardener for the well-off Hutchinsons. Hugo, small, underfed and dressed in worn clothes, was a natural target for school bullies. One day, a bully tore nine-year-old Hugo's shirt off and hung it up in a tree. Later, the same kid ripped a bat out of his hands during recess and pushed him down. When Hugo tried to fight back, he was hit so hard that he flipped over and landed on his back.

Fred found out and the next day at recess he told Hugo, "Those guys won't touch you anymore, Hugo." After school the previous day Fred had taken the big kid down to a local park and "beat the heck out of him." Then he "gathered all them guys that play ball together and told them, 'I'm gonna give you all a warning. I like Hugo. Him and me play catch and his dad takes care of our yard. Don't you guys ever touch Hugo again — or else.'"

"And from that day," concluded Mrs. Crist, "Fred was my dad's champion and no one ever dared bother him again."[19]

In his rough and tumble childhood, Fred engaged in his share of mischief at school and in the neighborhood. After some youthful indiscretion, he was excused from Emerson Elementary and forced to attend nearby Brighton.[20] "They were tough boys," says Charlotte. "Definitely not city boys." But Fred was always careful not to step too far over the line. "His father was pretty stern," adds Charlotte. "The boys had to march to the drum."[21] According to one story, once Fred went swimming instead of mowing the lawn as ordered. When he cut himself on a rock, the old doctor sewed it up for him — without an anesthetic — as a reminder of the perils of disobeying.[22]

Baseball soon made Fred stand out from the crowd. At the time, Seattle had an elementary baseball league and, as a catcher, he led both Emerson and Brighton elementary schools to city championships. His high school coach, Ralph (Pop) Reed, later told Emmett Watson for a 1957 *Sports Illustrated* article that he was impressed watching Fred as an elementary player. He remembered the way the ten-year-old stood with his catcher's mask pushed back over his curly red hair, arguing with an umpire. "When I saw him stand up and have it out with an adult umpire," said Reed, "I knew that here was a real competitor. The thing that impressed me was that he wasn't just shooting off his mouth. He was right and he knew it, and he had courage enough to say what he thought. He was already a tough, thinking ballplayer."[23]

As Fred got older, he played for various American Legion and VFW teams

The 1937 Johnson Paint team of Tacoma finished fifth at the national championships in Wichita, Kansas. Fred is in the back row, far left (courtesy Marc H. Blau
collection).

in Seattle and nearby Tacoma, pitching and catching. The Palace Fish team,
after his freshman year of high school, went undefeated through the city,
state and Northwest regional playoffs. The team was eventually defeated in
the Western U.S. playoff in Topeka, Kansas. With Seattle papers closely following the boys' success, Fred won the first game there as a pitcher (his four-
teenth in a row) and the next day went 4 for 4 at the plate. One of his catchers
on those teams, J.B. Parker, later said, "He had beautiful control. He wasn't
that fast, but he was fast enough.... He knew where he wanted to pitch each
batter. He wasn't just a flinger, he put it where he wanted." Fred never let hitters dig in on him. "If any batter walked into the batter's box and dug a hole
for his right foot, Hutch's first pitch would be under his chin."[24]

     At Franklin High School, Fred was all but unbeatable on the mound,
posting a 60–2 record over three years and leading Franklin to city championships from 1934 to 1937. Never developing blazing speed, he used his control, natural sinker, curve and change-up to keep batters off balance. He also
used his intense competitiveness. His scowl from the mound often melted
the will of batters. "If baseball wasn't a competitive sport — if it was just something you did for exercise — I don't think Fred would be interested," Pop Reed
told Watson. "Looking back on it, I think he may very well be the greatest
competitor baseball has ever produced."[25]

It was in high school that Fred met Patsy Finley, who would later become his wife. As a popular athlete, Fred had a lot of girls vying for his attention. "He was the star of the team," she later said. "My dad was a tremendous fan and he loved to go see Fred pitch. But I wasn't that crazy about baseball. In those days, we liked to dance. I wasn't crazy about sitting in a ballpark."[26]

"Fred was very quiet in high school," she says. "He always had a quiet way about him, except when something piqued him on the sports field. But he was so much more interested in baseball than girls in school. You would go out and he would just sit there, he wouldn't make conversation. Maybe he thought we weren't as interesting as baseball."

"But Fred seemed more grownup than other kids in school," Patsy continues. "All the boys followed him. He was definitely a leader back then."[27]

All the Hutchinson children grew up to be achievers in the classroom and on the athletic field. All were excellent baseball players. Bill enrolled at the University of Washington and became a star on the baseball team. As a senior third baseman in 1931, Bill was the captain of the team and hit .410. He was signed by the San Francisco Missions of the Pacific Coast League and played for them one year at $175 a month. He showed enough promise at that level to be invited to spring training by the Pittsburgh Pirates.[28]

But Bill had another passion besides baseball. He was accepted to McGill University Medical School in Canada for the fall of 1931 and had a choice to make: continue on the road to major league baseball or attend one of the more prestigious medical schools in North America. He called officials at McGill to explore the possibility of pursuing both. The answer was unequivocal. "You'd better make up your mind," he was told. "If you don't want to come here, just say so. We can take somebody else. We have plenty of people on our list."[29] So, like Moonlight Graham, the doctor in *Field of Dreams*, Bill chose medicine as a career and stepped over the baseline forever.

John Hutchinson played one season of professional baseball in the St. Louis Browns system. "He was great in the field but couldn't hit," is Patsy Hutchinson's scouting report.[30] John got out of baseball after one year and eventually became a professor at Columbia University.

Fred had choices to make also. Despite his great success in high school, major league scouts initially shied away because of his lack of overpowering speed. This confounded his proud high school coach. Once in 1936, when scouts told Pop Reed that Fred wasn't fast enough to win in the big leagues (after watching him strike out 18 in a game while yielding only one hit), Reed asked, "What do you want him to do, tap dance on his hands?"[31] The Detroit Tigers were the only team that expressed serious interest and they signed Fred to an option with the understanding that he would report in 1938. When his father demanded that he get a $5000 bonus, the Tigers felt that was too steep and let the option lapse. Fred enrolled in the University of Washington for the fall semester. The Seattle Indians of the Pacific Coast League had long coveted Fred, however, and now events evolved that set up the perfect opportunity for both the team and Fred.

The Pacific Coast League of the first part of the twentieth century was as close to the level of major league baseball as one could get without actually being a major leaguer. It was sometimes called the third major league. Many of the immortals of the game, such as Ted Williams, Joe DiMaggio and Lefty O'Doul, got their start in the PCL. The PCL was a mix of former major leaguers and rising stars. Quite a few players had the talent and offers from the major leagues, but elected to remain on the West Coast rather than go east because the lifestyle, the weather and the salaries were so good. PCL teams routinely outdrew major league clubs such as the St. Louis Browns and Boston Braves. Unlike the two other Triple-A leagues of the time, the International League and the American Association, which were interwoven geographically with major league cities, the PCL was separated by more than a thousand miles and two time zones from their professional rivals for fans' attention. In the 1930s there were no televised baseball games. The only time residents of the West Coast saw major leaguers was on newsreels before movies or during postseason barnstorming tours. The only real baseball actually seen live was at their local ball park.

Seattle had been one of the founding teams of the Pacific Coast League in 1903 and had a rich history. There were hard times in the 1930s, however. Owner Bill Klepper kept the Seattle Indians afloat through the Great Depression, but just barely. The games were played in Civic Stadium, a ramshackle facility with a rock-hard, all dirt playing surface. "If you'd put a horse out there to graze, he'd die," old-timer Edo Vanni liked to tell newspaper reporters years later. "There wasn't a blade of grass in the place."[32] Attendance was sparse. One infamous doubleheader in 1933 had a paid attendance of seven. Players staged a sit-down strike before a game once to collect a portion of their missing back pay.[33] Between games of a late-season doubleheader in 1937, federal and state agents seized the gate receipts for money due on taxes.[34]

In December 1937, Emil Sick, owner of the Seattle-based Rainier Brewing Company, bought the Seattle Indians team. Sick, a shrewd and successful business man, was a friend of Colonel Jake Ruppert who had used the profits from his brewing company to build the New York Yankees empire. Sick set out to do the same thing in Seattle. He renamed the team the "Rainiers" to promote his beer and immediately went to work renovating the team and its image. While Sick knew beer and business, he knew nothing of baseball, but he was smart enough to know where he needed help. He hired an equally shrewd, energetic local sports entrepreneur named Torchy Torrance to be his general manager. Torrance helped guide him to Jack Lelivelt for a manager.

Lelivelt was one of the best baseball men on the coast and had piloted the Los Angeles Angels to PCL championships in 1933 and 1934.

Sick soon announced that the team would be leaving their dilapidated park for a new facility in the Rainier Valley. The state-of-the art, 14,600-seat stadium, built at a cost of $500,000 (with Sick's own money), was scheduled to open in June of 1938. The new park would be named Sicks' Stadium (rather than Sick's to emphasize the involvement of his family).[35]

The new owner's biggest bonanza, however, came when Torchy signed Fred Hutchinson. Fred left the University of Washington behind to pursue his baseball career. The hometown baseball hero joining the hometown team was "the coalescing of sports in Seattle, when a town first fell in love with a team," wrote Blaine Newnham in the *Seattle Times* in 1999.[36]

John Hutchinson helped negotiate Fred's contract which called for a bonus of $2500, a salary of $250 a month and 20 percent of whatever his future selling price to the majors might be.[37] "John knew about the baseball business and contracts and he helped Fred with that," says Patsy Hutchinson. "John was the one who insisted on the clause to pay Fred when they sold him to the major leagues. Of course, at the time Fred was 18 so it seemed really far in the future."[38] The clause would turn out to be profitable for Fred much sooner than anyone expected. The entire contract was a very good one for an 18-year-old just out of high school. To put it in perspective for the time, just two years earlier, the San Diego club of the PCL had enjoyed the services of a pretty fair hitting skinny San Diego kid named Ted Williams for only $150 a month.[39]

If Fred had any ideas of entering the medical or academic fields like his brothers they quickly passed as he plunged into life as a professional baseball player. The PCL in 1938 included the San Diego Padres, Los Angeles Angels, Hollywood Stars, San Francisco Missions, San Francisco Seals, Sacramento Bees and the Portland Beavers. Life in the PCL for an 18-year-old was grand—full of new and exciting adventures. The Hollywood Stars, owned by Bob Cobb, proprietor of the famed Brown Derby restaurant and inventor of the Cobb Salad, were the biggest attraction in Hollywood other than the movies. Stars such as Jack Benny and Groucho Marx were frequently seated near the field and the games were often a who's who of Hollywood personalities. In San Francisco, the Seals' stadium was close to a large brewery and bay winds frequently blew foam from the brewery onto the field. Veterans often conned rookies into eating the foul tasting foam by telling them it tasted just like beer.[40]

Because of the distance between cities, teams played a seven-game, six-day series before moving on. Games were played Tuesdays through Sundays, with a doubleheader on Sunday ending the series. The team would then board a train for the next city. Former players remembered the long rides in sleeper cars through the Sacramento Valley. With no air conditioning, hot summer rides with open windows ended with everything covered in soot.

Fred's multiple talents initially caused some questions as to where he would be best suited, but Lelivelt decided that he wanted Fred mostly as a starting pitcher. Fred made his pitching debut in San Diego in the second game of the season. He lasted all of one-third of an inning before he was yanked after giving up three runs. Undaunted, Fred came back to win five straight. Thereafter, the "schoolboy wonder" was a sensation. The team won often and was entertaining. Fans remember a team without a lot of power but winning on hustle, running, bunting, stealing, pitching and defense. Attendance soared.

Fred was accepted and fit in with his teammates. It was largely a veteran team that Torrance had put together — six starting fielders and the other three main starting pitchers were more than 30 years old. As an 18-year-old with a large contract and an even larger stack of newspaper clippings, Fred may have caused some initial resentment from the older, less well-paid men. The headlines he had generated would swell the heads of many players his age. More than one young star has made the mistake of showing up with the wrong attitude and causing jealousy and hatred. This was not to be the case with Fred. He appeared quietly modest and humble and his team-first attitude allowed him to fit right in with the older players. Rainier players quickly learned to respect the fact that this youngster was a tough competitor who would not back down from anyone and would back up his teammates.

In one early game against the Padres, "they'd knocked me down two or three times," recalled outfielder Edo Vanni. "Fred was pitching for us. He said, 'I'll take care of that. Wait till he comes up.'" When the opposing pitcher stepped in the batter's box, Fred gave him a not-so-subtle message about knocking down Rainiers. "That pitcher got his control in a hurry," Vanni continued. "That's the kind of guy Fred was, a hard-nosed guy."[41]

Older opponents surely tested him early to find out how he would respond at the plate to being brushed back and on the mound when taunted from the bench. In those days it was not unheard of for a batter to drag bunt down the first-base line with the sole purpose of running up the pitcher's back with his spikes. Pro baseball was a man's game — a player could not show weakness. Every rookie was tested. Heralded rookies with big contracts were favorite targets. Needless to say, Fred passed these tests.

Fred impressed everyone with his precocious poise. Newspapers soon gave him the nickname "The Iceman" for appearing so composed on the field. "He was a sensation that season," veteran pitching teammate Hal Turpin later recalled. "And he was so cool about it. We were playing Portland one day and he was a little wild and having a little bad luck. So he just called time, walked to our dugout and got a drink of water. He went back and shut them out the rest of the game. That was something for a young guy like that."[42] The incident was much celebrated in the press and has been repeated often as an example of Fred's unflappable nature.

After the game, a Portland reporter asked if he had called time to soothe his nerves. "I was thirsty," the somber faced youngster replied.[43]

When the Rainiers played their first game at Sicks' Stadium on June 15, 1938, it was to a near-capacity crowd of 11,000. In addition, a large number of kids, unable to come up with the $1.15 for a box seat (or 42 cents for a bleacher ticket), gathered to watch the game from a vegetable farm on a hill just beyond the leftfield fence. Even though the home team lost the game to the Portland Beavers, spirits were not dampened. It was considered one of the finest minor league ball parks in the country. Fred Hutchinson was the winning pitcher the next night; the first Rainier victory in their new stadium. He pitched a six-hitter for his tenth win of the season.

Rainier games became events for the entire city. Bumpy trolley rides provided access to the stadium from most of the city's neighborhoods. Mount Rainier looming in the distance beyond the right field fence was a majestic sight. The spot behind left field came to be known as tightwad hill and was a frequent viewing spot for hoards of kids, many sitting atop large garbage dumpsters and banging on them with their feet in support of their team. A Seattle florist, Charles E. Sullivan, sat in a third-base box and rewarded Rainier players for home runs and shutouts with ten-dollar bills. The radio home run calls of Leo Lassen of "back, back, back ... it's over" were soon imitated by schoolboys throughout the northwest. The Rainiers were on their way to leading the PCL in attendance for the season with 437,161.[44]

No star shown brighter for the Rainiers than Fred Hutchinson. Winning game after game, he was built to near-mythic status by the three competing Seattle newspapers from which hyperbole fell like so much Seattle rain. Baseball fever gripped the city. On August 12, Fred faced the San Francisco Seals in Seattle, going for his 19th win of the season on his 19th birthday. A PCL-record crowd of 16,354 crammed into the stadium. Fans unable to find a seat filled the bullpens or lined the outfield fence, standing behind ropes. A ball hit into the roped-off area of the outfield was a ground-rule double. The fans used this ground-rule necessity to help the home team. "When we were up the fans pushed in toward home plate," Edo Vanni later said. "When San Francisco came to bat, the fans would move back."[45]

The Seals leadoff batter and future Red Sox star, Dom DiMaggio, singled to open the game and roughly two hours later flied out to end the game. In between, Fred thrilled the crowd by giving up only five hits, striking out three and walked away with a 3–2 victory.

It is impossible to overstate the enormity of the sentiment at that particular time, in that particular place, for Fred Hutchinson: the homegrown boy, humbling much older professionals in front of the hometown crowd. That sentiment was still illustrated 62 years later when *Seattle Times* writer Dick Rockne picked the ten greatest Seattle sports moments of the twentieth century — topping the list was Fred Hutchinson winning his 19th game on his 19th birthday.[46]

While Fred was taming the baseball world, he was still very much under the influence of his father. Emmett Watson later wrote that rumors circulated soon after the big game that Fred was being encouraged by some acquaintances to demand an increase in his salary in view of the profits he was generating for the club at the turnstile. According to Watson, when Dr. Hutchinson heard this, he "thundered" to Fred: "By the lord, you're a Hutchinson. You made a bargain and you'll stick to it — or you can pack up and move out right now."[47] The extent to which Fred actually entertained thoughts himself of demanding an increase is not known, but it remains a fact that he did not request any increase and finished the season according to his original contract.

Fred won his twentieth game August 17 with a three-hit shutout in which he struck out 12 and went 3 for 3 at the plate with a three-run home run. Major league teams were definitely showing interest now. The Dodgers, Red Sox, Indians, A's, Yankees, Pirates and Tigers all made inquiries. It was reported that some coast scouts believed that Fred was better than Cleveland's young pitcher, Bob Feller.[48] A Seattle official announced that the price for Hutch should be at least $50,000 and four major league players. "And by players, we don't mean putty-armed pitchers or washed up outfielders," he clarified.[49]

The Rainiers won 28 of 31 games down the stretch and finished in second place behind the L.A. Angels. "Always a good baseball town — when it had anything to cheer about — Seattle has gone baseball-mad over the stirring victories of Emil Sick's Rainiers," the *Seattle Times* proclaimed on September 12, 1938.[50] The top four teams in the league then played a best of seven semifinal and championship series in the Governor's Cup Playoffs to determine the PCL champs. The Rainiers were defeated by the Seals four games to one in the semifinals to conclude their season. Fred finished the 1938 season with a record of 25–7 and an earned run average of 2.48. He completed 29 of the 35 games he started and had 145 strikeouts in 290 innings. He also chipped in at the plate with a batting average of .313 and 13 doubles. He was named the league's Most Valuable Player and later *The Sporting News* named him Minor League Player of the Year.

After the season, Sick dealt with the numerous offers from major league teams for his prized pitcher. On December 12, 1938, Sick completed a deal with Detroit in which Seattle got four players and $50,000 in exchange for Fred Hutchinson. The Pirates had desperately stayed in the bidding war to the end and thought they had a chance with their offer of cash and five players. Afterwards, disappointed Pittsburgh manager Pie Traynor sourgraped to reporters, "Why does the American League have to get all the promising young ball players?"[51] With the four players said to be worth $50,000, it was called a $100,000 deal. It was the biggest deal for a minor leaguer in ten years. Again, to put it in perspective, two years earlier the Yankees had purchased Joe DiMaggio from the San Francisco Seals for $25,000 and five minor leaguers.[52]

The deal concluded a beautiful relationship between Fred and Seattle. The mutual benefit to city and player ensured lasting affection for both. The four players obtained by Seattle for Fred helped form the backbone of three consecutive PCL championships from 1939 to 1941. They would set the all-time minor league attendance record in 1939 with 517,657. The years from 1938 to 1941 would forever be cherished as the golden age of baseball in Seattle.[53] As for Fred, he was headed east to the major leagues and, in Fred, the young growing city of Seattle had its first national sports figure.

3

Detroit

THE DETROIT TIGERS which Fred joined in 1939 were a very good baseball team. The offense was led by future Hall of Famers Hank Greenberg and Charlie Gehringer. A pitching staff was being built which would bring Detroit the pennant in 1940, led by Bobo Newsom and Schoolboy Rowe. The additions of Hal Newhouser and Dizzy Trout to the staff as rookies in 1939 would pay big dividends the next year. However, the Tigers' investment in their prize rookie pitcher of 1939, Fred Hutchinson, would end up taking a little longer to pay off.

With newspapers all over the northwest following his progress, Fred struggled in spring training in 1939. Major league hitters are much more difficult to fool with location and change-of-speed than Triple-A hitters. A difference of one inch in location or a few miles per hour of speed can be the difference between success and disaster for a pitcher. And Fred did not have the kind of velocity which could make up for mistakes. No doubt pitching in Sicks' stadium helped a control pitcher such as Fred, as its dimensions of 335 feet down the lines and 415 to center were larger than many major league parks, helping turn long fly balls into outs instead of home runs. In smaller fields against stronger hitters, he no longer had the luxury of nibbling the corners with confidence. As a result, he walked many more batters than usual in spring training and, when he did throw the ball over the plate, was hit hard.

Fred made the team as it headed north but did not appear in a game until two weeks into the season on May 2, 1939. Unfortunately for Fred, it turned out to be a good day for the hitters of the powerful world champion New York Yankees. Entering the game as a reliever in the middle of a 22–2 bloodbath, he gave up eight runs in two-thirds of an inning, with four hits and five walks. An interesting sidenote to this game is the significance of a name which did not appear in the boxscore. For the first time in 2,131 games, the name Lou Gehrig was absent from the Yankee lineup.

The next day, the Tigers sent Fred to their farm team, the Toledo Mud

Hens. "He needs regular work to regain his control," said manager Del Baker. "And he'll get it at Toledo."[1]

"I'll be back," Fred told reporters. "Just as soon as I get some control."[2]

Fred gradually regained his form and confidence in Toledo and was named to the American Association All-Star team. He was recalled by Detroit on July 21 and finished the season there with a 3–6 record. On the positive side, Fred outhit American League batting champ Joe DiMaggio that season: .382 to .381. Of course, Fred's average was achieved in only 13 games.

In the spring of 1940, Fred looked forward to getting his shot at the majors again. "All I need is more work," he told reporters. "I've got more experience now, and I won't have that 'most expensive rookie' reputation to live up to every time I walk out to the pitching mound this year.... I know I'm a lot better than my record showed last season."[3]

Unfortunately for Fred, his record did not show much improvement. The next two seasons brought frustration with brief unspectacular stints with Detroit and longer stretches in the minors. Fred was labeled by the press "the biggest disappointment of the rookie crop"[4] of 1939, "the $100,000 lemon,"[5] and "the $100,000 pitching disappointment."[6] Some in the press questioned whether he would ever be a success in the majors regardless of having the greatest "nothing ball in the business."[7]

Despite his struggles in the field, Fred fit in with his teammates and was accepted and well liked. "Fred really liked Hank Greenberg," says Patsy Hutchinson. "Hank was so kind to him when he first came to Detroit. He just took Fred under his wing, showed him where he had his suits tailored and stuff like that. Fred thought he was the greatest. Fred's best friend with the Tigers was outfielder Hoot Evers."[8]

Catcher Birdie Tebbetts was also a close friend. "When Fred arrived to the major leagues he was noted to be rugged, handsome and well mannered," Tebbetts later wrote. "He was competitive as hell. He had a narrow-beam focus on winning."[9] Tebbetts, seven years older than Fred, helped him adjust to life in the majors. The friendships Fred formed with Evers and Tebbetts would last a lifetime as they became near-constant golf partners in the off-season in Florida.

The Tigers won the American League pennant in 1940 but lost to the Cincinnati Reds in the World Series. After posting a 3–7 record during the season for Detroit, Fred appeared in one game in the series, giving up one run on one hit and a walk in one inning. In 1941, Fred had a great year at Buffalo in the minors with a 26–7 record and he was named Most Valuable Player in the International League. He only appeared in two games for the Tigers that year, however. At 22 years old, coming off his best year, Fred was looking forward to the 1942 season — confident that he was finally ready for the majors. Then the world went to war.

Fred struggled in his early years pitching for the Detroit Tigers from 1939 to 1941 (courtesy Fred Hutchinson Cancer Research Center).

Fred received orders that he was to report to the Army on November 3, 1941, but decided to join the Navy instead and signed up for a four-year tour on October 24. Eventually rising to the rank of lieutenant commander, he spent some time as a shooting instructor (he was awarded a Navy medal for expert pistol marksmanship) at Norfolk Naval Training Station in Virginia.

He explained to reporters that he had acquired shooting accuracy from his many hunting trips in Washington and Alaska as a youth and he thoroughly enjoyed this part of military duty.[10] Most of his service, however, was spent as part of the Navy's physical education program. Former world heavyweight boxing champ Gene Tunney had been commissioned by the Navy to set up a physical conditioning program. He recruited a large number of famous professional athletes such as Bob Feller, Dom DiMaggio and Phil Rizzuto to serve as instructors. Eventually so many prominent athletes were gathered that they were formed into teams that competed with other base teams and often with college teams. The Navy's brass considered it a tremendous aid in recruiting and morale-building. They were called Tunney Fish (pronounced like tuna fish) by the other sailors, not always as an endearment, since some resented their relatively light military duty.[11] As with many pro baseball players, the only unfriendly fire Fred faced during his military time was from a distance of 60 feet, 6 inches. Playing baseball was his main contribution to the war effort. He played on base teams in Norfolk, Seattle and Honolulu. He was selected to play in the Army-Navy game at the Polo Grounds in June of 1942 and played on the service All-Star team that faced the American League All-Stars in Cleveland in July of 1942. He pitched in the Navy World Series in September of 1943 and was selected to play in an All-Star series organized by Lieutenant Bill Dickey in Honolulu in 1945.

Fred's Norfolk team in 1942, which included Bob Feller, compiled a record of 92–8. In addition to pitching, Fred was the team's hitting star with an average over .350.

In 1943, Fred paused long enough to marry his former Franklin High classmate, Patsy Finley, in St. Augustine, Florida. "I was in the Women's Army Auxillary Corp there," says Patsy. "Fred hurt his arm pitching that spring and so he had a little time off. He came down to Florida where I was and said, 'Well, I guess it's time to get married.' I didn't argue too much.

"At the same time, they were changing things over to the Women's Army Corp and they offered anyone who had been in the WAACs the chance to get out if they wanted, so I did," Patsy says. "It was nice that it happened to work out so I could go with Fred."

Patsy left the service to follow Fred to his stations. They went from Norfolk to Seattle, "but I didn't get to go with him when he got stationed in Hawaii," she says with a hint of disappointment. "I stayed in Seattle then.

"But it was really pretty good," she continues. "He pitched all the time he was in the Navy, he was never really out of shape. He felt bad about losing those prime years from his career, but that was what happened to all the players then. He played against a lot of big league players. They were all quartered in those locations. They were given fairly light duties and in the afternoon they would have a baseball game for the sailors. We would have a lot

The 1942 Norfolk Training Station team had a record of 92–8 and won the service championship of the United States. Seated left to right, Maxie Wilson, Hooks DeVaurs, Ted Rosa, Lt-Comdr. DeLong Mills, Morale Officer Captain H. A. McClure, Commanding Officer; Gary Bodie, coach; Ace Parker and Charles Stephens, assistant coach; Middle row, left to right, Jimmy Brown, Bob Feller (cut out of original photo), George Wolfman, Hank Feimster, Vincent Smith, Fred Hutchinson and Jim Kane; Back row, Jimmy Ewell, trainer; Charlie Metelski, Jim Carlin, Fred Collins, Mel Preibisch, Jack Conway, Doug Hautz and Carl Ray. (courtesy Hampton Roads Naval Museum).

of the players over to the apartment for dinner. Most of the players didn't have their wives with them, so they would come over for dinner and just sit around and talk baseball."[12] Fred and Patsy welcomed their first son, Fred Jr. (Rick), in 1944. He was followed in 1945 by John (Jack). They would later be joined by Patty Jo in 1948 and finally Joseph in 1953.

The time in the military allowed Fred to mature mentally and physically. Playing regularly against major league players was invaluable to his development. Players in the military developed a camaraderie which would not have normally been possible: competing side by side were former Red Sox, Indian and Yankee players. The friendships they formed would be carried back to the major leagues.

After the war, Fred was discharged on October 18, 1945. He eagerly rejoined the Detroit Tigers for the 1946 season. At 27 years old, he was ready to firmly take his place in major league baseball. The Tigers had won the World Series in 1945. Their pitching staff was now led by Hal Newhouser, who had won 25 games in 1945 and would win 26 in 1946. Hank Greenberg

Fred singles against the Boston Red Sox in an exhibition game at Hampton Roads Naval Station, 1943, in front of an appreciative crowd of sailors (courtesy Hampton Roads Naval Museum).

returned from the service to renew his assault on enemy pitchers and the Tigers added future Hall of Famer George Kell at third base in 1946. The Tigers had good teams throughout the next five years, but never quite as good as the powerful Yankee, Indian and Red Sox teams of the era.

Listed on the roster at 6–2, 200 pounds, Fred was now physically imposing. He had enormous hands and his scowl from the mound became famous. Fred was recognized as one of the more dependable pitchers in the league. In the five years from 1946 to 1950, Fred had a record of 77–47, with a high of 18 wins in 1947. Overall, he would finish his career with a 95–71 record. A good hitter, he was often used as a pinch hitter and he hit better than .300 in three seasons. He ended up with a lifetime .263 batting average and was used 91 times as a pinch hitter with four home runs. Known as one of the best control pitchers in the league, he was routinely near the top of the American League in fewest walks per nine innings and four times led the league in strikeout-to-walk ratio. Fred and the Yankees' Eddie Lopat were viewed as the premier off-speed pitchers in the league. He used his brains to nibble at the corners, setting batters up with a variety of changeups and curves. He was also generally considered to be one of the best fielding pitchers in the league. He appeared in the All-Star game at Detroit's Briggs Stadium in 1951. His manager during that period, Steve O'Neill, was quoted as saying, "If I needed one game on which my whole season was based, if my career depended on that single victory, I'd pick Hutch to pitch it for me."[13]

It was not Fred's talent, however, that most impressed fans and players around the league. His most lasting impressions were formed by his ferocious tenacity and intense competitiveness. Fans could see how much winning meant to him and they appreciated the sentiment. Losing killed him. His temper and post-game tantrums became the stuff of legend. His temper was mostly remembered as being directed at himself and inanimate objects such as furniture, equipment and umpires. "I always know how Hutch did when we follow Detroit into a town," joked Yogi Berra. "If we got stools in the dressing room, I know he won. If we got kindling, he lost."[14]

Long-time Tigers trainer Jack Homel later said, "The most serious pitcher we ever had was Fred Hutchinson. He was strictly business on the day he was to pitch. One day Hutch lost a two-run lead and was taken from the game. He ripped the water fountain loose in the dugout and spilled all the bats. In the tunnel to the clubhouse he smashed every light bulb. He locked himself in the trainer's room and wouldn't come out or let anybody in. We left him in the clubhouse. He finally came out after everybody else was long gone, and instead of driving to his home, about 21 miles out in the suburbs, he walked every step home. His wife was frantic. She had called the police to hunt for Hutchinson.... He finally got home about 4 A.M."[15]

George Kell provided excellent insight into Fred's nature during the Tiger years when he discussed him for the book *We Played the Game: Memories of Baseball's Greatest Era*, a collection of interviews with retired ball players published in 1994:

> I knew Fred Hutchinson mostly as a brilliant scholar who came from a family of intellectuals.... I liked to think I was the biggest reader in baseball because I never made trips without a couple of books.... Fred was the first other reader I ever knew in baseball — he also carried books with him. He studied all kinds of fields. He also studied baseball. He had a plan the night before on how he would pitch and usually it worked. He was just a tremendous competitor who was a good hitter and fielder and could have played anywhere.... He'd finesse batters to death. I remember him beating the Yankees in a day game in Detroit, 1–0, in about 90 minutes. He didn't throw a ball hard all day.
>
> Unlike Newhouser, Fred was liked despite having a terrible temper. Fortunately, his tantrums lasted only a few minutes. Once, in Briggs Stadium, he had the Browns beat 2–0 with 2 outs in the ninth inning. Then they got 4 or 5 straight hits ... and he was the losing pitcher. When he walked down the runway, under a row of unguarded light bulbs, he just took his glove and whacked about 15 of them.... One day he walked home mad, 7 or 8 miles from the Stadium. But the next day he was fine. I could go to the mound to calm him down. Probably a lot of other players couldn't. I was the captain of the club, roomed with him, ate with him every night on the road. He might even grin at what I had to say. I knew him better than to give him any advice or tell him to get the ball over the plate. We understood each other and respected each other. ... Evers [Hoot] and Hutchinson were my best friends on Detroit ... and would run together [after games]. There was very little drinking among the group that I ran with. I didn't drink. We went to movies instead of bars.[16]

Speaking of after-game liquid refreshments, Fred later said, "I never tasted the stuff until I'd quit pitching. When I was with Detroit, I roomed with Birdie Tebbetts and he didn't drink either. It must have seemed strange when we went on the town together that two big guys, strong guys like us only drank cokes."[17]

If Fred was ever tempted to drink to excess as a player, it would have been when he achieved a dubious immortality at Fenway Park on June 9, 1946. Pitching to Ted Williams, he gave up a 502-foot rocket to right field. The home run was the longest of Williams' career and is believed to be the longest in the history of Fenway Park. The seat where the blast landed, 37 rows up in the right-field bleachers, is painted red to this day as a memorial. Speaking of the hit later, Tigers catcher Paul Richards told the *Atlanta Journal*: "I'd caught the first game of the double header and Williams had got four hits.... Birdie Tebbetts was catching the second game and Hutchinson was pitching. Between games we're in the clubhouse and Hutch is saying that he doesn't care if Williams is the superstar. He's not going to let him hit like that. He's going to brush him back. Well, the game starts now and Williams comes up. He stomps his foot and digs in and Hutch comes inside and Williams leans back. Next pitch, Hutch really comes inside and Williams hits the dirt. He gets up and digs in again. Williams hits the next pitch out of sight.

"By the third inning, Hutch was out. He's back in the clubhouse and he's really fuming, but I can't resist. I sneak back there and leave the door open so I can get back out. I said to Hutch, 'You really showed that Williams.' Here comes a chair, flying at me, but I beat it to the door."[18]

Fred acquired the nickname "The Bear" during these years. While the nickname fit his body and temperament, the name reportedly was the result of an incident in spring training in Lakeland. According to the story, undoubtedly embellished over the years, a circus sideshow bear made the mistake of wrestling the wrong member of the Detroit Tigers. After the bear landed a slap to the face, Fred grabbed the unfortunate bruin in a headlock. The bear's trainer became upset when Fred wouldn't let go and the bear had to be rescued.[19]

Along with the respect of bears, Fred earned the respect of teammates and opponents alike. *Baseball Digest* in 1951 summed up the general feeling in baseball when it stated that "Fred Hutchinson of the Detroit Tigers is known as the friendliest fellow in the league, but the fiercest competitor on the mound."[20]

Fred's Tiger teammates elected him their player representative in 1947. A year later he became the representative for the entire American League. At the time, the player's union was in its infancy and had limited leverage. The owners held all the cards in their dealings with players. Before the establishment of the pension plan, many players—good players, great players—put in years of service in the major leagues only to become destitute once their skills had left them and they were no longer needed. Every player at that time regularly saw old-timers hanging around training camp, glad-handing veterans and offering menial tips to rookies, looking for handouts. It was a sad sight and a sad statement on the status of labor relations in the major leagues. Fred worked hard at his post, often lugging a typewriter with him on road trips to complete work. He testified before Congress at a hearing conducted by the House Monopoly Sub-Committee on antitrust laws regarding baseball. While most felt that players wouldn't be able to contribute enough in an eight to ten year career to make a retirement plan work, Fred saw the vast potential of All-Star revenue and television fees. Fred was able to help secure some positive changes such as meal-pay in spring training, a $5,000 minimum major league salary, and the designation of radio and television All-Star Game and World Series money to the players' pension fund.[21] "The owners had everything their way in those days," says Patsy Hutchinson. "Fred worked very hard to try to get some improvement. He went to a lot of meetings. Once he got so mad because the owners wouldn't let the players bring a secretary into the meeting to take notes. All the while the owners had their secretary there."[22]

While having some success off the field in meetings with owners, Fred was finding success on the field harder to come by. A series of arm ailments limited his effectiveness. It was time for the next stage of his career.

4

Manager Hutch

THE DETROIT TIGERS' fortunes started poorly in 1952 and things quickly got worse. In January, Walter O. Briggs, Sr., died. Briggs, 74, had been running the club since 1935. A good baseball man and a good manager of people, he was a tough act to follow. Unfortunately, his son Spike, who succeeded him as club president, was not quite up to the task. Team members and officials noticed an enormous change in attitude which engulfed the organization. A series of disastrous multiplayer trades tore the team apart. Fan favorites and All-Stars such as George Kell, Dizzy Trout and Hoot Evers were dealt away, with the Tigers receiving little or nothing in the way of talent in return.

Manager Red Rolfe, an Ivy League man who had played at Dartmouth and coached at Yale in addition to playing for the Yankees, had been the American League Manager of the Year in 1950. As the team declined he became bitingly sarcastic and caustic toward the players. He further irritated his team with a list of petty, bothersome rules. When the Tigers lost their first eight games, Fred called a team meeting of players only. Led by Fred, the players gave manager Rolfe 100 percent backing.[1] It did not help the team win many more games, however.

On July 5, with the Tigers off to a 23–49 start, Red Rolfe was fired. His replacement was announced as Fred Hutchinson, who would function as player-manager. The announcement surprised many. The 32-year-old Tiger pitcher had not figured prominently in the speculation as the vultures had circled the previous week. Several Tiger coaches and other currently available ex-major league managers had been mentioned in the press as possible replacements for the doomed Rolfe. Fred himself admitted to reporters that he was unaware he was even being considered until the day before the announcement. "I was down in the clubhouse, only half dressed when Spike called and asked me to come right up to his office," he said.[2] There, Briggs asked Fred if he would consider taking the post. Briggs told reporters that

Fred would finish the season as manager but would not comment on whether he would be retained for the next season.

Although the announcement surprised those on the outside, it seemed an obvious choice to those close to the team. Fred had experienced a rapid decline in the health of his right arm and knew his days as a pitcher were numbered. His record in 1951 had dropped to 10–10 and he had been demoted to a relief role. The numerous trades had left Fred as one of the elder statesmen on the team and he was a natural leader who inspired trust and respect. The announcement was met with "jubilation in the Tigers clubhouse"[3] according to the Associated Press. Tiger slugger Vic Wertz voiced the sentiments of the players when he said, "The players are all for the guy. They couldn't have picked a better man. We'll play for that guy."[4]

By becoming manager, Fred automatically had to give up his position as American League player rep. He also gave up most of his playing time on the field. He would pitch and pinch-hit in only 21 games in 1952 and 1953, devoting most of his energy to managing the team. "You can't do both," he later said. "You've got to think about too many things out there on the mound."[5]

It is often difficult for players or low-level coaches to make the transition from one of the guys to the boss on the same team. Fred made this transition in status fairly easily. He dealt with problems directly and was regarded as a straight shooter. He was also physically imposing enough to enforce his rule if necessary. He treated players as the professionals they were, doing away with the petty rules. The players responded well to this treatment. "I liked Hutchinson," pitcher Fred Hatfield later said. "He was the first one to praise you when you did well and the first one to jump on you if you did something wrong.... He knew how to get along with players. Plus, he put a little fear in us. Nobody who knew him would have wanted to be in a dark alley with him."[6]

"I loved playing for Fred Hutchinson," Tigers outfielder Jim Delsing said in 1994. "I would describe him as very sincere, very frank, very loyal to the players, and very involved with the players. I think everybody really liked playing for him.... I thought he was an excellent manager."[7]

Fans appreciated Fred's passion and players appreciated the way he backed them up, especially in disagreements with umpires. It was not unusual for Fred to get the thumb in order to keep one of his players in the game. The lack of talent he inherited was considerable, however, and the first season Hutch faired little better than his predecessor as the club limped to a 50–104 record, becoming the first Detroit team to finish in last place since the team joined the American League in 1901. Fred showed enough promise as a manager, however, that he was given a one-year contract to manage the Tigers for 1953.

The next two years brought a constant struggle to overcome front office decisions which further weakened the team. There were promising young-sters, such as future AL batting champs Harvey Kuenn and Al Kaline, but the pitching continued to dwin-dle. Kaline joined the team as an 18-year-old in 1953, having never played a day in the minors. He would go on to a Hall of Fame career as perhaps the most popular Tiger of all time. Kaline was aided in his early years by Fred's guidance and patience as he gained a reputation as a good man-ager for young players. Fred recog-nized the obvious potential in Kaline, but brought him along slowly the first year. He advised him to sit near vet-erans on the bench, observe the strat-egy on the field and ask questions. Fred introduced Kaline to Ted Williams before a game, knowing that Williams would jump at the opportu-nity to expound upon hitting with a young phenom as only Teddy Ball-

Manager Fred Hutchinson Topps baseball card, 1953 (Topps Company, Inc.).

game could. Speaking of Fred, Kaline later said, "The one thing he demanded was a 100 percent effort, no alibi-ing at all. He was a guy who didn't like to be embarrassed, and maybe that one word might be what he really stood for. He wanted his teams to be competitive and not embarrass themselves when they play.... When you played for him, you knew what to expect. There was no behind the back. He let you know, and you knew where you stood all the time, which is really what anybody really likes to know. He was an up-front type guy."[8] The Tigers slowly improved from the disastrous 1952 season, mov-ing up to sixth place in 1953 and fifth in 1954, within a few games of the first division.

However, Fred became increasingly frustrated by what he saw as a lack of involvement in personnel decisions by the club. He was the one who had to play with the hand dealt him by the front office and it was clear the trades were not benefiting the team. Fred was making $30,000 a year — a good salary for the time. The Tigers offered him $35,000 for 1955, but he insisted on a two-year contract, wanting more stability. When Spike Briggs informed him that one year was all the team would offer, Fred turned it down and concluded his business with Detroit.[9] Although disappointed to be leaving the team he had been with since 1939, Fred would not criticize the Tiger front office. When pressed for the reason he left, he told reporters, "It's personal." When prodded further, he said he left because "I wouldn't compromise my principles."[10]

"The Tigers had long-range plans," Fred later told a Seattle friend, "and I wanted assurance that I was included in them. It was a matter of principle."[11] Principle, true, but perhaps Fred also could sense a sinking ship and realized that with their front office, the Tigers had no hope of winning any time in the near future and he knew the manager would eventually be the one to take the blame.

Fred returned home to Seattle and soon took the job of managing Emil Sick's Rainiers. He had been offered a chance to stay in the majors as a coach with Baltimore, whose manager Paul Richards was a friend, but he turned it down. When asked later why he preferred to manage in the minors over coaching in the majors, he said, "Ask any fan to name six coaches in the big leagues and you'll see why."[12]

The general manager of the Rainiers by then was Dewey Soriano, which made things easier for Fred. Soriano was a close friend and former sandlot and high school teammate. Soriano, who in 1969 was instrumental in bringing the short-lived Pilots major league team to Seattle, had taken over as GM of the Rainiers in 1951 and, coming off a fifth place finish in 1954, jumped at the opportunity to have his buddy return to the scene of his greatest triumph. He knew what a boost this would be for both the team's success and attendance.

Fred was given a unique contract for 1955. The contract was for three years, but was only binding to the club. Fred was given a personal letter from Sick permitting him to deal with any major league team he desired if an offer of a major league managing position came up. His salary was a dollar a year "with considerations" covered by an oral bonus plan based on attendance.[13]

The announcement of Fred Hutchinson as the manager of the Rainiers sent a wave of expectant electricity throughout Seattle. Fred was given a hero's welcome back to the city. The 1955 season turned out to be everything Soriano and Sick had hoped. With Fred's help, Soriano made an incredible 67 player transactions and they cobbled together a championship team. KTVW Channel 13 in Seattle telecast every one of the Rainiers' 86 home games—handily dominating the local ratings. Even with the games televised, the team still led the league in attendance. "The 1955 season was the most magical of all Rainier seasons," William Arnold wrote for the *Seattle Post-Intelligencer* in 1999. "Without a single .300 hitter or 20-game winner, Hutch simply out-managed and out-fought the competition and won the pennant in a climatic series with Seattle's loathed arch-rivals, the Los Angeles Angels."[14] In a related article, Arnold wrote, "Seattle nailed down the pennant on September 11, and the celebration was like V-E day and Mardi Gras put together."[15]

Pitcher Larry Jansen later told Emmett Watson of that season: "I never saw a better man with pitchers. Hutch saved half a dozen games by moving his pitchers at the right time. He was almost psychic."[16] For his efforts, Fred was voted PCL Manager of the Year by baseball writers. The bonus plan turned out to be pretty good as the Rainiers drew more customers than any other minor league team in baseball. Fred collected nearly $25,000, making him the highest paid baseball figure outside the major leagues that year.[17]

The season further cemented Fred's legacy in Seattle. As Arnold wrote, Seattle had experienced "two fairly-tale bookend seasons—'38 and '55—both dominated by a hometown hero who looked like Dick Tracy, played with the determination of Knute Rockne.... In baseball, that kind of legend lives forever."[18]

The managerial success in Seattle and Fred's reputation ensured that he would return to the majors soon. The St. Louis Cardinals, although one of the best franchises in major league history, had fallen on hard times. They were very bad in 1955. Manager Eddie Stanky was fired after 36 games and Harry Walker took over. Walker could do no better and was fired after the season. On October 10, new Cardinal general manager Frank Lane announced that Fred Hutchinson was his choice for manager for 1956. "I knew we were going to have to build with young players," said Lane, "and I needed a manager who could handle them."[19]

Fred was the only person Lane had considered for the job and actually had the job sewn up before Lane took over with the Cardinals. At the conclusion of the 1955 season, Fred had stopped in Chicago on his way to Anna Maria Island for the winter and met with Lane over dinner. "Trader Frank" Lane, one of the most flamboyant general managers of the era, was famous for his numerous trades and dominating personality. He had just left the White Sox after a blowup with the owner, Chuck Comisky. Lane asked Fred if he would be willing to manage the Cardinals if Lane took the general manager's position in St. Louis. It was kept quiet until Lane finished his own negotiations with the Cardinals. Fred was announced as the new manager less than five days after Lane took over. Fred was given a two-year contract at a reported $30,000 a year.[20] "I had my eye on Hutchinson a long time ago," Lane later said. "I wanted a young manager who would work hard and Hutch isn't afraid of work." Lane said he remembered seeing Hutch in Florida during spring training with the Tigers in a meeting room off the hotel lobby in a session with a dozen Detroit players at eight o'clock in the evening. Lane was impressed that Fred would spend an extra two hours at night after exhibition games teaching the young players the finer points of the game.[21]

Once in St. Louis, Fred soon discovered that, as so often happens, the team's struggles were not entirely the fault of the previous managers. Team owner, beer-baron August Busch, Jr., was a gambling, womanizing, hard-drinking man. Despite these virtues, he had some bad habits. The most annoying one for members of the Cardinal organization was that he could not resist constantly meddling in the team's affairs even though his baseball knowledge was extremely limited. In three years of his ownership, the Cardinals had slipped from third to seventh place. Added to this was the fact that general manager Frank Lane, while firmly in Fred's corner, was also a hands-on executive and was somewhat of a loose cannon in his remarks to the press. Lane loved to deal players, frequently selling or unloading popular stars. He later reportedly tried several times to move St. Louis icon Stan Musial but was restrained at the last minute (probably by the fact that St. Louis fans would have lynched him). Lane was frequently heard, by writers and fans alike, screaming from the press box at his players and managers.[22] This was a very difficult environment for a young manager to step into.

Fred approached the job in his usual straightforward manner, however. The Cardinals improved by eight games in 1956, then enjoyed a much improved year in 1957, staying in the thick of the pennant race with the Milwaukee Braves of Hank Aaron, Eddie Mathews and Warren Spahn. Fred's managerial style was developing as one which inspired loyalty and respect from players. He gave players freedom to do their jobs but they always knew there was a limit and took care not to provoke his anger. "Fred Hutchinson, the Cards' new manager, was one of the best guys I've known in my life," slugger Hank Sauer later said. "He had a philosophy that I wanted to remember if I became a manager. He never had fun with the everyday player. He had fun only with the guys sitting on the bench. He said, 'Hank, if you keep those guys happy, then you'll have a successful ballclub.'"[23]

The success of this philosophy is illustrated by the fact that even non-starters appeared to like and respect Fred. Dick Schofield was a fiery young infielder who had hopes of being the everyday shortstop in 1957, but Hutch went with the veteran Al Dark instead. "However, I didn't dislike Hutchinson," Schofield later said. "He had some rules, but he treated his players like grownups. He was a decent guy and a good manager. He was also a tough guy no one wanted to mess with."[24]

In St. Louis, the legend of Fred's demeanor grew. It was during this period that Joe Garagiola, former Cardinal catcher and broadcaster, famously said of him: "He's really kind of a happy guy inside, only his face doesn't know it."[25] Watson wrote that, following losses, Fred broke water coolers, stools, light bulbs and once, in 1956 in Cincinnati, pounded his fists against a board-covered concrete wall until his knuckles were bloody and swollen.

"But his rages are rarely directed at an individual player; knowing his own temper, Hutchinson makes it a private rule to wait until the next day to chew out a player for his mistake," Watson continued. "Sarcasm, the goading tool of many baseball managers, is no part of Hutchinson's nature. His bluntness is deceptively simple."[26]

Players sometimes reached back for more effort, fearing Fred's displeasure more than they did failure. Pitcher Jim Davis told *Sports Illustrated*, "You get in trouble out there, and suddenly, out of the corner of your eye, you see him in the dugout. He's leaning forward on the bench or pacing up and down like a bear, and he's glaring at you. And suddenly you think: 'Good Lord, if I don't get the ball over the plate, he's going to come out here.'"[27]

Some more famous managers of the era, such as Casey Stengel and Leo Durocher, loved attention and played to the media, taking as much or more credit for success than their players. They gave the impression that the players were merely interchangeable parts deployed by a great master. These managers were often disliked by both their own players and those on opposing teams who could see through the act. Other managers were so combative or manipulative they were seemingly hated by everyone in the league. Charlie Dressen, who managed the "Boys of Summer" team in Brooklyn in the early fifties and later managed a number of other teams, memorably told the Braves in a team meeting his first day on the job, "I know you guys hate my guts, but I don't care."[28] Hutch was the polar opposite of these types.

Stan Musial told Watson, "Hutchinson is patient (with young players), knows how to use them. You'll never hear him taking credit. He never does that. But he brings out the best in us, because everything's out on the table with him." He added, "Let's put it this way: if I ever hear a player say he can't play for Hutch, then I'll know he can't play for anybody."[29]

"As a manager Freddie Hutchinson was very very fair," says shortstop Al Dark. "He remembered a lot of how things were when he was a player and that helped him know how to handle people. Everybody loved the guy. He was very strict and demanded certain things out of you but we all had a lot of respect for him. I gave him everything I had because he was such a good person."[30]

An incident in St. Louis gives insight into the kind of action which endeared Fred to his players. During the tense pennant stretch of 1957, after Fred rested Dark in the ninth inning of a close game which the Cardinals eventually lost, he was openly criticized by fans, media and the front-office. Richard Meyer, the team's executive vice-president was quoted in papers complaining, "You know that Dark is the glue that holds the infield together and keeps the pitchers on their toes."

Dark later admitted, "I saw where the front office blasted him for taking me out of that game in Brooklyn. I had this bad finger. It was the only time I ever asked to be taken out of a game in my life. So he got blasted for taking me out. But he never once opened his mouth to explain. That's the kind of a man he is."[31]

Fred appreciated players who, like himself, worked hard, were intense competitors and were team players. "I want men. I want big leaguers, guys who grind and fight until somebody gives in, guys who can play every day under all kinds of conditions," he told Watson in 1957. "There's no secret to it, a man is what he is, way back. I don't mean when he's 18 or 19, but long before that. It's deep in his makeup and nobody is going to do much about changing it." He added, "I try to make a ballplayer believe in himself, and the only way you can do that is to give him a chance. If he plays his way out of the lineup, then you try somebody else.... The ones who work hardest are the ones who make it, the ones who win. Sometimes that's the only difference. If you don't work hard at this game, you might as well hang them up. Sweat is your only salvation."[32]

Even though the Cardinals experienced success on the field, there was an ever-present struggle with front office meddling and second-guessing. Early in the 1956 season, owner Busch found out what kind of a man he had hired. The Cardinals had spent $125,000 on a rookie first baseman named Tom Alston. Tall and awkward, Alston had a flamboyant manner in the field which fans appeared to enjoy. His actual results were anything but crowd-pleasing, however. He was obviously not a major leaguer. Busch called Fred into his office and all but ordered him to play Alston more regularly. "Mr. Busch," he replied to the wealthy owner who was accustomed to nothing but yes-men, "do you want me to say what I really think, or what you want to hear? If I wanted to play a clown, I'd go hire Emmett Kelly."[33] (Kelly was the famous sad clown of the Ringling Brothers and Barnum and Bailey Circus at the time.) Fred did not play the owner's man.

In July 1957 the Cardinals held a 9–4 lead in Brooklyn in the ninth inning, when the Dodgers loaded the bases with one out. Fred left pitcher Wilmer Mizell, a left-hander, in the game to face the dangerous right-handed hitter Gil Hodges, rather than removing him for a right-hander as is common baseball practice. Hodges responded with a grandslam and Brooklyn went on to win the game. Afterwards, there was a storm of angry comments by club officials to the media. Vice President Meyer publicly called the game "pitiful, tragic and disastrous." General Manager Frank Lane openly second-guessed the decision and complained to reporters. Fred ordered a meeting in St. Louis with Busch and the two executives. He angrily told the men, "You all want a pennant, and we can have it. We've got an outside chance. But I've got to be left alone to do my job. It's hard enough to fight the opposition on the field every day without answering to my own front office in the newspapers. Criticize me all you want. Second-guess me in private. I get paid to take that. But when your criticism hits every newspaper in the country, it can wreck the morale of this ball club. That's one thing we can't stand."[34]

Left alone to do his job, Fred guided the team to a second-place finish, a big improvement from the previous year. The Cardinals were in contention until the end of the season. Fred was named National League Manager of the Year.

Coming off the success of 1957, the Cardinals approached the next season with optimism; however, the team struggled from the start. Lane, tired of the owner's meddling, resigned from the front office and jumped to the Indians. This infuriated Busch and, as a "Lane man," Fred's days were probably numbered at that point. Several Cardinal hitters slumped badly and the pitching staff proved to be one of the worst in the league. Most observers felt that Fred was an innocent bystander in the demise of the team. Roy Terrell wrote in *Sports Illustrated* in mid–May: "Neither does anyone seriously blame Fred Hutchinson, a man of stoic mien who has the grand misfortune to be the Cardinal manager. The plain truth of the matter is that the Cardinals have been losing on sheer talent; the pitching is pitiful, the hitting bad and, as a matter of fact, the base running and defense haven't been so hot, either."[35]

In explaining the bad pitching and lack of timely hitting, Fred said, "Multiply our ERA by the number of men left on base and it would equal the national debt." But he tried to offer some optimism — if the players' attitude could just be improved. "I sometimes think that mental attitude is the most important thing in the game. You have to go up there knowing you can hit or knowing you can throw that ball and get somebody out."[36]

Unfortunately for Fred, it was the opposing pitchers who were always confident in the knowledge that they could get out the lackluster Cardinals. The team finished in fifth place, six games below .500. Asked for his opinion on why the team was playing so poorly, Fred memorably replied: "A team finishes in fifth because it's a fifth-place team."[37]

Someone had to take the blame for the bad season, however, and it certainly wouldn't be the club's owner. When Bing Devine, the new general manager, was forced by Busch to fire Fred, he had a hard time coming out with it at their meeting, but Fred handled it well. Devine kept fumbling for words and finally Fred said, "Bing, I know what you're trying to do and why you have to do it. It's okay. I know it's not you. These things happen."[38]

Fred refused to dwell on the front-office problems publicly. When asked by reporters if he felt he had been treated unfairly by the Cardinals, Fred replied diplomatically, "No, I didn't get a raw deal. This is just baseball."[39] Regardless of Fred's public pronouncements, the move disappointed Cardinal players, including Stan Musial, who were angry with Busch for letting him go.

As before, Fred returned to Seattle to manage the Rainiers in 1959. The Pacific Coast League had changed greatly in the previous four years, however. The migration west of the Giants and Dodgers in 1957 had been the death knell for the golden age of West Coast minor league baseball. To avoid the inevitable drop in interest, attendance and revenue, the teams were aligning themselves with major league teams to be their AAA farm clubs. The Rainiers were now the top minor league team of the Cincinnati Reds. At the press conference announcing his plans for the 1959 season in Seattle, Fred quipped, "All you people probably heard that I lost my job in St. Louis, but that's not true. They just offered me another job. They handed me a shovel and told me to walk behind the Clydesdales."[40]

Fred and friend Dewey Soriano set about running the team in 1959, however it was not to be a long run this time. The Reds got off to a slow start under their manager Mayo Smith. With the team ten games under .500 in July, Smith was fired and Fred was called to Cincinnati to take over the team. Fred Hutchinson was back in the major leagues for good.

5

Cincinnati

THEY'VE BEEN PLAYING baseball a long time in Cincinnati. The local club formed the very first professional baseball team in 1869. The "Red Stockings" hired New York brothers Harry and George Wright, along with seven others, in an effort to challenge the powerful teams in the East. Harry was a managing genius as well as a great player and George was the best baseball player on the planet. The team did not lose a game for almost two years. Most true Cincinnati baseball fans will tell you that it is Harry and George and not Wilbur and Orville (those two guys who spent their time playing with bicycles and airplanes just up the road in Dayton) who should be the most famous Wright brothers in Ohio history. Legend has it that a very large, wealthy local kid, William Howard Taft, was a powerful hitter in his younger days before he gave up the game for politics and eventually landed in the White House.

By 1959, the Reds had been playing professional baseball at the same location, the corner of Findlay Street and Western Avenue, for a long time. In 1884 the Reds turned an abandoned brickyard on the site into a baseball field. After some improvements, it was called League Park. When a fire ravaged the wooden stands of League Park, a remarkable new stadium was built and opened in 1902. Given the ostentatious name of the Palace of the Fans, the elegant stadium had Corinthian columns adorning the top of the grandstand. When it was also affected by fire, it was demolished and a bigger stadium was built in 1912. Originally called Redland Field, it was renamed Crosley Field in 1934 when local businessman Powel Crosley, Jr., bought the team.[1] Redland Field had been the site of the 1919 World Series in which the infamous Black Sox had allegedly thrown the series. Most true Cincinnati baseball fans will tell you, however, that the series was not thrown, the team from Chicago was simply outplayed by the great Reds.

Cincinnati was the smallest major league baseball city in 1959. It was also generally recognized as one of the best baseball cities. There was a small-town atmosphere with players and fans knowing one another. Many Reds

41

players settled in the city after their playing days were finished. The fans were supportive and knowledgeable. As with any supportive, knowledgeable fans, they much preferred winners to losers. Unfortunately, the Reds had not been to the World Series since defeating Fred Hutchinson's Tigers in 1940. By 1959, every National League team had won a pennant since 1940 except the Reds and Pirates (the Pirates would win in 1960). It had been a long and frustrating drought. The city was starving for a taste of victory again.

The Reds faced a continuous struggle to compete with larger-market teams. In the early sixties, for example, the Reds spent $800,000 for player development one year, while the Dodgers spent $2.5 million in the same year.[2] Compounding the problem was the fact that the Reds had the oldest and smallest field (capacity around 29,000) in the league. This severely restricted revenue potential. In 1958, when the Dodgers and Giants fled west to make their fortunes, there had been pressure on owner Crosley to move the Reds to New York to fill the void left by the departed teams.[3] This thought had horrified Cincinnati citizens for whom the Reds provided a large sense of their civic identity. The nervousness caused by the speculation was still present when Fred Hutchinson arrived. Winning big in Cincinnati was going to be a challenge but would be very much appreciated by the locals who viewed a pennant as one way of saving their beloved team.

The Reds of the 1950s were known as a team with plenty of slugging, but not much pitching. They were often entertaining and occasionally contended for brief periods but were never seriously close to a pennant. The Reds were also a team with a number of hard-nosed men who played as hard off the field as on it. In 1957, "Manager Birdie Tebbetts didn't want to be too strict about curfews," pitcher Johnny Klippstein later said. "The Reds had a lot of characters and guys who liked to have a good time. One time he told us that if we were going to miss curfew because some family member was in town that we should leave a note in his box. He said, 'I want to know about it because if a writer says he saw a player out late I want to be able to say that he had my permission.' Well that plan lasted about a month. A couple of players stayed out all the time claiming they had all kinds of cousins."[4]

Discipline was not much better in early 1959 with manager Mayo Smith. Smith was a smart baseball man and would later win the World Series with Detroit in 1968, but in 1959 he was simply too easygoing for that particular situation. Players felt that general manager Gabe Paul was actually making most of the decisions. The team, which had considerable talent, seemed rudderless. Frank Robinson later wrote that Mayo Smith was a nice guy but "was among the most uninspiring leaders I've ever met."[5]

Jim Brosnan remarked in *We Played the Game*, "Mayo Smith was a kind, gentle man and I couldn't figure out how he ever got to be a big league manager. He wasn't the type. He didn't have any idea how to control his ballclub. Players talked about him behind his back. Ed Bailey, never one to hold back, told Smith to his face, 'You don't know shit!' whenever Smith came to the mound to say how he wanted a batter pitched to."[6]

The days of that kind of behavior were definitely over as a new marshal rode into town. "When Fred Hutchinson took over from Smith, his reputation preceded him," said pitcher Jim O'Toole. "We knew Fred was tough because both Jim Brosnan and Eddie Kasko had played for him in St. Louis. We were glad when he came because we had talent but needed discipline. Everybody respected him and was scared to death of him.... He'd look you right in the eye and when he said you had to do something you'd do it."[7]

"I liked Mayo," said pitcher Bob Purkey later in the 1959 season, "but I guess he was too easygoing. You lost a game, and it didn't seem to be important.... With Hutch, when you lose, you *know* it's important. He says, 'We're going to win tomorrow'— and you can tell he means it. We *are* going to win. We'd better."[8]

The Reds had a very unique player in right-handed pitcher Jim Brosnan. A member of that elusive breed of creatures on professional baseball teams which were occasionally talked about but rarely spotted — the intellectual — his tastes ran to classical music, martinis and literature with more words than pictures. He not only knew a lot of big words, but he wrote them down with considerable talent. In the Pre-Brosnan Era, most sports books "written" by athletes were ghost-written formula books in which "gee whiz, we would play this game for nothing" was the prevailing sentiment. These sugar-coated books were directed mostly at adolescents and never, ever peeked into athletes' private lives. With his diary of the 1959 season, *The Long Season*, Brosnan became the first athlete to provide a true look at a team and its players. He wrote about what players really did in their spare time (albeit in a PG-13 fashion) and what they talked about and did in the bullpen and clubhouse. And he wrote it entirely by himself. He essentially invented the athlete-diary genre which laid the ground work for Jerry Kramer's *Instant Replay* and Jim Bouton's *Ball Four* and forever changed the landscape of sports books. Brosnan followed *The Long Season* in 1961 with another book, *Pennant Race*. These books provide insight into the speech and mannerisms of his manager, Fred Hutchinson, along with the players' feelings toward him.

Brosnan recorded new manager Hutchinson's opening address to the Reds in *The Long Season*: "Most of you know me. I like to win. That's the only way to play this game. To win. We're all like that. From now on I'm running this ball club. If you have any problems come to me. I'll handle them or get somebody to do it for me. On paper this club looks better than the standings indicate so far. I don't know why, yet." He concluded by saying, "I'm glad to be up here with you. We're going to start winning. We might as well start tonight."[9]

Under Fred, the Reds began playing better and finished 39–35. Fred impressed observers with the quick turnaround and he began to receive more national attention. "Apparently everyone in baseball respects Hutchinson," wrote Roy Terrell in *Sports Illustrated* late in the 1959 season. "He is sincere and, above all, he is honest."

"To strangers, Hutchinson sometimes seems unapproachable," he continued, "Actually, however, he is a warm, friendly man, with great character, strong opinions and intense loyalties. With those he knows well, the eyes twinkle and the scowl is replaced by a strange little lopsided grin and the voice is full of salty humor. And this, in turn, inspires loyalty among those who have worked with him."[10]

The Reds had good hitting, led by Frank Robinson and Vada Pinson. Robinson had already proven to be a consistent 30 home run, 100 RBI man, and the athletic Pinson had more than 200 hits in 1959, his first full year in the majors. Both were younger than 25. However, other hitting stars, such as rugged second-baseman Johnny Temple, who hit .311, and Gus Bell, who had 115 RBIs in 1959, were over 30 and appeared to be on the downside of their careers. Shortstop Roy McMillan, one of the slickest fielding shortstops in the league and a perennial All-Star, was hurt much of 1959. The Reds' pitching was a problem, as they gave up the most runs in the league, but there were signs of hope with Bob Purkey, Brosnan and rookie Jim O'Toole. Tough and brash, left-hander O'Toole won only five games in 1959, but he had a live arm and loads of untapped potential. He only needed someone to help bring it out.

"I had a real good year in the minors in 1958, winning 20 games in my first year of pro ball," O'Toole says. "Then after spring training in 1959, I didn't pitch for a month. They had a bunch of older pitchers and I think Gabe Paul was calling the shots, having them pitch more. Hutch came in midseason. He saw what I had and he gave me the ball. He sort of gave me the confidence I needed."[11] Along with confidence, Fred gave O'Toole the advice to not make his fastball too good over the plate, but to keep it outside.[12] O'Toole would become one of the most consistent winners in the league over the next five years.

The next season, 1960, the Reds took a step back. Front-office troubles threatened to haunt Fred again and the club struggled to a 67–87 record and finished in sixth place. It was a very frustrating year for both the players and their manager. "In 1960 we were just a bunch of ballplayers, we weren't a team," Jim O'Toole later said.[13] Hutch struggled to hammer the club into shape with a combination of fines, talks, discipline and patience. Compounding Fred's frustration was the fact that general manager Gabe Paul had an

Fred (left) and Reds owner Powel Crosley, spring training 1960 (Cincinnati Reds).

annoying habit of traveling with the team and demanding long explanations from the manager after losses. The stress of that long season caused some of the more memorable explosions in the clubhouse by the Bear, which added to his growing legend.[14] Nothing seemed to help though. It was clear that the Reds' talent was either too young or too old. Some changes were needed.

6

1961

GENERAL MANAGER Gabe Paul resigned after the 1960 season to join the new Houston Colt 45s (whose name would later be changed to the more twentieth-century-sounding Astros in 1965). Owner Crosley, looking for a someone with good baseball knowledge who also knew how to squeeze a dollar, hired Bill DeWitt as general manager in November. When Paul, the man who had hired him, resigned, Fred may have initially feared a repeat of the front office troubles which had sabotaged his two previous managerial stints. These fears would prove unfounded as DeWitt would come to be a valuable ally, a good baseball man and, in time, a good friend.

The 57-year-old DeWitt had gotten his start in baseball at the age of 12 selling soda pop at St. Louis Browns games. He had worked his way up the baseball ladder, starting as office boy for the Browns' Branch Rickey at $3.50 a week. DeWitt proved to be worth the money and when Rickey moved across town to the Cardinals, he took young Bill with him. Bill, following Rickey's advice, learned bookkeeping and typing and attended college at night. He eventually became Rickey's secretary and then the treasurer of the Cardinals. After earning a law degree, he was made assistant vice president and put in charge of player procurement for the vast Cardinal farm system — which, at the time, was the envy of all of baseball. DeWitt went on to become general manager of the Browns in the forties and later was part owner of the Browns in the early fifties, eventually selling out to Bill Veeck. The experience of juggling the books with the sad, underfunded Browns would prove valuable in the small market of Cincinnati.

Powel Crosley died in March of 1961 and the team was put up for sale. DeWitt seized the opportunity, put together the financing and bought the club for $4.6 million. A portly, serious man, DeWitt wore horn-rimmed glasses and combed his slicked down hair straight back in the manner of all serious men of power of that era (see Nixon, Richard and J., L.B.). Hard-working and ambitious, frank and demanding with his employees, DeWitt was an admitted baseball junkie. He had no hobbies or interests other than baseball. He had no other financial resource. His business was baseball. He was a tireless promoter and shameless shiller of his product. Reds fans were treated to a number of special days such as Senior Citizens' Night, Safety Patrol Night, and Farm Night, as well as promotions such as a rotten egg-tossing contest before a game. When 650 fans showed up with real and toy trumpets to get in free on Trumpet Night in the early sixties, DeWitt quipped, "How about a Piano Night next?"[1] DeWitt repainted Crosley Field from top to bottom and installed brand-new rest rooms. "The Cubs *used* to have the best rest rooms [in baseball]," he proudly told *Sports Illustrated* later.[2]

Rest rooms were not the only thing DeWitt needed to improve. He realized that paint and special promotions could only go so far to get fans in the seats. To keep them coming back, he needed to field an exciting, winning team. On paper, the Reds did not appear to have much hope of improving tremendously over their mediocre 1960 season. There were major question marks at second and third base, the pitching staff was weak, and the catching, first base and shortstop positions also appeared to be below average. The roster was comprised of players who were either too old and past their prime or too young and in need of a few more years experience. Outfielders Vada Pinson and Frank Robinson were the only Reds remotely considered to be All-Star candidates.

DeWitt, who would later incur lasting infamy for his 1966 trade of Frank Robinson, initially struck gold with his first trades for the Reds. He dealt two of the older players, Roy McMillan and Cal McLish, and got pitcher Joey Jay and third-baseman Gene Freese in return. In April, he traded aging catcher Ed Bailey to the Giants for second-baseman Don Blasingame and two minor players. These moves did not generate much enthusiasm from the masses initially as none of the players received was an established star, but time would show that these were very good deals indeed.

A large pitcher at 6 feet 4 inches and 225 pounds, Joey Jay was a hard thrower. By 1961, however, he was widely considered to be a pitcher who had not lived up to his potential. The first Little League alumnus to play major league baseball, Jay had been a bonus baby with Milwaukee as an 18-year-old in 1953. Rules at the time mandated that, because of the bonus, he had to remain on the major league roster for two years, and so he had not been permitted the luxury of learning his craft in the minors. Not developing as the Braves hoped, Jay played for several managers in Milwaukee, none of whom believed he was worthy of the regular rotation. His confidence damaged, he became moody and developed bad habits. As reported in *Sports Illustrated*, "Jay quickly won himself a reputation as an eater and sleeper of championship caliber. He seldom was seen awake without a candy bar or a soft drink, often with both. He would eat in the bullpen during ball games.

At one point he weighed 245 pounds."[3] There were several incidents of missing team practices and meetings because of oversleeping. One Braves manager, Fred Haney, complained about Jay: "He just won't do anything in pregame drills. He's fat and he's too lazy to get in shape."[4] At 25 years old, Jay was a veteran of seven major league seasons but had never won ten games or pitched more than 140 innings in a season. In short, he was a flop with a questionable attitude who had not justified his large bonus.

Fred Hutchinson was instrumental in obtaining Jay. Looking for pitchers, Fred talked to veteran Milwaukee pitcher Lew Burdette about several of the Braves' young pitchers. Burdette, the hero of the 1957 World Series, owned a cottage on Anna Maria Island like a lot of the Braves because of the proximity to the Braves' spring training site in Bradenton. He was a frequent visitor to Hutchinson cookouts on the island. Burdette convinced Fred that, in the right hands, Jay could still become a very good pitcher.[5] In the first meeting with his new manager, Fred told Jay he was going to get a lot of work. "That's all I did for him — let him pitch,"[6] Hutchinson later told *The Sporting News*. Jay would respond very well to the confidence of his new manager.

Gene Freese was a rugged, hard-hitting third baseman with a reputation for being a butcher in the field. His erratic arm kept fans in the seats behind first base at risk for their lives. At 27-years-old, he had played for four different teams in the past four years before coming to the Reds from the White Sox, never quite finding a home. He had hit 23 home runs in 1959 for Philadelphia but otherwise his career had been unremarkable. Freese would room with first-baseman Gordy Coleman who was also known for his misadventures in the field. It became a team joke that there was no use in calling their room because neither of them would be able to successfully pick up the phone. In an attempt to defend his roommate's honor, Coleman once said of Freese's arm: "The nice thing about (Freese's throws) is that they were over my head. Some guys are always skipping them into your shins."[7]

Coleman was another player without much of a pedigree. At 27-years-old, he had never been a starter in the major leagues. He had only six games of major league experience before being traded to the Reds from Cleveland before the 1960 season. In a trade for other principal players, he had been a throw-in, an afterthought. In 1960, he had hit six home runs in 251 at bats for the Reds. Along with his troubles in the field, the left-handed Coleman could not hit any left-handed pitcher in the league except, for some strange reason, future Hall of Famer Warren Spahn. Coleman's unorthodox bucket-footed swing at the plate was sometimes ridiculed as looking like he was falling out of bed.[8] On the positive side though, Coleman was a great guy to have around. Always smiling, he was a very likeable guy with a good sense of humor who seemed to get along with everyone.

Getting Blasingame would turn out to be a key for the team. A major league-quality glove man up the middle, he was a consistent, though not spectacular hitter. "Don has knitted the infield," Fred told reporters later in the year. "I had him in St. Louis, and I knew what he could do."[9] As with Brosnan and Kasko, Fred brought in a former player who he knew to be reliable.

The Reds gathered in Tampa for spring training, picked by writers to finish no higher than sixth place. Fred later admitted that he began the year with the lofty goal of getting into the first division.[10] "Nobody gave us much of a chance to be very good in 1961," says Jim O'Toole. "No one thought we had a shot."[11] The team did nothing in March to convince anyone otherwise.

After one particularly poor showing in spring training, Bill DeWitt said, "Don't tell me these fellows play that way during the summer. I think I was misled when I signed some of these players I'm seeing. They aren't the players they told me they were when we talked contract."[12]

Jim O'Toole beat the Cubs on opening day and the Reds won five of their first seven games. Joey Jay's first start was against the Cardinals in St. Louis and he began poorly. He walked the first four batters he faced. With no outs, one run in and the bases loaded, Jay saw his manager lumbering out of the dugout. Fred walked slowly to the mound while Jay waited, expecting the inevitable hook and possible banishment to the bullpen. "Here we go again," he thought.

When Fred reached the mound, he glared at Jay and snarled, "Don't walk yourself out of there, for crissakes. Make 'em knock you out."[13] He turned and went back to the bench. Jay, surprised and grateful, pitched his way out of the jam. Jay lost his first three decisions in 1961 but his manager stuck with him. He responded to this confidence by turning into one of the best pitchers in the league.

The Reds were surprisingly near the top of the standings early in the year when they went into Los Angeles and lost a particularly sloppy doubleheader to the Dodgers. "We got killed. We played like a bunch of high school kids," Jim O'Toole remembers. "After the doubleheader, Hutch calls a meeting. We had been there from ten in the morning, now it's seven at night and he says, 'Guys, don't take your uniforms off.' We all looked at him; we were worn out. He said, 'We're going to go back out there and I'm going to teach you how to play this game.'" The enraged players trudged back onto the field grumbling under their breath. "He made the pitchers who didn't pitch in the series throw batting practice. He said, 'Don't tell them what's coming.' The catcher was calling signs, just like a game."[14]

"We played under simulated game conditions until dark," said Coleman. "I think that convinced everyone Hutch meant business; that he felt we were better than we'd played."[15]

"Everybody was bitching but he taught us a lesson," continues O'Toole.

"That night we said, 'There's no game tomorrow, let's go out.' So we all went out together as a team. It brought us together because we were all tired and mad at Hutch. So we all went out and had a good time."[16]

To make one further point, Fred had a bed check that night. "I don't think he had bed check more than twice the whole time I was there," says Eddie Kasko, "but that night he checked."[17] O'Toole was scheduled to pitch the first game of the next series and went back to the hotel a little before midnight and did not get caught. The rest of the team wasn't so lucky. Gene Freese shared a ride back to the hotel with O'Toole but went to the hotel bar instead of going up to his room. As a standing rule, players were not allowed in the hotel bar — it was the exclusive domain of the manager and coaches.

"The first guy Freese sees when he goes into the bar is Hutch," says O'Toole with a laugh. "Not knowing what else to do, Freese bought Hutch a drink." Freese didn't know that his manager had just called up to his room. Coleman, contrary to his teammates' beliefs, had indeed fielded the phone cleanly and, covering for his roomie, told Fred that Freese was in bed and he didn't want to wake him. "Hutch said, 'Hey Gene, good to see you, tough game today. Oh, by the way, I just called your room and your roommate said you were sleeping.'"

"Out of the 25 guys on the team, I think he caught 20 of them out that night," says O'Toole. "He fined everybody a hundred bucks. After that, everybody got the message. You lose a doubleheader, you should feel so bad that you go to bed early."[18]

"I was one of the guys he caught," says Kasko. "I gave him a check for $100. But after the season, I got a check from the club for $100 saying Fred Hutchinson wanted this returned. I guess after the way the season turned out, Hutch felt we deserved the money back. The funny thing is that he had never cashed my original check, so I figure I made $100 by being caught out late."[19]

From June on, when the Reds visited another city for a series, they were met with a headline in the local sports page with some version of "How much longer can the Reds hold on?" or "Are the Reds for real?" This provided further motivation to the players. Because of the number of previously unheralded players who seemed to have been thrown together to form the club, someone in the press called the team the "Ragamuffin Reds" and the name caught on. "I don't know at what point they called us the Ragamuffin Reds," said Robinson later, "but we took it to heart. We knew nobody was giving us a chance ... but we knew we were better than everybody thought."[20]

The Reds slumped in late June and a players-only clubhouse meeting was called to clear the air. The players spoke their piece about each other, holding nothing back. "For instance," said O'Toole, "some of the guys pointed out that I was overreacting to errors—I'd throw my glove or curse the fielder. After that I bit my lip when someone blew one."[21] Robinson later said he got a lot off his chest and challenged the team to stop making excuses. The meeting seemed to "cleanse our souls," he said.[22]

According to O'Toole, another turning point in the season came soon after the meeting in a game against the Braves. In the early sixties, the Cubs and Braves were notorious for stealing signs to help their hitters. At their park in Milwaukee, the location of the bullpen in the outfield helped the Braves accomplish this bit of skullduggery. Someone in the bullpen with binoculars would watch the catcher's signs. He would then relay the information to the hitter by a prearranged signal, such as standing or crossing his legs, to indicate whether a fastball or a curve was coming. A major league hitter, confident in the knowledge of which pitch to expect, can be very dangerous. Opposing pitchers, as expected, found this little ruse somewhat annoying. "We went into Milwaukee and I'm throwing pretty good but they're hitting line drives all over the place," says O'Toole. "Mathews hit a homer down the line in left and he's a left-handed pull hitter. There's no way you can hit that kind of a curve that way unless you know it's coming. I get to the bench and I'm hot. I said, 'What the hell's going on?'"

"And Jay says, 'I just saw [Milwaukee pitcher Bob] Buhl. He's got binoculars down there and he's relaying the signs.' So we changed the signs but I'm still pretty hot. The next inning I got on first base and I told Adcock [Milwaukee's first baseman], 'You guys are stealing signs, there's no way Mathews hits that curve ball out to left.'

"And he says, 'Now you know we wouldn't do that.'

"And I said, 'Tell Mathews the next time I see him digging in like he knows what's coming, I'm going to stick it right in his ear.' So I guess he must have relayed that to Mathews. A few innings later, I'm on first base again and Kasko hits a double off the wall. I round third and try to score but I slipped and fell down. Then I got in a rundown between Mathews and Torre." Mathews, a tough guy and one of the league's most ready brawlers, took exception to O'Toole's polite elbow in his face as he tagged him. Mathews jumped on O'Toole's back, they rolled over and both benches cleared.[23]

Fred Hutchinson was soon in the middle of the pile, pulling players off O'Toole and tossing them out. As he pulled Mathews out of the pile away from his pitcher, Hutch said, "What are you trying to do to my pitcher, Ed?"

Mathews, also a frequent Hutchinson-cookout attendee in Florida, said, "But Hutch, he tried to knock the ball out of my glove."

Hutch looked at him and replied, "What did you want him to do, give you a kiss?"[24]

O'Toole's father, seated in the first row of the box seats, almost joined the fight. He had one leg over the rail when one of Jim's brothers grabbed him and pulled him back.[25]

"That fight kind of brought us together," says O'Toole. "We felt like it was us against the world."[26] Coleman eventually won the game with a home run in the 13th inning. The Reds won the second game of the doubleheader on a late Robinson home run. They ended up sweeping the series and returned from the road trip to a big cheering crowd at the airport. The Cincinnati fans could sense that something special was happening.

The Reds continued to roll. The pitching staff, always a Cincinnati weakness, was suddenly one of the toughest in the league. Joey Jay, after struggling his first few games, was seemingly winning every time out. Jim O'Toole, gaining the ability to go with his confidence, and veteran Bob Purkey were not far behind. The bullpen, led by lefty Bill Henry and righty Jim Brosnan, who was writing another book, was unhittable.

The Reds battled the Dodgers all year. The Dodgers pulled ahead by one game in August. Many expected the Reds to collapse. They went into the L.A. Coliseum for a crucial series with the Dodgers in mid–August and lost the first game. That made six losses in the last seven games for the Reds. The next day, in front of 70,000 fans, the Reds bounced back to sweep a doubleheader with Purkey and O'Toole both pitching shutouts. After that series, "I remember thinking 'God, we're gonna do it,'" O'Toole later recalled.[27]

Shortly after that, Bill DeWitt announced that Fred Hutchinson had signed a two-year deal that would keep him in Cincinnati in 1962 and 1963. There was no announcement on salary, but DeWitt and Fred both admitted, "it was sweetened a little." DeWitt called Fred "the outstanding manager in baseball."[28]

The Dodgers did not give up easily, however. They came back into Cincinnati late in the season with one more chance to take away the lead. The Dodgers won the first two games of the series, bringing up a doubleheader. If the Dodgers swept both games, they would be back in first. The Reds fell behind 5–1 in the first game, but Gene Freese, the career journeyman no one wanted, hit a three-run home run in the seventh to start the comeback and the Reds won 6–5. The Reds then took the second game as well.

On September 26, the Reds played in Chicago, needing to win one game to clinch at least a tie for the pennant. Jerry Lynch won it with a three-run homer in the eighth inning. Rather than fly to their next game in Pittsburgh, the Reds flew back to Cincinnati where a big downtown reception was planned in Fountain Square. A wild, cheering crowd greeted the Reds at the airport when they landed. "We rode on a bus to Fountain Square from the airport and the place was crazy," says O'Toole. "People were on top of the bus, shaking it."[29] Fans lined the highway and were gathered at intersections along the route from the airport to Fountain Square, waving pennants and screaming madly. The Reds' radio network carried the Dodgers game in Pittsburgh. An estimated 30,000 fans in Fountain Square listened to the game on loudspeakers which had been set up. When the Pirates won the game, Cincinnati fans released 21 years of pennant-less frustration.

"Bedlam broke loose," wrote Brosnan. "Bands played, sirens wailed, fans hugged each other and danced in the street. Hutchinson was carried about on the shoulders of the crowd."[30]

The Reds had won the pennant. The Reds players were celebrities. "We owned the city," says O'Toole. Fred Hutchinson hosted a huge party for the Reds players at the Netherland Hilton Hotel in Cincinnati. "Hutch even got up and sang," says O'Toole.[31]

Grabbing the microphone at the party, Fred became uncharacteristically emotional as he thanked the players for the great season. He then turned loose his inner crooner and belted out the song "I'll Understand." For the amazed players, this was a side of Fred they had never seen.

Fred called his wife to deliver the news. "Unfortunately, I had to take the kids home to start school in Florida, so I missed the celebration when they won the pennant," Patsy says with disappointment. "Fred called up and said, 'Well, I guess we won it.' Winning that pennant was the biggest event of his life."[32]

Many of the Reds' unheralded players had turned in the best years of their careers. Henry and Brosnan combined for 32 saves which led the National League as a twosome. Coleman and Freese each hit 26 home runs for the season. Jerry Lynch, living up to his billing as "the world's greatest

Some of the big guns for the 1961 Reds (Topps Company, Inc.).

pinch hitter," inspiring the phrase "Lynch in the pinch," had numerous late-inning heroics and finished the year with 13 home runs in just 181 at bats.

Eddie Kasko, a utility infielder before Hutchinson made him an every-day performer in 1960, took up the slack at shortstop for the departed McMil-lan and made the All-Star team in 1961. "I knew he was a good ballplayer,"[33] Fred told reporters midway through the season. Jay, the castoff from the Braves, ended up with a league-leading 21 wins. O'Toole won 19 and Purkey, 16. During the tense pennant race, O'Toole had won 13 of his last 15 starts and was 5–0 in September down the stretch.

But it was Robinson and Pinson who had the most remarkable seasons. Pinson hit .343, second in the league to Roberto Clemente, with 208 hits and 87 RBIs. Robinson hit .323 with 37 home runs and 124 RBIs and won the league's MVP award.

Unfortunately for the Reds, their opponent in the World Series was the New York Yankees. The powerful 1961, Yankees led by Roger Maris's 61 home runs and Mickey Mantle's 54 are generally ranked in the top five among all-time best teams. The Reds were prohibitive underdogs going in. Before the

Yankee manager Ralph Houk and Fred at Yankee Stadium for the 1961 World Series (National Baseball Hall of Fame Library, Cooperstown, New York).

series, Fred told everyone, "The Yankees can be beaten; they have been beaten." When someone told him the odds against the Reds were 12–1, he replied, "So what? Weren't the odds against our winning the pennant something like 60–1?"[34]

Jim O'Toole started for the Reds at Yankee Stadium against Whitey Ford in the opener. O'Toole pitched very well but the Reds could do nothing with Ford and lost 2–0. The Reds came back to even the series by winning the second game 6–2. The game was put out of reach when backup second-baseman Elio Chacon broke from third and scored on Elston Howard's passed ball which had not seemed to roll far enough away for the runner to score. Joey Jay was the winning pitcher. After the game, Fred cracked, "Where is the expert who picked the Yankees to win this series in 3 games?"[35]

With the series back in Cincinnati, Bob Purkey held the Yankees in check for most of game three and the Reds took a 2–1 lead into the eighth inning. But Purkey gave up a home run to pinch hitter John Blanchard in the eighth and another to Maris in the ninth and the Reds lost 3–2. Ford, who was in the midst of a streak which would break Babe Ruth's record for World Series consecutive scoreless innings pitched, threw another shutout in game four to win 7–0.

After the fourth game, reporters asked Fred if he intended to make changes in the lineup for the slumping Robinson, Pinson and Freese. "Why should I make changes?" Fred asked. "Who's not hitting? Robinson, Freese and Pinson. And who got us this far? Robinson, Freese and Pinson. We'll sink or swim with those guys."[36]

After the Yankees won the series clincher, Hutch took the loss with gracious equanimity. He quietly circulated through the Reds locker room, shaking hands with his players and wishing them well for the winter. He told reporters, "The turning point came in the ninth inning of Saturday's game. That homer by Roger Maris, the one that beat Bob Purkey 3–2, was the key to the series…. We were never the same after that. We had no spark, got no lift and went nowhere after we had evened the series in New York." He went on to praise the Yankees as a "real fine ball club" that deserved to win. "As for our good points, Jim O'Toole, Jay and Purkey all pitched well and Johnny Edwards … convinced me that he has a future with us." Edwards, a rookie catcher who had come up in midseason, had led the Reds' hitters in the series. Hutch concluded: "I know of no reason why we shouldn't win again in 1962."[37]

The World Series defeat did nothing to dampen spirits in Cincinnati. Fred Hutchinson was picked Manager of the Year for the second time. The Reds were the toast of the town. It had been a magical season. It would prove to be a watershed year. The Reds had had only one winning season (1956) since World War II but after 1961 they had the best record in the National League over the next forty years.[38]

Frank Robinson later wrote about that season: "I really had pride about this team ... because we weren't picked to win. People just didn't think we could do it and we went out and showed them."[39]

What did their manager mean to the Reds in 1961? "Everything," says Jerry Lynch.[40]

Jim Brosnan recalls a conversation with Frank Robinson at a team function late in the year in which Robinson talked about Fred Hutchinson's effect on the team. "Just out of the blue he said how lucky we were to have a man like that leading us—that he was just the kind of man needed for that club."[41]

"Hutch gave us the confidence we needed to win it that year," says Jim O'Toole.[42]

The Reds were an astonishing 34–14 in one-run games. In close games, especially in the late innings, every move seemed to work perfectly.

In response to the media's continued praise for his "miracle" work with the Reds in 1961, Hutch downplayed his role, saying, "It's a good ball club, a hell of a lot better than it gets credit for."[43]

The Reds and Yankees line up at Crosley Field during the 1961 World Series (Cincinnati Reds).

Fred Hutchinson meant "everything" to the pennant-winning Reds in 1961 according to ace pinch hitter Jerry Lynch (National Baseball Hall of Fame Library, Cooperstown, New York).

"It took a lot of things to win," Fred said. "First we had the players, good pitching was key.... Everything had to jell. All I had to do was to pull the string now and then."[44]

The Reds were optimistic in spring training in 1962, however things quickly soured. Gene Freese broke his ankle early in March and it was a sign of things to come. Freese, whose career year had helped so much in 1961, would miss the entire season and the Reds would miss his bat. The 1962 season was the year of Maury Wills breaking Ty Cobb's record with 104 stolen bases. The Dodgers' pitching tandem of Sandy Koufax and Don Drysdale were at full speed. But it was the Giants, with the power of Mays, McCovey and Cepeda, who took the flag. The Reds had a very good season, winning 98 games, but finished in third place, five games out.

That fall, while watching the Reds' Tampa Instructional League team play, Fred got his first glimpse of a hard-hitting, hustling youngster fresh from the Reds' Class A team in Macon. The youngster played baseball like nobody else had before; he attacked the game. Fred Hutchinson was immediately impressed with young Pete Rose. It was something he would remember over the winter.

7

Charlie Hustle

PETE ROSE had grown up living on baseball in a tough section of western Cincinnati. After a high school career in which he was overshadowed by the much-heralded shortstop Ed Brinkman (who signed with the Senators), he had been recommended to the Reds by an uncle who was a Reds scout. In 1960, as a 19-year-old in rookie ball in Geneva, New York, Rose played fairly well, but did not particularly stand out. It was evident that he could hit, but his play at second base was not good as he made a plethora of errors and struggled turning double plays.

But the famous Pete Rose work ethic and confidence were already there in 1960. Teammate Art Shamsky later recalled that even at that age, Rose approached the game differently than anyone else, getting in the batting cage and stroking line drive after line drive — not just trying to see how far he could hit it. "There were very, very few young players taking that kind of approach," he said. "It wasn't that Pete put in more time but he practiced right."[1]

The next year in Tampa, Rose was a star, setting a league record with 30 triples. He was even better in 1962. Whenever old-timers in Macon, Georgia, gather to talk about the good old days of the Macon Peaches minor league baseball team, Pete Rose is the first name to come up. He was very popular with the fans (and their daughters) and led a great Macon team which included future Reds teammates Mel Queen, Shamsky and Tommy Helms and was managed by Dave Bristol. The Peaches ripped through the South Atlantic League and Pete Rose was the driving force. "Pete put out electricity when he played," Peaches general manager Bob Bonifay later recalled. "If you watched him play, you knew that this boy was not going to be denied from reaching his goal."[2] Rose hit .330 with 17 triples, and scored 136 runs, the highest total in the South Atlantic League since 1940, but he was still considered by most in the Reds' organization to be at least one year, maybe two, away from the majors. However, the man in the Reds' organization whose opinion mattered the most, Fred Hutchinson, thought otherwise. He could

Pete Rose of the Macon Peaches, 1962. Sliding feet first? (courtesy of the Middle Georgia Archives, Washington Memorial Library, Macon).

see the talent, the drive, the potential star quality. And he was determined to give him a chance in 1963 to see what he could do for the Reds.

"I can clearly remember in the fall of 1962 my father telling my brother and I, 'If you want to see how the game of baseball should be played, come over tonight and watch one of our minor leaguers, Pete Rose,'" says Jack Hutchinson who was 17 at the time. "My father really liked his attitude, his demeanor with other teams, just the way he played the game."[3]

"As soon as Hutch saw Pete play, he fell in love with him," Earl Lawson of the *Cincinnati Post* later said. "At the winter meetings that year he told me, 'If I had any guts, I'd stick Rose at second base and just leave him there.'"[4]

Rose's constant energy on the baseball field was something to see. Rough in the field at second base, it was obvious, nevertheless, that he possessed excellent baseball knowledge. He always threw to the right base and was always in the right place at the right time. As a hitter, he ripped line drives to all fields from both sides of the plate, had a great eye for the strike zone and rarely struck out. Daring on the bases, he was constantly looking to turn singles into doubles, doubles into triples. And on close plays when he slid — well, he didn't exactly slide; he launched himself head first, arms stretched in front and, before crashing back to earth, seemed suspended horizontally several feet off the ground. If you look at old pictures of what became the most famous slide in baseball in the sixties and seventies, it is not a stretch to add a red cape and put an S on his chest to resemble a certain man of steel in midflight.

In spring training Fred bragged about Pete to a fellow manager. "Can he run?" the other manager asked. "He goes to first in 4.1 seconds," answered Hutch. Then, grinning, added, "But that's only after he has drawn a base on balls."[5]

"Rose was a great player," O'Toole later said about 1963. "He went about his business on the field like nobody I'd ever seen."[6] There was no doubt about Pete Rose's ability and effort on the baseball field. Legend has it that early in the spring, while most veterans were still easing back into shape and not exerting too much effort, Whitey Ford, after watching the rookie sprint to first base after a walk, leaned over to Mickey Mantle on the Yankee bench and said sarcastically, "Look at Charlie Hustle." The name stuck. In late spring, Fred Hutchinson announced that Pete Rose would be the Reds' second baseman.

With his nonstop hustle, youthful face topped with a crew cut and ready quips for interviews, Pete was an immediate hit with the press and the hometown crowd. Not so with his teammates. The initial problem for Pete was that the Reds already had a pretty good second baseman in Don Blasingame. "Blazer" was a veteran who had been a starting major league second baseman for the past six seasons. He had been one of the key players on the 1961 pennant-winning team. He was a scrappy player, a pretty good (.260 to .280) hitter and a slick-fielder. He was well schooled, graceful, and efficient in the dance around second base for turning ground balls into double plays known as the pivot. And, most significantly, he was one of the guys. He was generally liked by all the veterans and part of a large crowd that often hung out together away from the field. Suddenly, Blasingame was in danger of becoming unemployed. The knowledge of one's limited playing-lifespan is universal in baseball and that knowledge makes the owners of the few jobs available very resentful of would-be job-stealers. It would be normal to expect some resentment among his buddies, especially for an unproven rookie. However, that resentment seemed to take on exaggerated proportions concerning Pete Rose.

"Don was my roommate on the road and Pete was taking his job," says Jim Brosnan, "so I kind of resented it. He was the guy taking my roomie's job."[7]

"Don Blasingame had his best year in 1962 and he should never have lost his second-base job," O'Toole later said. "As a pitcher, I didn't like that Rose couldn't make the double play like Blasingame."[8]

Rookies normally are not immediately accepted into social circles on most teams. Some veterans are nice and welcome rookies, but most are indifferent and prefer to stick with proven friends and teammates more their age. Occasionally, veterans are downright rude and insulting to rookies. "I wasn't accepted right away, rightfully so because when I joined the ballclub, that meant somebody had to be let go. The other players looked at me as someone taking a spot on the 25-man roster.... I was an outcast. I couldn't go have a drink with the guys, and they wouldn't invite me to dinner."[9] This statement of the hard facts of life for a rookie was spoken by Al Kaline not Pete Rose, but it could easily have been said by any rookie of the era when describing his first year. In addition to the natural problem of being a rookie, Pete Rose's personality certainly aggravated the problem. The personality which was famously on display throughout the seventies and eighties in good times and bad was already present in 1963. He was brash, extremely confident — some would say arrogant — and he didn't really seem to care what other teammates thought of him, on or off the field. This, perhaps, was the thing that was most infuriating to even those who silently supported him or those who tried to give him hints on how to be accepted by the team; he just didn't seem to care what anyone else thought. He was Pete Rose and he was going to do as he damn well pleased. With his mannerisms on the field, he was viewed by many as a hot dog. Pete hustled as hard off the field as on it and some teammates resented this as well (or resented his success).

As O'Toole said, the Reds' pitchers certainly preferred the comfort of having Blasingame at second for double plays. Rose struggled on pivots and sometimes seemed in danger of being crippled by opposing runners. "He was such a good player, they had to find a place for him," says Kasko, "but it was obvious second base wasn't going to be his best long-term position."[10]

Another factor in Rose's difficulty in 1963 was the fact that there were very few other rookies that year. The only rookie on the Reds for any length of time other than Rose was outfielder Tommy Harper. Harper, who was black and from Oakland like Pinson and Robinson, naturally hung around them. Rose had moved up faster than his similar-aged friends like Mel Queen, Tommy Helms and Art Shamsky, who were still in the minors. At 22-years-old and unmarried, Rose had a different agenda away from the field than his older, married teammates. Rose was definitely not interested in sitting around a bar and talking to the guys after games.

After a while, Rose found acceptance in Robinson and Pinson. Robinson wrote in 1988: "He (Rose) was a cocky little dude who moved chest out like a bantam rooster.... A lot of guys regarded Pete as sort of a hot dog.... When I saw that Pete Rose was being ostracized by most of my teammates — guys hardly talking to him, never inviting him out with them — I asked Pete one night if he would like to join Vada and me for dinner.... No other players warmed to Rose all season, so Vada and I became his friends and showed him the ropes around the league."[11]

"We were upset, too," Pinson later said about the reaction to Rose taking a spot on the team. "We couldn't understand why Blasingame was being edged out.... But the way Pete was being treated was not something we were going to go for. It upset me. He was a rookie, untried. But he had a uniform on, he was a teammate, and we were trying to win."[12]

As the best players on the team, it was natural that an eager rookie such as Rose would want to emulate Robinson and Pinson. He imitated the way they wore their pants tight and low, the way they shined their shoes and made sure their uniform was perfect before stepping out onto the field. He even imitated the way they talked. This appears to have rankled some of the veterans and executives.

By 1963, Frank Robinson was the longest-tenured Red, the best and highest paid player. He had gradually become more outspoken. The relationship between Robinson and owner DeWitt had never been good and it is likely that there was resentment from the front office because the man with the largest salary was not earning it in 1963. Robinson battled a series of injuries, played in only 140 games and hit 21 home runs, by far his worse season in the majors. Some executives questioned the attitude and work ethic of Robinson and Pinson.

Rose was advised by the front office to "stop hanging around with the colored players." The "colored players" only included Robinson, Pinson and Harper in 1963. Which exact members of management had a problem with Rose's relationships has never been explicitly stated; however, it apparently came straight from the top. Rose never implicated Fred Hutchinson in any of his books. In most, he wrote that team owner DeWitt called him into his downtown office and gave him this advice. DeWitt's assistant Phil Segui was also mentioned as attempting to deliver the message. Rose's mother later stated that DeWitt had discussed the matter with Rose's father also and he had spoken to his son about this. The "advice" was not taken — Rose continued to hang out with whomever he pleased.[13]

There was another aspect of young Pete's off-field behavior which apparently bothered Fred Hutchinson. One of Rose's neighborhood friends from his early days told author Michael Sokolove in 1990: "Freddy Hutchinson told him (Rose) not to go to the track anymore. He really got on him about it as I understand it, because he didn't think it looked good for Pete to be there all the time. Pete did quit going for a while, but (after 1964) he started going back."[14]

On the field, Pete Rose struggled early, but his manager had faith in him and stuck with him, even when others doubted him. Rose started the season 0 for 11, then was 3 for 23. Hutch benched him a short time, but let him know it was only temporary — to get some extra batting practice and find his stroke, "not to be impatient, but to observe how big leaguers act, especially at the plate."[15] Back in the lineup in late April, Rose went on a tear. The job belonged to Rose for good. Blasingame was eventually sold to the Senators on July 1. Rose played in 157 games, hitting .273 and scoring 101 runs. At the end of the season he was elected National League Rookie of the Year.

Several other veterans, in addition to Robinson, battled injuries and had unexpectedly poor seasons in 1963 as the team struggled to an 86–76 finish, 13 games behind the league-leading Dodgers. Nevertheless, the team and their manager were optimistic looking toward 1964. Robinson would surely have another good year and the farm system was loaded with promising players, some of whom could be expected to help a great deal in 1964. And so, as Fred Hutchinson prepared to return to Anna Maria Island, he was indeed looking forward to the 1964 season.

8

"Dad's home and
he blew another one"

THE EARLY SIXTIES were great years for Fred Hutchinson and the Cincinnati Reds. The team was a legitimate contender each season and drew well at the box office. The farm system was stocked with excellent players which in the not too distant future would form the backbone of the Big Red Machine. Fred had the support of management and the fans of Cincinnati loved him. The team was stable. The Reds players were comfortable with their manager. They respected him and knew what to expect. There was no doubt about who was in control.

Fred was popular with writers, especially those who spent a large amount of time covering the Reds, like Si Burick of the *Dayton Daily News*, Earl Lawson of the *Cincinnati Post* and Ritter Collett of the *Dayton Herald-Journal*. These writers, not unlike modern day reporters embedded with the military, traveled with the team, lived with them on the road, and ate and usually drank with them. Lawson, whose career covering the Reds would span 34 years from 1950 to 1984, and Collett, whose career would last more than 50 years, both would eventually be elected to the National Baseball Hall of Fame. They developed a special friendship with Fred Hutchinson. He enjoyed their company away from the field and allowed them to see him in a light rarely seen by his players or the public. He often confided with them and they, in turn, proved trustworthy by not printing "off-the-record" material (at least not until their memoirs were published 20 years later). Lawson wrote that during spring training, they used to haunt the Island Club in Tampa and "after closing, Hutch delighted in going to the bandstand, grabbing the mike and making like Frank Sinatra as the jukebox blared."[1]

What was Fred Hutchinson like? What were the secrets of his success? How did his players feel about him? The following stories help answer these questions.

Fred receives good luck wishes at Crosley Field, ca. 1961 to 1963 (Cincinnati Reds).

Fred was credited as being a good handler of men and a good manager to play for. He understood that different players respond to different methods. He seemed to have the ability to know when to push a player and when to leave him alone; when to change something in a players' technique and when not to. "As a general rule," he told a reporter in 1962, "I let a man work out his own problems. It's easier to say too much than too little, and ordinarily you won't complicate matters by keeping your mouth shut. Besides, there's such a thing as over-teaching. However, there are times ... when you have to do something."[2]

"Hutch leaves you to work it out," Frank Robinson told a reporter in 1963. "He doesn't bug you." He went on to explain that although Hutchinson chewed the team out, he didn't ride individuals, didn't make personal remarks and didn't interfere in a player's affairs.[3]

"The main thing is he is very understanding," O'Toole told the same reporter. "He leaves you to work out your problems for yourself."[4]

Jim Maloney was a bonus baby who came up to the Reds in 1960 as a

20-year-old with a great arm and little control. Fred treated him with a mixture of patience and discipline. After spending the entire 1960 and 1961 seasons with the Reds, Fred sent him down to San Diego in early 1962 to work out his problems. Initially, as one might expect, Maloney did not welcome the move. "He was mad," Hutch later told a reporter. Fred explained what he wanted Maloney to work on and soon Maloney was back in the majors for good and blossomed in 1963 with 23 wins.

"Sure I was mad," Maloney told the same reporter. Noting that, looking back, it had been for the best, he continued, "I wouldn't want to pitch for another manager. I hope I never pitch for any other manager."[5]

Similarly, when Joey Jay, after back-to-back 20-win seasons, struggled in 1963, he appreciated the fact that Hutch stuck with him. "There's no manager in the majors like him," said the man who had bounced from the rotation to the bullpen and never found a home in Milwaukee. "I know that every five days I go in there, and it's up to me. Before Hutch handled me, I never knew when I'd pitch. You lose confidence. But Hutch has the faith to put you in after five days rest and you really do your best."[6]

"He was a good manager to play for because he would sort of let you go, he wasn't on you all the time if you made a mistake," says Kasko. "You knew you made the mistake. He might walk up to you and say, 'That was a bonehead play wasn't it.' And you'd agree. And he'd say, 'I don't expect to see it again.' He expected the most of the players but it was almost like a self-policing thing. You knew what you had to do and he treated you like an adult."[7]

Players appreciated being treated like adults. Because of his tough exterior, the players knew there were limits and were wary of crossing the line. But Fred rarely held bedchecks or worried about curfew if the team was going well. The players appreciated this as well. Johnny Klippstein recalled an incident with one of Fred's favorite players, Jerry Lynch, for *We Played the Game*: "One night when I had just joined the ballclub, we were sitting and having a drink on an off-day in Cincinnati. It was about 20 minutes before midnight curfew. And in walks Hutchinson, who sits down at another table for a nightcap. I didn't know him at all then. I said, 'Jerry, we've got to get out of here.' He said, 'Hutch doesn't want us to leave.' Jerry wrote him a note that said, 'The Klipper and I know not what we do. We may be a few minutes late.' We sat there for about another hour. Hutch left before we did and never said a word. That's the kind of guy he was. He knew we were just having a few beers and talking and that we weren't out carousing. I really liked Hutchinson."[8]

"He had a good feel for handling people without saying a whole lot," says Sam Ellis. "He wouldn't need to call you in and talk for an hour. He would have done it in a few words. He had a real presence about him."[9]

"Hutch knows just the right approach with each player," Pete Whisenant told *Sports Illustrated* in 1962. "With Pinson, it's 'Vada, don't you think.'

When Coleman gets down on himself you have to remind him what a great hitter he is. You can kid Robinson. Kasko doesn't need anything. Jay has to be handled with kid gloves. Hutch knows how."[10]

"Fred Hutchinson understood every one of our ballplayers," says Johnny Edwards. "He managed on personalities. He knew how to handle people. For instance, I don't think he ever told me 'good game' because I was the type of person who always wanted to be pushed and I would play harder because I was trying to please him. A lot of managers handle everyone the same. But he handled Joey Jay a helluva lot different than Frank Robinson or Pete Rose a lot differently than me. He just had that ability in him to get the most out of his ballplayers."[11]

Jim Brosnan had been a pitcher of modest talent with intermittent success as a starter. He had a bad habit of running out of gas in the middle innings and blowing games. Fred felt he would be much better suited for the bullpen. In those days, every pitcher wanted to be a starter. The bullpen was often seen as a demotion. There were no terms such as "closer" to make late-inning relievers feel special. Saves were not a big statistic. Fred invited Brosnan to his hotel room, offered him several drinks to help him understand the situation better, and they talked things over. "He didn't tell me a thing I hadn't heard before," Brosnan said later. "Other managers had said I couldn't go nine innings and that I ought to relieve, but from Hutch it sounded different. I had always resented the bullpen and it affected my work. But after that session with Hutch, I was a relief pitcher and liking it."[12] Brosnan became one of the best relief pitchers in the league.

"He urged me to think of it as an important job," Brosnan told another reporter. "He urged me to think of it as satisfying him. And that was something a lot of players playing for him wanted to hear."[13]

Jerry Lynch was a good hitter but a poor fielder in the outfield. In 1961, the Reds outfield was crowded. No one was going to take Pinson or Robinson's spot and the Reds also had Gus Bell and Wally Post competing for playing time at the other outfield postion — all proud men with impressive hitting years in the past. It was a delicate situation which could have turned into a serious morale problem for the team. Lynch had complained about wanting to be traded to a team he could start for. Fred explained his role — splitting time in the outfield with the aging Bell and Post and pinch hitting — then proceeded to tell anyone who would listen that Jerry Lynch was the world's best pinch hitter. Lynch may have still wanted to start, but being the best of anything is a distinction. He responded by truly being the world's best pinch hitter for several years. It is unlikely the Reds would have won the pennant without Lynch's numerous late-inning heroics.[14]

"I remember one time I was at the park and my dad was working with Tommy Harper," recalls Rick Hutchinson. "The night before, Tommy had allowed a run to score on a sacrifice fly by catching the fly ball over his non-throwing shoulder, instead of over his throwing shoulder which allows you to get rid of the ball a lot quicker. The runner had barely scored — if he had caught the ball on the right side, the runner would have been out. My father had a coach hit him some balls and Tommy caught each one over the left side, he just wouldn't catch it on the right side. After only a few balls, my father said, 'Okay Tommy, that's good' and stopped. That night driving home, I said to him, "You know, he never did get what you were trying to tell him."

"And he said, 'Oh yes he did. I shouldn't have done that because I'm afraid I showed him up. I made a mistake.' He knew Tommy wasn't going to respond after a few swings of the bat so there was no use in staying out there and making it worse."[15]

"One time, maybe in 1962, we were playing the Dodgers and I'm ahead 3–2 in the ninth and the first batter gets on with an error," says O'Toole. "The next batter breaks his bat and the ball comes floating at me in slow motion and goes right through my legs. I'm really steaming. Hutch comes out and growls, 'Gimme the ball, field your damn position.'"

"I said, 'No way, I'm finishing the game, our bullpen hasn't gotten anybody out in a week.'"

"And he says, 'Gimme the damn ball.'"

"And we argued back and forth calling each other names and cussing at each other. Kasko and Blasingame are right behind me adding up the fines, saying 'That's a hundred dollars, that's two hundred dollars.'"

"Finally I said, 'Here's the damn ball,' and I walk off the field."

"He goes, 'I'll see you after the game.'"

"So I go in the clubhouse and cool down. Brosnan gets them out and we win. Hutch comes in and walks by me and doesn't say a word. I'm starting to feel bad for acting that way and I'm sure I'm going to get hit with a huge fine. So I go into his office and say, 'I'm sorry for blowing my stack out there, but I just didn't want to come out of that game.'"

"He looks at me and says, 'O'Toole, if you weren't like that I wouldn't have you on my team. I'd of done the same thing. Now get the hell out of here.' That's the kind of guy he was."[16]

"One time in the early sixties, we were playing in Philadelphia," recalls Johnny Edwards, "and Callison hit one up in the scoreboard in right-center field and the ball ricocheted off and was still playable. He came all the way around trying for an inside-the-park home run. I went up the first-base line to get the ball and when I came back I had time to get him out but he crashed into me and I dropped the ball. It cost us the game. I was really upset. I normally didn't get like that but I broke the water cooler and a few bats and that sort of thing. Hutch could tell I was upset, he had never seen me that upset. We took the bus into New York that night to play the Mets the next day. When

Fred skeptically looks over some rookie hopefuls (Cincinnati Reds).

we got off the bus, Hutch says to me, 'Come on, you're coming with me.' He took me to dinner to Toots Shor's. He was good friends with Toots. And we sat there and talked. He was just trying to get me to forget it. I had caught a lot of doubleheaders that year and was pretty tired. He really invigorated me. So you can see why I thought he was a great manager."[17]

But Fred didn't always see eye to eye with his players. "In 1960, I decided to get married during the season," says O'Toole. "We planned it for when the team was in Chicago, our home town. There was a big party and we were out late. The next day I get to the park feeling pretty bad. I didn't think I would have to pitch but Hutch goes, 'You're starting.' It was hot and humid and miserable. I was dead just after warming up. The first batter fouls off about 25 pitches and finally I throw one on the black and the umpire, Jocko Conlon, calls it ball four. Conlon was known for his quick temper. I called time out and got right in Conlon's face and called him all sorts of names.

"He took off his mask and said, 'O'Toole, I've heard enough of your bullshit. I know you got married last night and you want to get thrown out.

But if we all have to suffer in this heat, you do too. I'm not throwing you out, now get your ass back out there and pitch.'"[18]

After the game, when asked why he had pitched O'Toole the day after his wedding, Hutch said, "I didn't set O'Toole's wedding date."[19]

The famous temper was always a potential threat. Every former player recalls the time in 1962 when the Reds lost a doubleheader in New York to the hapless Mets. Losing two sloppy games to an expansion team was more than Fred could bear. He stewed in the dugout for a few minutes, then picked up the dugout phone and called into the clubhouse. "Tell everyone to be outta there in ten minutes. I don't want to see any of them sonsabitches when I go in there," he growled. Grown men flew through the clubhouse, changing clothes without showering. Everyone was on the bus in five minutes.[20]

"I had never seen him so mad as that time," adds O'Toole. "We couldn't wait to get out of there."[21]

"There were no showers taken," says Edwards. "The next day when we came in for the game there was no furniture in the clubhouse, only kindling."[22]

"I remember one time after a bad game, we had these big trunks lined up that we carried everything in on the road," says Eddie Kasko. "We had blown the game in the late innings. Hutch came in and he hauled off and kicked that trunk really hard. Of course, the trunk didn't move. He didn't say anything, he just turned and went on back to his office. The next day I was in there early and he was in the whirlpool and his leg was black and blue from the knee to the toe. He acted like nothing had happened."[23]

Earl Lawson recalled the appearance of the clubhouse in Milwaukee after a frustrating loss. It included broken light fixtures and an overturned table of food. "Hutch's uniform lay tattered and torn on the floor in front of his locker stall. He had ripped it from his body."[24]

Pitcher Johnny Klippstein who played for the Reds in 1960 recalled a famous postgame tantrum. "The maddest I ever saw him was when Jim Brosnan pitched against the Cardinals with a 3–1 lead and 2 men on.... He [Hutch] went to the mound to make the change, but Brosnan must have talked him into letting him pitch to Sawatski (the next batter). Hutch hadn't even gotten back to the bench when (Sawatski) hits it into the stands ... and we lost. I walked into the clubhouse behind Hutch.... He goes to kick a bag of baseballs and slips and falls on his butt on the wooden floor. He was swearing like crazy. He got back up and kicked the bag of baseballs and hurt his foot. Then he grabbed the bag of balls and limped into his office and threw it through the glass window.... He wasn't mad at Brosnan. He wasn't mad at anybody but himself."[25]

If Fred could be rough on his team, no one else was allowed to. "Many times in 1959 and 1960 we would lose games in San Francisco late," says

O'Toole. "McCovey would hit one in the bay or something and we would blow close games with our pitching. The next day, Hutch would get on the bus and there would be scratches and cuts and bruises all over his face where he had gotten in a fight over us — some wise guy would say something bad about our pitchers and he would fight them."[26]

His disagreements with umpires were legendary. "When he got upset at the umpires, he was really mad," says Patsy Hutchinson. "He had quite a vocabulary."[27]

"Once Jocko Conlon called a game off because of fog with us behind in the sixth or seventh inning," remembers Johnny Edwards. "I thought Hutch was going to kill him. He chased him all the way to the umpires' locker room. Lucky they got in and locked the door before Hutch got them."[28]

"I remember one time Hutch got into a real argument with an umpire and got thrown out," says Jay Hook. "He came charging into the locker room. My locker was by the door and he said, 'Hey do you have a pair of tennis shoes?'"

"I said, 'yea'"

"He said, 'Can I borrow them?' He was on his way to fight the umpire and didn't want to slip with his spikes. I think he cooled down before he found them, though."[29]

"I remember one time Hutch got in an argument with an umpire and got thrown out," recalls Mel Queen. "He sent Bernie Stowe [the clubhouse attendant] back to the dugout to find out what size tennis shoe the umpire wore. He had Johnny Edwards ask him during the inning. We asked Bernie, 'What's this all about?'

"He said Hutch had boxing gloves and tennis shoes on and he wanted the umpire to get his shoes and gloves on and settle this with boxing gloves. Hutch was standing in the runway with the boxing gloves. Regie Otero and one of the other coaches got him out of there. In the training room there was a punching bag and Bernie said the last three innings Hutch was just wearing that bag out."[30] Same game as Hook remembered? Maybe, maybe not. For the record, Fred, for all his intentions when angry, never laid a finger on an umpire.

"A lot of times after games Hutch would be in the back of the clubhouse working out on that punching bag," says Hook. "You could hear it bouncing back and forth."[31]

It was reported that his temper mellowed in the sixties. Winning teams have a way of doing that. "Since 1960 I don't remember his losing his temper at all, smashing things," O'Toole told a reporter in 1963.[32] Apparently he failed to remember a few of the above episodes. But by all accounts, Fred was overall more mellow in the later years.

"They say I've got a temper, they're still riding that," Fred told the same reporter in 1963. "I've been that way, but only in baseball, I hate to lose. I'm not that way with my family or with my friends. The temper, everybody has that. It's what you get mad at. And I take it out on inanimate objects. My father had a temper. My wife and kids are all redheads."[33]

But Fred could poke fun at his own reputation. In 1961, after a particularly frustrating loss, Giants manager Al Dark tore the top of a finger off when it became caught in a chair he was attempting to hurl across the locker room. Perhaps feeling guilty he hadn't taught his former player better in the fine art of furniture tossing, Hutch said, "You gotta be careful. You haven't been throwing chairs that long. It takes practice."[34]

Baseball people on the after-dinner speaking tour and announcers in the early sixties needed at least two things in their tool kit: a Yogi-ism and a good Hutch story. What was truth and what was myth? It's difficult to say. Yogi Berra once said of the Yogi-ism: "I didn't really say all those things I said." Did he really say that? Or was that a Yogi-ism also? Similarly, some of the Hutch stories were more legend than fact. But, with both, truth isn't really the point. Even if the stories didn't happen, they certainly could have and that's all that is important.

In one story, Fred was playing golf in Florida. He hooked his tee shot into a swamp. His face reddened and he hurled his driver into the swamp behind the ball. After a few seconds, he turned to his caddie and said, "I'm gonna need that club."

"I'm not going after it," the caddie replied. "There's snakes in there."

"All right, I'll get it," Hutch said angrily. "And I'll kill the first damn snake that tries to stop me."

No snake dared.[35]

While playing for the Tigers, Hutch was introduced to the fiancée of fellow Tiger and good friend Birdie Tebbetts, who was also known for his temper and fighting ways. Afterwards, she was so impressed by Fred's courtesy and manners that she said,

The Bear (Cincinnati Reds).

"Birdie, he's such a gentleman. Can't you tone down a little and be more like him?"

The next day, sitting near the Tigers' dugout, she watched Hutch go storming off the field after being knocked out of the box.

"Did you get what he said?" Birdie asked her later, laughing.

"My heavens!" she exclaimed, rolling her eyes. "I never heard such language." She never asked him to be more like Hutch again.[36]

Once while pitching for the Tigers, Hutch was so upset after a loss that he charged out of the clubhouse and walked seven miles to his house. Only after he arrived home did he remember that he had left his car at the ballpark. He also remembered that his wife had come to the game with him and he had left her at the ballpark too.[37]

Once, after a rough game while pitching for the Tigers, Patsy was waiting for him in the car with their two young sons. "Now when Daddy gets into the car," she warned, "don't say a word to him. He just got his ears beaten off."

On the way home, Hutch sat silently fuming in the car until he noticed that the children were staring at him.

"What are you looking at?" he asked.

"Mommy, he's still got his ears," Jack said.[38]

Later, when Fred was manager, Patsy asked him why he didn't take the kids to the park to sit on the bench with him during games. "The ballpark is no place for kids that age," he said. "I don't want them to hear the language the players use around the locker room."

Not long afterwards, the kids came home after a youth game and Patsy asked them how it came out. The older son answered, "We'd have won if this little sonofabitch hadn't dropped a fly ball."

When Patsy told Fred what his son said, he smiled and replied, "See, I told you the ballpark is no place for them."[39]

Managing the Cardinals in 1957, Fred sent Del Ennis to pinch-hit in a tight spot. Ennis took a bad swing at a 2–0 pitch and popped it up. As Ennis walked back to the dugout swinging the bat like a cane, Fred sat with his elbow on his knee, chin cupped in his hand, seething. As Ennis flipped his bat toward the bat rack, Hutch erupted, grabbed the bat and began beating it on the concrete steps. He then threw it on the floor and stomped on it but the thing wouldn't break. Finally, his anger spent, Hutch picked up the bat and handed it back to Ennis. "Here," he said, "keep it. It has good wood in it."[40]

Once when Fred was having a rough day pitching in Boston, Bobby Doerr, an ex–Pacific Coast Leaguer and a good friend of Fred's, came to the plate after Dom DiMaggio had hit one of Fred's fastballs over the left field wall. It was the third Red Sox home run of the game. Usually in that situation, Fred's next pitch would put the batter into the dirt to send a message. Tigers manager O'Neill came to the mound to take Hutch out.

"Geez, Steve," Hutch pleaded, "just let me knock him down once."[41]

Another time after a rough day at the office pitching, Hutch stormed into the house and loudly slammed the door. His young son, playing on the floor, without looking up, said, "Mom, Dad's home and he blew another one."[42]

9

Patsy

THROUGH ALL the travels and trials of baseball life, there was one constant Fred could always count on: his wife Patsy. Attractive and outgoing, she was the perfect social compliment for the reticent Fred. She enjoyed the socialization with other players and coaches and their wives.

As a young wife, Patsy had sweated through Fred's playing career — good times and bad. It was not always easy to be a faithful fan of a struggling pitcher. "I used to spend a lot of time pushing the two boys around the neighborhood in Detroit in a baby buggy when he pitched," Patsy says. "I would get so nervous listening to him pitch. You could walk around the neighborhood and hear the whole game because everyone had their radios on. The announcer would say, 'Here comes a slow pitch,' then, 'Here comes a slower pitch.' It was very nerve-wracking."[1]

"If the [team] lost, mom would tell me, 'Don't mess with your father, go out and play.'" Rick later said.[2]

"It's true that he didn't want the kids to come to the ballpark and sit on the bench because he didn't want them to hear the swear words. They would roll their eyes and look at me — you could hear him all over the field, you didn't have to be on the bench."[3]

Their home on Anna Maria Island was the getaway, the permanent base for raising the family. "I think the people in Seattle resented me because I took him away to Florida," she says. "Hoot Evers was an outfielder with Detroit when Fred was pitching. He was probably Fred's best friend on the team. He and Nancy, his wife, moved to Bradenton, Florida, where her parents lived, then talked us into moving down there. Our kids really loved the beach so we built a house on Anna Maria Island. We moved there in 1949. It was very undeveloped then. You had to cross a rickety old wooden bridge to get to it."[4] In the fifties, the bay side of the island was largely wilderness, populated by snakes, mosquitoes and more than a few baseball players. Since their spring training site was across the bridge in Bradenton, many Braves had winter cottages on the island. Fred's good friend and catcher from the Tigers, Birdie Tebbetts, lived nearby in Bradenton.

"Anna Maria Island was special," says Rick, "we all loved it. It was basically a tropical paradise. As kids, we especially loved boating. We would go out with our friends and spend all day on the boat. Back then, there were fish everywhere. My father would go out on the boat with us, but his real passion was golfing."[5]

"Back then, the island was beautiful," says Jack Hutchinson. "It was unspoiled, wild, a lot of natural beauty. Our house was maybe a hundred yards from the beach. There was no television there until the mid to late fifties and even then it was maybe one station on for about three hours; but that was probably a blessing. We didn't miss it."[6]

"The kids loved it there — they went out on their boat and went all over the Bay," says Patsy. "In the off-season, Fred played golf as much as he could. After the kids got older I played about three days a week. We were both avid golfers." When asked if she ever beat Fred, she replies on cue: "I wouldn't dare."

"But we were good playing together in couples tournaments," she continues. "He would get me to the green and I would take it from there. I was a devil around the green."[7]

The kids attended the small school on the island and played youth baseball on the field their father helped build. In the late fifties, Fred and Patsy organized an All-Star fundraiser baseball game in Bradenton to benefit the Anna Maria Island Playground Society which helped build the baseball field and supported the Anna Maria Island Community Center. The game was attended by such luminaries as Paul Waner, Edd Roush, Heinie Groh, Early Wynn and Ewell Blackwell. Grateful islanders named the field after Fred.[8]

"Everyone knew each other on the island," says Rick. "My father was good friends with the local pharmacist and the grocer who ran the IGA. We would have a lot of cookouts and all these major league players would come, guys like Warren Spahn, Early Wynn, Eddie Mathews, Birdie Tibbetts and Earl Torgeson."[9]

Earl Torgeson was a behemoth American League first baseman in the forties and fifties who owned a house on the island. Also a Washington native, he became good friends with the Hutchinsons. His daughter later recalled her father and Fred Hutchinson frequently digging barbeque pits for parties.[10]

Joe Hutchinson, the youngest of the crew, recalled that everybody on the island knew the Hutchinsons. The get-togethers with celebrities from the sports and entertainment world were especially memorable. "We used to have parties at our house," he told a reporter in 2008. "There were people who would show up like you wouldn't imagine."[11]

While in retrospect it was exciting for the kids to see so many famous people, at the time they just thought that was the way things were and did not make a big deal of it. "When you're that young you don't think it is anything special," says Jack. "You become accustomed to it."[12]

But having a father who was a pro baseball player did give the kids a reason to feel special. "When I was little, I was always proud of my father," says Rick Hutchinson. "He was a big guy and all the neighborhood kids thought he was special because he made a living playing baseball. We kind of took it for granted because we didn't know any different, but we were all kind of in awe of my father and thought he could do anything."[13]

The family attended church in Bradenton and Fred even taught Sunday School — a sight which would have amused National League umpires. "Fred taught Sunday School at church one year," says Patsy. "There was a class of boys no one could do anything with, so he taught it. I think he taught mostly baseball though, but the kids really enjoyed his class."[14]

Once time for baseball arrived, the family would be separated. "When Fred would go over to spring training, we would go over on the weekends. Then when the season started, I'd stay until the kids finished school, then we would pack up and go to whatever city Fred was in, then come back to get the kids in school in the fall."[15]

In Cincinnati, a lot of the baseball families lived in an area called Swifton Village for the summer. It was a quasi-compound with houses which resembled Quonset huts. "The kids had a wonderful time there because there were a lot of other kids their age to play with during the day," Patsy remembers. "There was a big pool near there. The kids of all the players spent a lot of time together. Then we would go to the games at night. My daughter had taken Spanish in high school and she would take Regie Otero's wife and a couple of others down to the ten-cent store and help them buy things because they didn't know how to speak that much English."

"We would get together a lot with the coaches and their wives, especially Dick and Dottie Sisler, and play cards. We had a lot of friends in baseball. I hated when Joe Garagiola would come to town to do games. He and Fred were good friends. He would keep Fred out late talking about baseball. I never had to worry about other women keeping Fred out late, only Joe Garagiola."[16]

When the two older boys became old enough for serious baseball, they stayed in Florida for the summers to play on an American Legion team there. "Joey, our youngest son, had the run of Crosley Field. He got to know all the ladies that worked at the concession stands."[17]

The Hutchinson kids were active in school. Patti was captain of the cheerleaders at Manatee High School. The boys, like their father, were very good athletes. Rick and Jack both starred in baseball and football in high school. In football, Rick was an end and caught eight touchdown passes in 1961 and was named honorable mention all-state. He missed one game that season, however. That was when he flew with Jack to Cincinnati for the last three games of the World Series. Jack helped the high school team to a state championship in baseball in 1963. Rick and Jack played together on the Bradenton American Legion baseball team and led them to the final round of the state tournament several times. Jack was good enough to be signed to a minor league contract with the Reds for 1964.

Because he was busy with the major league teams in the summer, Fred didn't have time for a lot of hands-on help with the boys' baseball careers. "He sometimes offers suggestions, but usually works on the presumption that if we really want to become good baseball players, we'll pick up enough talent on our own," Jack told reporters in 1962.[18]

"My father never insisted that I become a ballplayer," Jack later said as a minor league player. "It was entirely my own idea. He didn't care what I did as long as I was happy."[19]

"But when you have a famous father you do pay a price," says Rick. "We didn't get to see him as often as I would have liked and we had to move around quite a bit, especially early on."[20]

All the work behind the scenes was very hard—for Patsy. "Unlike today where the economics have changed and players can have people do things for them, back then all the work of getting the house in order at the end of the spring, packing up the kids and moving them around and taking care of things fell to the women," says Jack. "And when the team was on the road, it was the mother's job to be the sole entertainment for the kids. So there was a lot of work for her to do and I'm sure it wasn't easy."[21]

"My mother was a very strong person," says Rick. "It's not easy getting four kids packed up and moved around during the season. Of course, my father couldn't help because he was playing so she had to do a lot by herself. And, you know, kids are going to fight and complain sometimes. We didn't appreciate it as much as we should have at the time. But she never really complained. She did it all."[22]

10

Bill

WHILE FRED was climbing the ladder of success in baseball, his older brother Bill was similarly climbing the ladder of success in the medical field. After graduating from McGill University Medical School in 1935, Bill performed an internship and surgical residency at Baltimore's Union Memorial Hospital. With his bride, Charlotte, he returned to Seattle to begin practice in 1940. They would eventually have five children: Charlotte, William Jr., John, Stuart and Mary.

Although slightly smaller with hair that was not as black, Bill shared a strong family resemblance with Fred. He also shared the charisma and way with people. "They both always seemed to have time for other people," says Charlotte. "My father was very dedicated to his profession and his patients. That's really where the love of his life lay. He was very compassionate and understanding and always available to his patients."[1]

"Bill really was a good guy," says Patsy. "He had a short fuse, like all Hutchinsons, but he was an achiever. Hard work and long hours were nothing for him. This was what you're supposed to do."[2] Like Fred, Bill had this work ethic firmly ingrained from their childhood watching their father.

"I admired my uncle, Dr. Bill Hutchinson," says Rick Hutchinson. "Uncle Bill was probably the person in my life I most admired. He was a great person."[3]

Bill was recognized for his compassion, hard work and benevolence. Former Seattle baseball player and longtime resident Edo Vanni called Bill a saint for the good will he spread. "He would help all these old-timers who couldn't pay for services," Vanni later told a reporter for the *Seattle Times*.[4]

Bill became very involved and well known in the community. He retained his love for baseball and coached numerous Little League, Babe Ruth and Connie Mack league teams and promoted youth baseball in the area. "His real love other than his profession was baseball," says Charlotte. "In the summers, there was a game every night."[5]

Bill and Fred remained close through the years. "His brother Fred was so important in his life," says Charlotte. "He was his little brother. They were extremely close. There was a great deal of love between those two brothers. They were always in communication." Bill had watched proudly as his younger brother achieved success in the baseball world and closely followed his career. "Dad tried to listen to every single baseball game Fred managed," says Charlotte. "That was the only reason we got a TV. We were the last kids in the neighborhood to get a TV. We were finally able to convince Dad that he could watch Fred's games if we had one."[6]

The admiration was mutual. Fred later wrote of Bill, "We've a lot in common. He likes baseball and I like medicine. If he hadn't been dedicated to his profession and I to mine, our positions might have been reversed."[7]

As their children grew, the two families stayed close and enjoyed being together. "When all the family got together it was crazy," said Bill's son William, Jr. of the crowd which would eventually include nine children. "Somebody was always fighting about this or that or wanted a different toy."[8]

Charlotte recalls an incident at Thanksgiving in which she, as a four- or five-year-old, argued over a toy car with the other kids and eventually ripped it out of her brother's hand, taking a large chunk of his finger with it. "Dad had to take him in and sew up the finger. We all had to wait around for Thanksgiving dinner. The adults weren't too happy about that."[9]

Minor mishaps aside, they created many fond memories together. "It was fun because Bill and Fred had great senses of humor," said Charlotte.[10]

When Fred managed in Seattle in 1955 and 1959, the two families melted into one. "Our families just hung out together all the time," says Charlotte.[11] Fred's two oldest sons, Rick and Jack, played on the same baseball team with Bill's sons—with Uncle Bill as the coach.

"There was a Hutchinson at almost every position," laughs Patsy.[12]

The two summers were an endless blur of dogs, kids, boating on Lake Washington, barbecues and baseball games—all together. "It was fantastic," says Charlotte.[13]

The oldest of Bill's children, Charlotte, was enamored with her famous uncle. "I just adored Fred," she says. "He was so much fun. He was just such a gorgeous big man. When I was in high school, he'd come over sometimes and when dates would come to the door he would answer it. The kids would stand there with their mouth open."[14] There was no doubt they would be on their best behavior for the evening.

"He was amazing," she said, speaking of Fred's popularity in Seattle. "We would go out to dinner and people would hover around him. Fred had time for everyone. It used to drive me crazy, but he was always chitchatting."[15]

"Fred was so good to me," Charlotte continues. "He used to pick me up if I spent the night with a friend and he was staying with Mom and Dad. He would just get in one of the cars and come pick me up. What kind of a well-known sports figure would do that? It meant a lot to me. He was such a fun-loving guy. He was always available and loved his fans and always had time for them." Charlotte remembers Fred driving her and friends in the car singing loudly along with the radio: "the bird's the word, bird, bird, bird"[16]— a scene which surely would have amazed National League players and umpires.

With his Hutchinson work ethic and superb surgical skills, Bill became one of the more prominent surgeons in the region. He operated on many cancer patients and, according to friends, was affected deeply by the disease. He considered cancer to be the medical scourge of humanity. He became frustrated by the lack of success experienced by all doctors of the era. At the time, radiation and chemotherapy were primitive and often not very effective. The only treatment for most cancers was surgical excision and this was all too often not enough to help. Bill became convinced that extensive research was needed for the prevention and treatment of cancer. This became a consuming passion and the driving force for his career.

By the mid–1950s, Bill began voicing his dream of a center — a nationally known and respected independent center for the research of cancer. He realized that it would take influence and money to achieve this dream. He began the tireless work which would continue for years to help this dream come true. He butted heads with politicians, other doctors and university officials. He schmoozed and glad-handed wealthy benefactors in the name of his cause. The well-known Hutchinson family name helped the projected center gain local and regional support.

One of Bill's chief allies was Warren Magnuson, a powerful Washington senator. With his help, the dream began to take shape and appear possible. In 1956, with additional help from the U.S. Department of Public Health, Bill founded the Pacific Northwest Research Foundation which had the initial goals of providing funds for basic and clinical research devoted to improving patient care. The foundation, which provided for heart surgery and endocrine diseases such as diabetes as well as cancer, was a start; however, Bill would not turn his sights from the ultimate goal: a center devoted solely to the treatment and research of cancer.

Bill was adamant that money should be committed to "one good cancer center ... and not a lot of fragments."[17] He was able to wear down resistance by peers who believed the startup cost was prohibitive and that sustaining funds might not be available. Also, he fought those who thought the University of Washington Medical School should run the center. Bill wanted to avoid university politics which might take away from the focus of the center. By 1963, Bill had forged the political alliances and procured enough funding from federal grants and private sources so that his dream of an independent cancer center was within sight. The opening was hoped for within two years.

Fred Hutchinson arrived at Bill's house in Seattle shortly after Christmas in 1963 and placed himself under his brother's care. Christmas decorations still hung in the house, however the mood was anything but festive for Bill who had not liked what he heard on the phone when Fred initially called him. "My father was very concerned when Fred was coming up," says Charlotte.[18] He had heard these symptoms too many times before and knew what they meant.

While Fred later admitted that the fact that Bill told him to immediately fly up to Seattle made him realize the concern, he tried to downplay the whole thing. In fact, the night before he left Florida, he and Patsy had hosted about 80 people at their house for a Christmas party with Fred acting like nothing was wrong for most of the guests. The only ones he shared his plans to go to Seattle with were close friends Hoot Evers and Birdie Tebbetts.[19]

While at the airport in Florida on his way to Seattle, Fred spotted Jimmy Mann, a writer for the *St. Petersburg Times* who was a friend and golfing buddy. Fred intentionally shouldered into Mann, almost knocking him down. "Get your clubs, let's play golf," Fred laughed. Fred bought Mann a cup of coffee as they awaited their flights. Mann asked Fred about a recent hole-in-one he had made.

"I hit a driver on the hole," Fred happily told him. "I think the last roll carried it into the hole."

Mann asked Fred where he was headed. "West Coast," was the only answer. The reporter's instinct got the best of him and he asked if Fred was working on a possible trade or team business, which Fred casually denied. Mann asked, "How long are you going to be there?"

"Dunno, but when I get back I'm headed to Europe for the Air Force. Sort of a goodwill trip." Fred happily wished Mann goodbye and boarded his flight.[20] Mann would not discover the real reason for Fred's trip until the rest of the country found out a week later.

Fred stayed at Bill's house, trash talking with Bill's kids over the pool table in between tests at the hospital. Bill directed the testing. Fred was examined and x-rayed, then examined and x-rayed some more. A biopsy was scheduled for New Year's Eve. Fred later recalled that when he came out of the anesthetic, he asked his brother, "How does it look?"

"Not good," was the answer.

"Have I got it?" Fred asked.

"Yeah, you've got it," said Bill.

"Well, what do we do now? How do we fight this thing?"

"We don't know yet," replied Bill. "All we have is a preliminary report. We'll have to study the situation further before deciding."

That evening, Fred got a phone call from Patsy, who told him, "I'm flying out there tomorrow."

"What for?" Fred replied. "I'll only be here a few weeks. Why disrupt the whole family?"

"The kids are following me out in a couple of days," Patsy said. "They can go to school there."[21]

Bill had called Patsy and told her he thought she should be there and Patsy made plans for Jack to follow with the two younger children in a few days. Fred later admitted he was concerned that first night. Not knowing the full extent of the disease yet, not entirely knowing the prognosis, not knowing how long they would be in Seattle — there were a lot of unknowns, but if Bill had felt that Patsy and the kids needed to come to Seattle then it must be serious. Very serious.

"He [Bill] would tell me everything he thought I should know without waiting for me to ask," Fred later wrote. "I wondered vaguely if this was the ball game.... I'd better make sure my affairs were in good order, I thought, as I lay in bed that night. I didn't want Patsy to have any worries. With four children to think about, this would be a bad time for me to leave.... I tried not to think too much about myself, but I guess I couldn't help it. There really wasn't anything I could do except follow doctors' orders and pray to God that everything would come out all right. If it didn't, it didn't, I'd have to face it, and I'd like to think I was ready to.... You're never sure about anything like that. We all want to face things with courage and dignity, but who can know for certain that we will? People you think might calmly accept inevitable disaster sometimes crack up when they're face to face with it. And people you think might blow apart keep their heads right up to the very end. How could I know what I would do? I couldn't until the chips were actually down, until death was actually imminent?"

"What was the sense of worrying about it?" Fred continued. "If I was going to die of course, worrying wouldn't save me. And if I was going to live, worrying was a waste of time. One thing was sure. I wasn't going to worry myself to death.... I prayed. I always have prayed. I'm not terribly religious, but I have a strong faith in God. I figured from the beginning He would do what He thought best. I think that first night after Bill told me I had cancer was the only one in which I thought much about it.... I never lost any sleep over it."[22]

When Patsy arrived, Bill sat down with her and Fred at his house and delivered the news. It was not good. The additional tests had shown the cancer was in Fred's lungs, was at an advanced stage and had already spread. In 1963, the prognosis for this condition was uniformly, invariably fatal. Fred might have one year to live at the most. The only thing medicine at that time could offer was radiation treatment, which might shrink the tumors temporarily, and pain control.

Fred Hutchinson, 44 years old, a man near the top of a profession he loved — husband, father, ex-baseball player, major league manager and legend — was now a man who knew exactly what his fate would be. Exactly? Bill knew. Bill had spent 25 years caring for too many patients like this. He knew exactly what the course would be. "My father told him, 'Give it to me straight, I want to know, and he told him,'" says Rick.[23]

One can only imagine the anguish Bill faced upon discovering his brother's condition and then having to tell him and his wife the prognosis. It must have taken extraordinary strength to be able to tell his brother the entire truth. The temptation for a lesser man would be to somehow sugarcoat the news, make it not seem so bad, to put off the painful truth until later. At the time, some in the medical community favored keeping patients in the dark so as not to discourage them, telling them only good news. Of course, that was not the Hutchinson way. "Bill laid it right on the line," says Patsy. "He didn't hold anything back. Bill balled like a baby."[24]

"He looked as if he wanted to change places with me on the spot," Fred wrote of Bill breaking the news. "He had spent his life cutting tumors out of people, and now here was his own brother with one. It shook him up pretty good."[25]

Fred Hutchinson knew he had probably less than a year to live. He knew the end would most likely be painful. And there was nothing either he or his brother could do about it. What would most people do in that situation? Hide the truth from employers and the public? Sink into depression and give up? Go home, rest and wait for the inevitable? Take off around the world with a "bucket list?" Psychologists say that most would at least go through the steps of denial, anger, bargaining, depression and acceptance.

There had been speculation among acquaintances and in the press about Fred's health. It was impossible to keep secret the presence of such a celebrated city figure as Fred Hutchinson in a local hospital for extended testing. Bill told Fred, "People are asking questions. I got a long distance call from Si Burick of the *Dayton Daily News* today. He wanted to know if it was true you have cancer. I'm sure others will be calling too."[26]

Never one to dodge the truth, Fred decided to call a press conference to set the record straight. "Let's tell them," Fred told Bill. "What the hell, it's not syphilis or anything to be ashamed of.... We'll have one press conference and tell them as much as we can."[27] Fred wanted to enjoy the New Year first with family. The press conference was set for January 2.

11

January: "It's Cancer"

THE PRESS CONFERENCE was scheduled for January 2, 1964 in the Seattle office of Fred's old friend and current Pacific Coast League President Dewey Soriano. Soriano made all the arrangements. Newspapers, wire services, television and radio were all represented at the conference. Charlotte Hutchinson, after graduating college, had recently taken a job in Soriano's office, working for the PCL. She would have a front-row view of her uncle as he dealt with the news. Fred also called his boss in Cincinnati and informed him. Back east, Bill DeWitt issued a press release in Cincinnati before Fred's press conference on January 2. The story became national news.

The headline in the January 3 edition of the *Cincinnati Post* told Cincinnati residents the bad news: "Hutch Sick, Out for 2 Months."[1] The statement from the club read: "It was announced by William O. DeWitt, president of the Cincinnati Reds, that with deepest regret the recent illness of Fred Hutchinson, manager of the Reds, has been diagnosed as a malignancy. This information was revealed to DeWitt by Dr. William Hutchinson of Seattle, Washington, Fred's brother, under whose supervision the tests were made. Dr. Hutchinson advises that Fred will remain in Seattle for the next two months, taking treatments for his illness, which we hope will prepare him for the spring training period and the 1964 season."[2] DeWitt told reporters that no changes would be made as a result of the news. "We don't know how it will come out, but we are going ahead with spring training plans on the premise he will be there. Of course, you never know how these things will come out."[3] It was noted by reporters that DeWitt tiptoed around the truth a bit, stating that Fred had been diagnosed with a "malignancy."

In Seattle, dressed in a coat and tie, sporting a Florida tan and appearing slightly nervous, Fred stepped into the room crowded with reporters and photographers. Bill Hutchinson accompanied him. Fred was much more informative at his press conference than DeWitt. And more direct. "It's cancer," he said.[4] He proceeded to tell reporters the story of when he first noticed the problem, how it was diagnosed and what the doctors had told him. He offered one of his crooked grins and made a few lighthearted remarks, but he did not sidestep the truth. He was completely open and honest — the Hutchinson way.

Reporters noted that Fred spoke dispassionately while discussing his condition. "Agonizingly casual about the announcement," wrote Arthur Daley of the *New York Times.*[5]

"Only perspiration beading the brow beneath black hair beginning to tinge with gray betrayed inner apprehension as Hutch, with a thin grin, agreed it was the toughest press conference he ever faced," *Seattle Times* sports editor Georg Meyers wrote.[6]

Fred admitted the diagnosis shocked him. "It's like having a rug jerked out from under you. I've been feeling fine. My weight is up — about 220. But I felt around my neck a little soreness and swelling. The doctors thought at first it might be an infected lymph gland." He explained that the biopsy, performed New Year's Eve, revealed the cancer. "Brother Bill told me the biopsy showed malignant tissue in the right lung, apparently in the early stages but very active.... I had had no previous knowledge of what to expect. You're feeling fine, then the doctors tell you, 'You have a malignancy.... You don't know what to think.'"[7]

"But the doctors are optimistic — at least, they say they are," he continued. "The doctors said it's a very active cancer of the right lung, but they think they caught it early." Treatments were scheduled to start in two days at the Swedish Hospital Tumor Institute in Seattle.

Fred explained that his family had joined him in Seattle except for Rick who was at Florida State. Fred also mentioned that he had cancelled two planned trips. He had been scheduled to visit Venezuela to look at Reds prospects playing in the winter league along with the ten-day trip to Europe for the Air Force.

Fred said that he was planning on being back in time for spring training. "After about two months of treatment, through late February, I will be able to go to spring training ... at least the doctors have given me no reason to think I can't." He concluded by saying he had not let "this thing get to me. There's nothing I can do.... But you know you're not alone in it. Lots of others have gone through it. I think I can too."[8]

Reporters across the country were impressed and moved by his straightforward approach, but as one wrote, "You wouldn't expect anything else from Hutch."[9]

New York Herald Tribune syndicated columnist Red Smith, the preeminent baseball writer of the generation, wrote, "It was characteristic of this blunt, honest man that when he got word, he made the plain, hard fact public, mincing no euphemisms. It also was typical that the announcement would be accompanied by one of his rare grins."[10]

John Carmichael, sports editor of the *Chicago Daily News,* wrote, "It's always hard to believe that a big man like Hutchinson, with the strong, shambling gait of a bear from which he derives his nickname, can be leveled by something he can't see.... Hutchinson is somebody you don't hear too much of anymore: A man's man ... his voice is deep, his laugh rumbles and he has the quiet confidence of a self-made man."[11]

In *The Quality of Courage,* Mickey Mantle and Robert Creamer stated, "Reporters were politely trying to find out more information. Instead of hiding, or staying out of sight ... and letting his brother or some other doctor talk to the press, Fred Hutchinson talked to the reporters himself. He told them what the doctors had told him, what treatment he would undergo, what his chances were."[12]

In 1964, cancer was a dreaded word. People avoided it. In polite company, ladies whispered the word when talking about the afflicted. Very few public personalities had openly discussed their cancer with the world. Fred had no problem with this.

Fred later wrote, "They tell me it's unusual for anyone in the public eye to announce he has cancer.... What else could I do? I was in a hospital in my old home town, going back and forth every day, constantly running into people I knew.... That made me a hero to say what I had? I think it's senseless to go around whispering that a guy has cancer.... What's wrong with letting it be known that Fred Hutchinson has cancer?"[13]

The public appearance and attitude was consistent with that seen privately by his family. There were no tears from Fred Hutchinson, publicly or privately. He would continue to not let "this thing" slow him down. For the family, the news was met with shock and disbelief. "There had been no warning — it just came out of the blue," remembers Jack Hutchinson. "I don't ever remember my father being in bed sick a single day. I just always thought of him as being so strong. So it was certainly a surprise. Initially there was some confusion because they said there was a chance of remission and things like that, but my Uncle Bill told me right out that it didn't look good, that we should prepare for the worst. But when you're 18 you don't really comprehend that at first."[14]

"It certainly came out of nowhere," recalls Rick Hutchinson. "Initially, I thought 'So it's cancer, he'll beat it.' My father had basically lived a charmed life. He always came back no matter what happened. We thought he could do anything. I'm reminded of a time when we were very little and he took us to the circus. They had a sideshow with a really huge wrestler and they asked the audience if anyone thought they could stay in the ring with the guy for five minutes. And all us kids pointed to my father and shouted, 'He can, he can.' And he was going 'Shut up, shut up.' But we just thought he could conquer anything or anybody. He was just that kind of person. So we didn't think something like cancer could stop him."[15]

Charlotte echoes the sentiment, "We all thought 'He's such a tough guy, he can beat anything.'"[16]

Reporters shared a similar view. Jimmy Mann of the *St. Petersburg Times* wrote: "If you really know Fred Hutchinson, then your impression has to coincide with mine—cancer has overmatched itself."[17]

Fred didn't discuss the issue unless asked, even with his family. He just talked about getting back to spring training and working with the team. "I never heard him say one word complaining," says Rick.[18]

"He didn't really talk about it much," says Patsy. "He never complained. I never heard any 'Why me?' or anything like that. He just didn't say anything. He was that kind of person, though. If that's the way it was, that's the way it was and he would take it."[19]

The news was met with anguish and tears by his loved ones, but Fred was determined to remain a rock. "When Bill told us the extent of the condition, he told us everything," Patsy continues. "He knew what the course would be. He said it was inoperable. He laid it right on the line. He couldn't help crying. After we left, Fred kind of smiled and said, 'My brother's a big baby.'"[20]

One day, early in his treatment, Fred was being driven home from the hospital by Charlotte. Considering the whole situation and overcome with emotion, Charlotte started crying. Fred put a huge hand on her shoulder and, very softly, told her, "It's okay Charlotte, I can handle it. I'll be allright."[21]

"He just felt that whatever happens is what's going to happen. You just deal with it," says Charlotte. "I wasn't taking that very well. But it was strange him consoling me — it should have been the other way around."[22]

Another time Fred told Charlotte, "I've lived a great life and I've never left anything undone. I've got no regrets."[23]

Fred had smoked, sometimes more than two packs a day, since his days in the Navy. Undoubtedly this was a factor in his disease. But he could hardly be blamed at the time. Look at old movies from the forties and fifties. Everybody smoked. In the military during World War II, the rate of smoking was more than 90 percent. Most major leaguers smoked. Joe DiMaggio had a standing order for a rookie or clubhouse boy to light up a Chesterfield in the dugout when the opposing team was batting with two outs so it would be ready for him when he jogged in from the outfield.[24] Everybody smoked. There was no conclusive medical evidence condemning smoking. Who knew it was that bad for you? Bill Hutchinson knew.

"I can clearly recall when I was little, being at a cookout at my Uncle

Bill's house and my father was smoking and Uncle Bill saying, 'Fred, you better get rid of those things. They're going to kill you,'" says Rick Hutchinson. "He said, 'I've got too many patients not to know that there's a very definite connection between smoking and lung cancer.' And my dad would just laugh."[25]

Medical literature reports in the fifties had suggested a link between smoking and various diseases. In 1957, the Surgeon General had declared that evidence pointed to a causal relationship between smoking and lung cancer. These warnings had been largely ignored by the public which didn't feel alarmed by words such as "suggested" and "causal relationship." Fred, like the rest of the country, would not find out with certainty until the Surgeon General released the landmark report on smoking. Ironically, it was released mere days after Fred's press conference. On January 11, 1964, the President's Special Commission presented the findings to the public. *Smoking and Health: Report of the Advisory Committee to the Surgeon General* reported unequivocal evidence for the link between smoking and lung cancer, along with emphysema and heart disease.[26] The news hit the country like a bombshell. A Gallup survey in 1958 showed that only 44 percent of Americans believed smoking caused cancer. This number rose to 78 percent by 1968. Congress would decree that all cigarette packages in the United States carry a health warning in 1965, and cigarette advertising was banned from television and radio in 1970. Unfortunately for Fred Hutchinson, the news came too late.

Fred continued to put on an optimistic public face in early 1964. On January 9, he told Gil Lyons of the *Seattle Times* that he was looking forward to many more seasons as a major league manager. "The doctors have been much more optimistic the past few days, since they've been taking tests," he said. He went on to explain how much he loved managing. "Some day I'll be fired, I know that," he said. "But I've hung in there for years and maybe will stay quite a bit longer.... It's a good living, it's been good to me."[27]

Bill told reporters, "It will be a month before we know what's happening." The plan was for daily treatments for a week, followed by an observation period and further treatment. The treatment was described as the "only one of its type available in the United States. A 2-million volt X-ray from a Van De Graf generator applied in a pressurized chamber."[28]

"I didn't care what the doctors planned as long as they'd get it done fast enough for me to return to Florida in reasonably good shape by March 1," Fred later wrote. To get back to his job of managing the Cincinnati Reds— that seemed to be the thing pulling Fred through this. "It never occurred to me, then or at any other time, that I wouldn't (make it back). He felt that the team looked like it could be a pennant contender. "If we could answer third base and relief pitching, it might be 1961 all over again.... This could be the Reds' year again. I didn't intend to miss it."[29]

"So we ended up being in Seattle much longer than we originally expected," says Patsy.[30] Two months. It was a long two months of treatment and tests. After staying with Bill the first few weeks, Fred and Patsy moved with the kids into the house of a friend who was staying in Mexico to spend the duration of their time in Seattle.

As Bill told reporters, the super-voltage radiation in the hyperbaric chamber was a relatively new treatment method. The patient was sealed into a large, round, metal chamber, similar to an altitude chamber. Fred's description of the treatment sounded like something out of the space program.

"You lie on a table, and they slide you in like a side of beef, then slam the door," wrote Fred. "The top is plastic or some such thing, so you and people outside can see each other. There's a built-in communications system. If you're inside, all you have to do is talk. If you're outside, you have to wear earphones and talk into a mouth piece. Once they get you into this thing, they pour on the pressure. They give you 30 pounds of oxygen so that you can absorb two million volts of radiation. This shortens the length of the treatment and practically eliminates the risk of hurting healthy tissue." The treatments usually lasted about 30 minutes—about ten minutes to get the patient "down," seven minutes of radiation and ten minutes to come "back up." The radiologist in charge of the treatment explained to Fred that it was not an easy thing to go through. There was a danger of getting the bends if the patient was taken out of the hyperbaric chamber too fast. Many patients could not take the psychological stress of the treatment. Patients who were apprehensive or prone to claustrophobia did not do well. Most patients experienced pain in their ears from the pressure and got headaches. Some patients got an intense feeling that they were going to burst into small pieces.[31]

The radiologist offered Fred the choice of having an anesthetic to make the treatments easier. After hearing the description of the treatment, Fred was tempted but he asked the radiologist which he preferred. "He said it was much better if I didn't [take the anesthesia]," wrote Fred. "That was enough for me. Why make it tougher for the doctors?... There was no sense throwing blocks at them. I'd go into that chamber conscious." The first treatment was unsettling.

> It was as bad as the doctor said it would be. When I was settled on the metal table I clenched my fists while they slid me in.... The technician kept assuring me that everything was going to be all right. I tried to believe her, but that still didn't keep me from wanting to try to bust out of there once she had slammed the door.... There was a hissing sound, but I didn't feel anything at first. Then my ears began to get tight, the way they sometimes do when you come down fast in an airplane. After that came a nagging little ache which grew worse and worse until I began to wonder if I really was as insensitive to pain as I had always thought. Pretty soon my ears were pounding and my head felt like a lopsided baseball and I wanted to fight the whole damn gadget, technician and all. Every

so often a doctor popped in, picked up the other earphone and talked to me. Patsy was in and out of the room or maybe she was there all the time, but out of my range of vision. She looked as if she thought the whole thing was going to explode.[32]

After reaching the appropriate "depth" the radiation was applied and the process repeated as he "came up." After finishing, Fred felt a complete freedom upon exiting the chamber. "They couldn't get me off that table fast enough.... The 40 minutes I had been in that chamber seemed a lifetime. When I looked at the chamber from the outside I wondered how I had stayed in so long. Worse, I wondered how I could make myself go back in there the next day." But Fred did go back in the next day, and the next — he had treatments six days in a row and then, after a three-week layoff, six more days in a row. He managed to take it a little better each day. "I had to give myself another pep talk in the morning [of the second treatment]," he wrote. "And this time I was really mad. It was ridiculous to be such a baby. That thing wasn't as bad as all that.... What the hell was the matter with me?"[33] The second set of treatments hardly seemed like an inconvenience. The treatment left a big scar on the upper right side of his chest where the deep radiation was concentrated. It also left him with a headache which persisted for months. After the treatments were concluded, he remained in Seattle for the doctors to check on his progress.

Doctors were initially optimistic after the treatment. Dr. Orliss Wildermuth, head of the Tumor Institute at Swedish Hospital, told reporters, there was "definite regression of the tumor."

"It is extremely graftifying," he continued. "Normally at this stage of treatment we are happy if the tumor has stopped growing."[34]

Fred was amazed at the outpouring of public sentiment and the number of cards and letters he received wishing him well. Dewey Soriano gave him space in his office to use and Charlotte helped him keep up with the correspondence. "He answered every single card and letter himself," says Charlotte.[35]

"I had no idea it would cause such a fuss," Fred wrote. "I got hundreds of letters from all over the country and they were still rolling in when I returned to Florida. It'll take me all season to acknowledge them. I think it's wonderful that strangers are so thoughtful, but I can't understand it.... A lot of people have cancer, maybe one out of eight. Some victims are pretty prominent, far more than I'll ever be. I'm not a world leader or a movie star or one of the Beatles. I'm just a baseball manager looking for a third baseman and maybe a relief pitcher or two."[36]

Earl Lawson wrote Fred in January offering encouragement and told him he was getting ready to set up some singing engagements in Tampa for spring training. "Just tell me one thing," he wrote, "how's your voice?"

He received an upbeat letter in reply which concluded, "My voice is a little raspy."[37]

But other than the raspy voice, Fred appeared to sail through it all. He finished the treatment and got the official clearance to go to spring training. He was feeling good when he left for Tampa in late February. He was looking forward to guiding the Reds through the season.

12

March: Spring Training

PITCHERS AND CATCHERS reported to the Reds' spring training headquarters at the International Hotel in Tampa on February 29. Manager Fred Hutchinson was there as usual to greet the returning players. He had endured a long month and a half of treatment but he was feeling pretty well. Bill had advised him to take things slowly and get plenty of rest and he planned to follow the advice as much as possible. As Fred climbed into his uniform in the clubhouse before the first day of spring training, it would have been hard not to feel a few butterflies and also a great sense of accomplishment. How many major league training camps had he attended as a player and manager? Almost twenty. Enough that it became routine — anticipated and enjoyed certainly — but not unique or special anymore. This was special, though. This was unique. He had never worked so hard, battled so much uncertainty just to make it to spring training. But he had made it. And he felt good. As he stepped into the sunshine for the start of exercises he told the gathered reporters: "Well, I made it here in time just as I said I would."[1]

Fred explained that he had actually arrived in Tampa with a week to spare, spending a lot of time on the golf course while waiting for his players to arrive. "I feel fine, but my golf has been lousy," he joked. When questioned about his treatment, he stated that he had finished the radiological treatments for the present and was awaiting his periodic checkups. "I had to hang around Seattle for two weeks for the X-ray pictures to tell if this damn thing is progressing or regressing. Fortunately it has been regressing." The reporters noted mild hoarseness in his voice, but otherwise he appeared fit. "I can't shout anymore," he added with a crooked grin, "and that should please a lot of people."

"I've quit smoking and this silly thing had nothing to do with it," he continued, referring to the cancer as if it were a mild annoyance like a common

93

cold. "About the middle of December — that was before I even knew I had this—I decided that I was smoking too much. I smoked at least two packs a day and on occasions like a baseball meeting where you sit up half the night, I probably smoked three or four packs. It was getting so ridiculous that I just quit cold."[2]

Earlier, when asked what his brother had told him before leaving Seattle, Fred replied, "Nothing he hadn't been telling me for a long, long time. He is one of those fellows who doesn't smoke or drink and he has preached it to me. This time I'll listen."[3]

The reporters were struck by the carefree, detached way in which Fred discussed his cancer. "If he is alarmed, he hides it well," wrote Arthur Daley of the *New York Times*.[4]

The headline in the sports section of the *Dayton Journal-Herald* on March 2, 1964, proclaimed the good news to Ohio fans: "Hutch Keeps Promise, On Hand For Training."[5]

Most of the returning players had no idea anything was wrong with their manager. A few had seen announcements in the paper in early January but most had not. And none of them had grasped the severity of the situation. Although they all grumbled as they went through calisthenics and conditioning, most players truly enjoyed spring training. It felt good to be out in the sunshine of Florida, away from the cold and gloom of places like Ohio, West Virginia and Wisconsin. Most of the married players brought their wives and rented cottages near the beach. Before the preseason games started, there was quite a bit of free time. It was fun to catch up with teammates not seen since October. And it was great to be playing baseball again, to be getting paid to play a game.

In those days, almost all baseball players worked winter jobs to help make ends meet. Even the team's stars rarely made enough money to allow the luxury of not working a second job. Jim O'Toole sold insurance during the off season one year, worked as a PR man for a hotel another.[6] Gordy Coleman sold season tickets and did promotional work for the Reds. Jim Maloney sold used cars in California and every spring joked with teammates about selling stick shifts to one-legged veterans.[7] Rookie Bobby Klaus worked at a bank in the off season in California and told reporters it was great for his coin collecting hobby — he took home a bag of coins each night, sifted through it for ones he needed and brought it back the next day.[8] Many players worked construction or other odd jobs. So in the spring, it was good to shed the yoke of common labor and return to the sunshine, outdoors and baseball. Amid the groans and complaints was genuine laughter.

Joe Nuxhall, a 35-year-old veteran, glanced enviously at a hustling group of rookies. "If I tried to do the same things today I did 10 years ago, I'd have a pulled leg muscle already," he joked with reporters. "I've got to be a little cautious now."[9]

"Any advice for a rookie pitcher?" a reporter asked ace Jim Maloney, nodding to a group of young pitching hopefuls.

"Yeah," he answered, "get your curve over, pitch batters high and tight and low and away and find a way to keep Hank Aaron out of the lineup."[10]

Maloney heard John Tsitouris talking to a reporter about his screwball. "You mean his 'Billy Williams pitch,'" laughed Maloney. "Williams put it into orbit at Chicago."

"What was that pitch you threw McCovey?" Tsitouris countered.

"You mean the one where the next day it said in the papers it was the longest ball hit at Crosley Field in 25 years?"[11]

The news in early spring training 1964, as every spring, concerned who was holding out, who hadn't shown up on time and why. Fred was happy that most of the players were in camp as scheduled. Pitcher Al Worthington was a notable hold out. Worthington, a 35-year-old veteran, was coming off a fine season in the Reds' bullpen. Unhappy with his contract offer, he hinted to newspaper men that he might just remain in Birmingham and enroll at Howard University to pursue a degree in physical education. Assistant general manager Phil Segui countered by hinting to newspaper men that Al had a better chance of finishing his college degree this year than getting a raise from the Reds.[12]

It was the time-honored dance of give and take employed by players and general managers. In 1964, baseball's infamous reserve clause was still very much in effect. The reserve clause, which had withstood several assaults in court, basically bound a player to the team which signed him for life. If the player was unhappy over playing time or money, he had two, and only two, options: (1) shut up and play, or (2) go home and find another source of employment. There were no agents to bargain for players, no playing out options, no free agency. A player was the property of the team which signed him, for better or for worse, until death, release, injury or retirement.

For their part, general managers and owners were dealing with far less baseball income in those days. Television revenue and merchandising were still in their infancy. Teams had to keep a very tight hold on the purse strings, especially in small markets such as Cincinnati. Owners were also aware, however, that unhappy players sometimes do not perform to their potential, so it was in the best interest of the team to make small concessions in salary to keep the morale up. Often these concessions were very small and not given without great struggle and gnashing of teeth.

Pitcher Joey Jay also did not report as scheduled. Jay, a veteran of several holdouts, was actually signed but he had unfinished loose ends in his oil well business in West Virginia to tend to and had permission to be a little late. Jay, after back-to-back 20 win seasons, had fallen to just seven wins in 1963. He had signed for 1964, but upon arriving in camp complained about being forced to take a $5000 pay cut from his 1963 salary of $36,000. "I don't think they did right by me," he told reporters when asked about his contract, "but I was too tired to argue with them."

"When you have a bad season everyone becomes a professor," he continued, discussing his plans to rebound from his 7–18 record of 1963. "DeWitt thinks you can get off to a better start if you work harder in spring training.... Seghi, the Reds assistant general manager, tells me that I should throw more fast balls."[13]

Jay voiced no concern of being demoted from the starting rotation after his poor season. "Hutch knows what I can do when I'm winning," he said. "I waited long enough for my chance to be a winning pitcher and I'm sure I can do it again."[14]

Among first-year pitchers trying to make the team in 1964 were three talented players, each with a different background. Billy McCool was 19 years old, less than one year out of high school. A left-hander with a smooth, graceful pitching motion, he had deceptive speed — referred to as sneaky fast by players — with excellent movement and control. His youthful face masked a very competitive nature and extreme confidence. Some of the confidence came from having rarely faced failure on any athletic field. He was quite possibly the greatest athlete ever to come out of Lawrenceburg, Indiana, a small border town 20 miles from Crosley Field. A star on both the football and baseball teams, he had thrown three no-hitters in high school and had been under the watchful eye of Reds scouts as early as 1961. After graduation in 1963, he had pitched well at Class A Macon and was promoted to Triple-A San Diego for four starts at the end of the season. There, pitching against men only one step removed from the major leagues, the 18-year-old won all four of his starts. Fred Hutchinson had seen him pitching in the Fall Instructional League and was impressed. "I was pretty confident going into spring training," McCool says. "I had a pretty good year in the minors in 1963 so I had a pretty good idea I would make the team."[15]

Although inwardly confident in his own ability, McCool was not cocky. He was described by Si Burick of the *Dayton Daily News* as having "the self-consciousness of a teenager trying to live as an equal among established big league players" early in the spring. He rarely made eye contact, kept his head down and "spoke hesitatingly and only when spoken to."[16]

Sammy Ellis was a right-handed pitcher who had attended Mississippi State. Signed by the Reds for a $60,000 bonus, he had been up to the majors in 1962 briefly at the age of 21 but had struggled and was sent to San Diego, where he promptly threw a no-hitter. He spent the entire 1963 season at San Diego, compiling a 12–10 record and leading the league in ERA with 2.62. He was a hard thrower with a good fastball and a pitch which reporters called a knuckle-curve but he called a spike-curve. "I wasn't sure I would make the

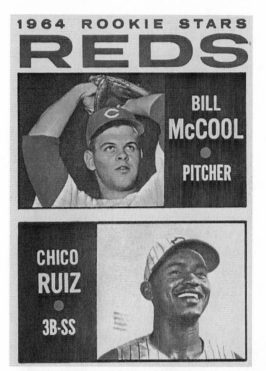

team in 1964," Ellis recalls. "I hadn't even been given a shot at making it in 1963. They had a very good staff. Back then, sometimes you had to put together three or four good years in the minors before you got your chance."[17]

Dan Neville was a self-described baseball fanatic. He had always loved everything about the game. Growing up across the Ohio River from Cincinnati in Covington, Kentucky, Dan spent many days at Crosley Field as a youth, walking across a suspension bridge to see his idols Ted Kluzewski, Wally Post, Joe Nuxhall and Gus Bell. When he wasn't at Crosley Field, he was playing

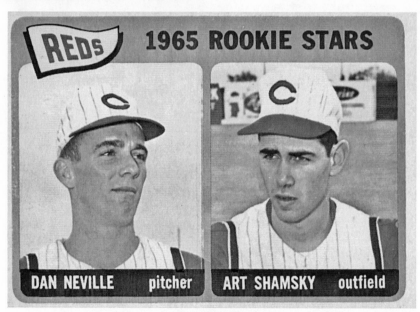

Top and above: Rookies in camp, 1964 (Topps Company, Inc.).

baseball, throwing a rubber ball against a wall or collecting baseball cards. He played on an amateur team in high school with a spunky infielder from Cincinnati's Western Hills High School named Pete Rose. Signed by the Reds after high school, Dan played in the Rookie League at Geneva, New York, in 1960, along with Rose and future major leaguers Art Shamsky and Tony Perez.

Dan had a great season in the minors in 1961, winning 15 and losing only 4, but at the end of the year he hurt his arm so badly that the Reds' organization considered cutting him loose. He convinced his coach, Johnny Van Der Meer (of double no-hitter fame), to allow him to hang around and be the clubhouse boy for the Tampa team in 1962 — anything to stay connected to the game. For five months Dan shined shoes, washed uniforms and cleaned up after the other players. Near the end of the season, he started tossing a ball against the side of the dugout and discovered that his arm didn't hurt anymore. He was able to get back in uniform and did well. He had a good year at Macon in 1963, going 13–9 with a 2.70 ERA, and entered spring training in 1964 full of both hope and apprehension.[18] "Realistically, in 1964, I thought I was probably one year away," Neville says. "But you never know.

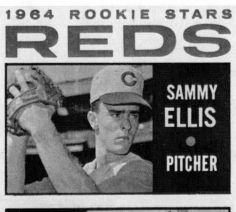

Rookies in camp, 1964 (Topps Company, Inc.).

I was probably a little intimidated in the spring because I had grown up watching a lot of those guys. All of a sudden I'm in the clubhouse with Joe Nuxhall, after watching him play when I was just a kid."

"It was difficult being a rookie in camp because you weren't quite sure you belonged," he continues. "You were anxious to show what you could do but there was a little bit of doubt. Also, some of the players weren't exactly friendly to the new guys. Some guys, I remember especially Nuxhall and Bob Purkey, were great. But some other guys could be downright you-know-whats. They let you know that they were major leaguers and you were just a lowly guy who was lucky to be there — and may not be there long."[19]

For the veterans who knew

they had the team made, spring training was less stressful and more about grinding old bones back into shape and losing some blubber gained over the winter. As the pitchers and catchers gathered for group pictures, Joe Nuxhall, pointing to 6 feet, 4 inch, 220-pound catcher Johnny Edwards, joked: "Don't put Edwards and me on the same side or we'll tilt the field."[20] The heaviest player on the team, listed (often optimistically) at 230 pounds, Nuxhall waged annual battles in the spring with his weight.

Along with the usual issues in spring training, Fred Hutchinson was particularly worried about pitcher Bob Purkey's arm. Purkey, a classy professional pitcher who kept hitters off balance with a variety of well-placed pitches, including a knuckleball, had been the Reds' big winner in 1962 with 23 victories. Arm troubles in 1963 had limited him to only seven wins. Purkey, who got along well with everyone and was the Reds' player rep, was a valuable member of the clubhouse as well as the pitching staff. Fred and pitching coach Jim Turner anxiously watched his early throwing sessions and planned to bring him along slowly.

Position players reported to Tampa on March 4. A notable absentee was Pete Rose who was finishing up his obligation to the National Guard at Fort Knox and was scheduled to arrive in a week. "I sure will be glad when young Pete Rose reports," Hutch lamented to reporters early in March. "He'll liven things up."[21]

Several players from the powerful Triple-A farm team in San Diego were in camp hoping for a job with the Reds, among them outfielders Mel Queen and Art Shamsky, and infielders Bobby Klaus, Tony Perez, Deron Johnson, Tommy Helms and Chico Ruiz.

Dave Bristol was scheduled to manage the San Diego team in 1964. He was in Tampa helping the major league coaches until the minor league camp opened later in March. "Spring training was great," remembers Bristol. "I was 31 in 1964 and had managed in the minors several years. I was only in camp to help out, but Hutch treated me just like I was one of the coaches. He gave me responsibilities and even told Otero [assistant coach Regie], 'When the games start, let him coach third base some,' to get me experience."

"Hutch was fantastic to work for," Bristol continues. "He let the coaches coach but he took full responsibility to make sure everything was done. He invited all of us over to his home on Anna Maria Island after we played in Bradenton. He just said, 'Stay over and we'll have a cookout.' On an off day he gave me his golf clubs and said, 'Go play.' The funny thing about those clubs was that the putter was bent in about four different ways. There was no doubt those were Hutch's clubs."[22]

As far as their manager, most Reds did not notice anything different in the spring of 1964. To the veterans, it was business as usual. To the young players like McCool, Klaus and Neville, in their first or second springs with

Fred keeps a watchful eye at the batting cage (Cincinnati Reds).

the Reds, things appeared pretty normal for a training camp. There was no mention of any illness from their manager. "He certainly still looked like the Bear that spring," says Klaus.[23]

"I didn't know he was sick in spring training," recalls Worthington, who had signed soon after camp started. "It seemed just like any other spring. Hutch and the coaches didn't mention anything about it."[24]

The men who had been through the wars of several years with Hutch, like Edwards and O'Toole, knew about the cancer but didn't talk about it in the spring. "I had found out about it in the papers in January," says O'Toole. "I couldn't believe it. But nobody talked about it in the spring. We had no idea it would get that bad. I was young back then, you don't think of death when you're that age. And he looked great in spring training."[25] Many of the old favorites from the pennant-winning team, including Lynch, Brosnan, Freese, Blasingame and Kasko, were gone by 1964.

If players looked close, however, they could see subtle signs of changes. Hutch had made a few concessions to help preserve his energy. A large wooden lifeguard chair was erected behind one of the backstops so he could see the whole field without walking around too much. Also, he had a golf cart to ferry him back and forth from the clubhouse to the five diamonds where the players were working out. He would take a pass on several long bus rides to away games during the exhibition season. Bill Hutchinson visited him from Seattle for a week to check on him and watched some early games from a box seat near the dugout.

To players, his energy level, demeanor and attitude seemed unchanged, however. He could be intimidating to rookies. "I was scared to death of Fred Hutchinson initially," says Sammy Ellis. "I later found out he was a very loveable guy. But he was intimidating. He was burly and almost a grumpy looking guy when you first met him."[26]

"He seemed to be everywhere," says Queen. "He didn't miss anything. I remember one day I was taking grounders at third base and somebody hit a rocket at me and I just got out of the way. Suddenly I hear somebody say, 'That doesn't happen on my club. Catch the ball.' I looked behind me and there he was. He could intimidate you, especially if you were a rookie."[27]

But the young players also saw signs of Fred's subtle humor. "Once later in the spring we had a game with the Braves, and we knew going in that mostly the veterans would be playing," recalls Neville. "It was a thrill just to see guys like Aaron, Mathews and Spahn up close. Tommy Helms and I were sitting down on the far end of the bench watching. About the seventh or eighth inning, Hutchinson yelled with a gruff voice, 'Helms, grab a bat and get over here.' Tommy jumped up, excitedly looked around and carefully picked out a bat, then hurried over to where Hutch was sitting on the bench. And Hutch said, 'Knock that dirt out of my spikes.' He didn't have any intention of putting him in the game, he was just messing with him."[28]

Joey Jay soon left camp and returned to Cincinnati. The papers noted that he "went AWOL" from Tampa after the team denied permission to leave. He told reporters he still had to finish business with his oil wells in West Virginia and to help his wife. When he returned to Tampa on March 13 after missing two days of workouts, he was fined by Fred Hutchinson. Hutch would not disclose the amount to reporters but said, "He knew he would be fined when he left camp."[29] Jay, the revamped pitching star claimed from the Braves, often seemed to have his own agenda. All business on the field with a serious nature off the field, he got along okay with teammates but was not a central figure in the clubhouse. In 1963, he had staged a prolonged, bizarre holdout during spring training in which he set up regular press conferences to air his side of the story, suggested to anyone who would listen that he was going to give up baseball, and then offered to buy his contract from DeWitt for $150,000. An unheard of practice, this would have allowed him to offer his services to any team — an early form of free agency. The offer was naturally turned down and he eventually signed, but the whole process had irritated some teammates who questioned his devotion to the team.[30]

Pete Rose reported to camp on March 15 with his customary zeal. He later wrote that he got to the International Hotel at 11 P.M. and immediately tried to get buddy Art Shamsky to go out and play catch, however Shamsky refused. The next morning Rose jumped in the batting cage and with his first swing of the spring, ripped a drive to deep left. "Hey, I'm back, Vada, I'm back," he shouted to Pinson.

"You didn't have to tell me, Pete, I noticed," Pinson replied.[31]

Reporters questioned whether Rose, who had received his 1963 Rookie of the Year trophy earlier in the day, would be able to avoid the dreaded sophomore jinx. Tommy Harper, himself a potential casualty of this nefarious malady, told them: "I don't think you're going to have to worry about the sophomore jinx getting Pete Rose. He has always been a hustler ... never satisfied with himself and he's not going to change. He won't let up."[32]

"I don't believe in any sophomore jinx," said Rose, coming out of the batting cage after driving several balls over the left-field fence. "I was a rookie here last year and now I'm a major leaguer. The skipper went along with me last year and I made quiet a few mistakes and got away with some. I can't do that any more."[33]

Asked if he resented being called cocky, Rose replied, "Naw, not at all. Lots of good players are cocky. There's nothing wrong with that. There's no fun being a blushin' Gussie. Remember, too, if you're aggressive they say you're cocky. Every league I've been in they said I was a cocky kid. But I don't try to be. Sure I run to first base because the faster I get there the faster I can get to second. They've ribbed me plenty about it everywhere; in fact, some of you newspapermen call it show boating. I don't care. I'm going to keep doing it. Anyone can do things the way everybody does."[34]

Lou Smith of the *Cincinnati Enquirer* proclaimed that Rose was now the most popular player on the Reds as far as fans were concerned. Smith noted that although other players may be annoyed by Rose's hustle and popularity, to them "he is the symbol of something they would like to be, but can't — an earnest, honest youngster who loves the game so much he would play for nothing."[35]

On March 10, in an intrasquad game, Billy McCool, pitching for the Sislers, blanked the Turners over the first three innings. The veterans were impressed with the speed and movement of his pitches, his control and overall poise. "I like what I've seen of the kid so far," Hutch told reporters, "he definitely has a major league arm."[36] Pitching well against teammates who were not quite in game-shape was one thing, getting proven major leaguers out was another, however.

The Reds opened exhibition play on March 14 against the White Sox with Billy McCool once again looking very sharp on the mound in a three-inning stint. Management was beginning to think they had the real deal in McCool. Two days later, Dan Neville pitched three scoreless innings against the Twins, boosting his hopes. Fred Hutchinson showed he was already in midseason form himself by getting thrown out of the game by the umpires on March 16. It was a meaningless game featuring only a few regular players, but that did not deter the Bear from looking at it like a pennant-race contest. "He (the umpire) just had a bad day," Hutch told reporters after the game. "All I said was, 'Keep your mind on umpiring.'" After the Reds' pitcher was also tossed, Hutch argued loud and long over how much time the next pitcher should get to warm up. "I told the umps he wasn't going to start pitching until we said he was ready," he stated.[37] Fred may have also been making a statement, to assure himself and his players that he was going to approach this season exactly like any other season. Or he simply could not resist complaining about a perceived injustice, no matter what the stakes.

The battles in the spring of 1964 were over third base, which was wide open, at first base between Gordy Coleman and Deron Johnson, and for the last few pitching spots on the roster. Left fielder Tommy Harper had shown signs of great potential as a rookie in 1963, but also had shown inconsistency, and he would battle speedy Marty Keough and several rookies for playing time. Third base was a particular worry. Rookie Chico Ruiz was fast and a slick fielder at third as well as the other infield positions but his bat was suspect. Tony Perez was a powerful hitter but was not felt to be close to the major league level with the glove at third yet, and he was sent to the minor league camp in late March. Harper and Johnson were considered at third also, but their primary positions were outfield and first, respectively. The

Reds had picked up little known Steve Boros from the Cubs over the winter. Described by the press as a "cast off," he turned out to be a great fielder. It soon appeared that if Boros could earn his keep with the bat, he could solve the problem at third base.

Gordy Coleman, one of the most likeable guys on the team, was coming off a poor season as the first baseman. Hutch felt that Coleman had listened to too much advice during his prolonged slump in 1963. Early in March, he told Coleman to "just cut and slash away. If you have any questions ask me or [hitting coach] Dick Sisler. Don't ask anyone else."[38]

Coleman had always needed a special brand of Hutchinson-psychology. Hutch had to frequently reassure Coleman that he was a good hitter and a valuable member of the team. During the spring of 1962, while coming off his best year, Coleman had explained his delicate psyche to a reporter for *Sports Illustrated*: "I'm a worry wart — when I hit, I worry I'll stop. When I don't, I worry I won't start." When the reporter told Coleman that he was the only first baseman on the roster that spring, Coleman replied, "I guess if I'm the only first baseman on the roster, he thinks I can do the job."

Later, Hutch told the reporter, "Coleman is the only first baseman, but we have two or three other guys who could play first base."

When Coleman was told of Hutch's remarks, he said, "That's why you have to worry. There are always guys looking over your shoulder who aren't even there."[39] Unfortunately for Coleman, in 1964 there was someone looking over his shoulder who was definitely there.

Deron Johnson was a 27-year-old well-traveled power hitter. Coming up through the Yankees system, he was originally hailed as another Mickey Mantle. Despite very good years in the minors, he never stuck with the Yankees, playing in a total of 13 games for them over several years before being dumped to that purgatory for ex–Yankees: Kansas City. It was implied that he had been exiled due to a zest for enjoying the nightlife too much. In Kansas City in 1961, he hit .216 as a part-time player and was cut the next spring. He later admitted he had been ready to give up baseball. "I figured if I couldn't play for Kansas City, then I just couldn't play baseball."[40] He wound up at Triple-A San Diego in 1963, where he regained his confidence and led the PCL with 33 home runs.

By 1964, Johnson had played a total of six seasons in the minors and had never hit fewer than 24 homers in a season. But all those minor league home runs had only earned him frustration and disappointment. With Cincinnati, Deron Johnson hoped to finally get a chance to show what he could do against major league pitching. He would also find some suitable running mates for after-game fun. His sense of humor allowed him to soon become a popular member of the team. "Deron was a gamer who loved to play baseball," said O'Toole. "Everybody thought the world of him. He and Nuxhall were roommates and a fun twosome."[41]

The young players toiled nervously throughout camp, wary of the dreaded news of being sent down. "Back then, the clubhouse guy would come by and tell guys they were going to get the ax, that Hutchinson wanted to see you in his office," says Ellis. "So when it got down to the last few days we would tell that clubhouse guy, 'Stay away from my locker.'"[42]

"When I went down for my first major league spring training in 1961 everything was nice," says Mel Queen. "There was a fairly large clubhouse. When they would break for lunch you would have cold cuts and stuff. When I got sent down to the minor league camp , the clubhouse was crammed with about five times the number of guys and you got a watered down cup of bullion and an orange about the size of a plum. So we definitely didn't want to go back to that."[43] Queen, friendly and gregarious, was the 23-year-old son of former major league pitcher Mel Queen, who had played for the Yankees and Pirates from 1942 to 1952. He had signed for a large bonus as an 18-year-old. As with many other players of the era, the bonus became a millstone around his neck. By the annoying and difficult-to-understand major league rules of the time regarding young players and signing-bonuses, he was "out of options" in 1964 — meaning that if he was not kept on the Reds' major league roster he could be plucked from their system by any team willing to pay a small price. This increased the likelihood he would make the team but probably cost him in the long run as there was not space in the outfield for him to get the playing time he needed to develop properly.

Bobby Klaus worked hard to compete with second-year man Pete Rose at second base and hoped to at least earn a spot as a utility infielder. His older brother Billy was already a major leaguer with the Phillies. "Spring training in the major league camp was a little rough but it was wonderful just being there for the first time," says Klaus. "It was exciting. My brother Billy was with the Phillies. The first time he came over, he pinched my Reds jersey and said, 'Nice job.' That was kind of neat. We got a picture of us together in our major league uniforms and I still have that up in my living room today."[44]

Relief pitching continued to worry Hutch. Several veterans were brought into camp to compete for jobs. Owner DeWitt was seen huddling with the presidents of the Braves and Phillies in an attempt to find more relief pitchers. Fred shared his concern with reporters: "It's tough to ask a kid pitcher to tackle short clutch relief on a contending team. Don't get me wrong, I hope one of my kids makes me eat those words, but I'd be kidding myself and you if I said I thought it would happen."[45]

Both Lou Smith and Ritter Collett questioned whether Sammy Ellis had the temperament to be successful in the bullpen.[46] Ellis, by his own admission, had experienced trouble controlling his temper on the field the past two years in San Diego and it had cost him more than a few wins. "It tears me up when I do something wrong or get what I think is a bad call by an umpire,"

Ellis said.[47] He told reporters he was determined to corral his temper and though, like all young pitchers, he wanted to start, he would gladly work out of the bullpen this season. "If it means getting my chance to stay in the big leagues right now, that's fine and dandy with me."[48]

Fred Hutchinson's son Jack was training in Tampa with the Reds' farmhands. He was slated to play in Cedar Rapids in the Rookie League — the bottom rung of the ladder. Early in the spring, Fred was asked by reporters to pose for a picture with Jack. "You'll have to clear it with him," Hutch replied. "I think he kinda wants people to forget he's my son."[49]

"If I make it, I want to make it strictly on my own," Jack later said. "I realize people are extra nice to me because I'm Fred Hutchinson's son. I appreciate that but honestly, I don't want it. I have to make a living on my own."[50]

Jack was mixed in with the other several hundred minor leaguers in Tampa. On the field, there was little worry about the appearance of favoritism being shown to the son of the boss. "I was pretty far removed from the major league level, so I didn't have much contact with my father in spring training," says Jack. "I was busy working as hard as I could to make the team. He was involved in the cancer treatment, but I was pretty oblivious to that. I didn't know how he was doing with it. He didn't talk about it much."[51]

Fred appeared to be in good spirits. He was available and open with reporters for the most part, even though Lou Smith wrote in the *Cincinnati Enquirer* that "Hutch is getting slightly irked at being constantly asked 'How do you feel? And do you think you'll be able to stay on the job all season?'"[52]

Fred maintained an optimistic outlook throughout camp. "I've never felt that I couldn't get over it," he told one reporter. "I'm just glad to be around."[53]

"I think I've got it licked," he told another. "I know they've arrested it."[54]

Fred also continued to act as a spokesman for cancer patients and cancer research. If his own affliction could help bring the condition more public awareness, so be it. "This is cancer I have," he said. "It's not some dreadful thing, some unspeakable thing. It's cancer. Folks hesitate to come out with it." When asked what he first thought when he found out, he replied, "You say to yourself, 'Well, it's happened to me. I got it. What am I going to do about it?'" Then, in a statement which surely brought a smile to his brother's face, he added, "You wish more of the money collected was finding its way into the research department. That's the pity of the thing."[55]

Fred's attitude and appearance were a frequent topic of reports sent back to Cincinnati by the writers — keeping the citizens updated on the condition of their favorite manager. Pat Harmon of the *Cincinnati Post* reported that Fred had given up smoking and was not eating highly seasoned food, or anything too hot to avoid irritating his throat. He was taking an hour's nap after work every day at 6 o'clock and making sure to get eight hours of sleep. He also was not supposed to shout to avoid straining his throat. Otherwise, he was still the "same intense, dedicated baseball man ..., the same tough, frank talker. His habits, only, have changed, not his personality." Harmon continued, "Hutch, the big man who has won every battle and won the nation's admiration, is in his toughest fight." He concluded by mentioning Hutch's family, which was with him, saying, "They love the guy. So do all of us."[56]

On April 1, Fred and Casey Stengel entertained reporters before the Reds played the Mets. "I thought I'd come over and see you. Care to take a ride?" Hutch said to Stengel as he pulled up to the Mets' dugout in his golf cart.

"Do the players get jealous of this cart?" Stengel asked. "You don't own this club now, do you? The way you're traveling, it looks like you own it. I hear you go as far as Clearwater in this thing."

"How do you feel?" Stengel then asked, turning serious. "Have you really been sick?"

"Feel great," Hutch replied.

"After what happened, I began to worry about my health," said Stengel. "Now I only smoke my coaches' cigarettes. So they won't lose their health. I'm helping them out." Then they sat on the golf cart together and posed for the photographers.[57]

The *Cincinnati Post* described an early spring meeting with reporters and the uneasiness friends and acquaintances had upon seeing Hutch for the first time since the news of his illness broke: "There is always an awkward, embarrassed reticence, wordlessly expressing sympathy, fondness, hope, consideration, even a kind of awe and timidity." It continued, "greetings exchanged, the Big Bear waits. He knows what's coming. The very words. With his sense of amusing ... it's not unlikely he privately savors the hesitancy, the hospital-like hush." Hutch turned on a "wide friendly smile that magically transforms his rough, craggy, forbidding features into a warm welcome."

"Okay fellows," he said, "let's raise the curtain on the first act. Yes, I've been treated for cancer. Yes, I was shook up when my brother told me the tests showed malignancy. That was last December. I've been taking heavy radiation treatments. My brother flew here to check further the other day. Said I was coming along fine. I feel fine, too and have picked up weight.

"Bill tells me one out of every seven or eight people contract cancer in one form or another. A lot of them beat it. My only worry right now is whether this team can bounce back."[58]

Late in March, team leaders Jim O'Toole and Frank Robinson put into words for reporters for the first time how the team felt about their leader and his illness. "You always want to win for a man like that," said O'Toole. "Now we're going to try all the harder. The guys don't talk about it, but you know how they feel about it and what they're thinking."

"Hutch's great fight against odds will make us all better players and better men," added Robinson. "All of us feel like we'd like to win the whole thing for him."[59]

As the Reds prepared to head north, they appeared, indeed, to be capable of bouncing back and possibly winning the whole thing. The roster finalized, the team looked good on paper and on the field in the final exhibition games. The pitching staff was very solid. Ellis and McCool were both kept by the Reds and would start the season in the bullpen. Ellis, ecstatic over making the team, would earn the major league minimum of $7,000 for 1964. In addition to his success on the field, he had also met his future wife during spring training, so it had been a very productive month.[60]

Klaus and Queen made the squad also and would provide bench help. Third base would be divided between Boros and Ruiz. Johnson had hit so well in the spring that it was impossible to keep him out of the lineup. He and Coleman would split time at first base, with Johnson also playing in the outfield. Dan Neville was one of the last players sent down. He, along with Tony Perez and Tommy Helms, would start the season in San Diego.

As for the Hutchinson family, 1964 would be much different than their normal season routine. Patsy would go north to spend the entire season with her husband. Rick, at Florida State, would join them in Cincinnati as soon as his classes were finished and would spend the season with his father also. Jack bid his father farewell and left with the Reds' rookie league team for Iowa. He noted that his father looked very good, pretty much normal.[61] Busy playing in the minor leagues, he would not see him again for four months. As they shook hands in early April, Jack did not realize how different his father would look the next time they met.

13

April:
Opening Day

OPENING DAY in Cincinnati is a spectacle unlike that seen in any other city in baseball. By 1964, the Reds had opened at home 86 consecutive years. In honor of being the first professional team, the Reds traditionally started one day before the rest of the league. Opening Day is a celebration for the entire city, part of the city's identity; not unlike the Derby Festival in Louisville or the 500 Festival in Indianapolis. Unlike the other two cities, however, in Cincinnati the masses are totally united in rooting for the same winner each year. The school board, wary of truant students (and teachers and principals), long ago declared the day an official school holiday. Opening Day parades date back to 1890. Jim O'Toole particularly appreciated the tradition, the excitement of the fans and the anticipation of Opening Day festivities in his adopted city. "Opening Day in Cincinnati always has a feel to it like the World Series," says O'Toole, who started three Opening Days between 1961 and 1965. "We all wanted to be the Opening Day pitcher because of the atmosphere."[1]

In the week leading up to Opening Day, virtually all the stores downtown ran baseball-related specials and filled their windows with Reds pennants and posters. Most also exhibited signs saying they would close at noon on Opening Day. The fans looked forward to a rebirth, when the errors and losses of the previous season were forgotten. Sellouts were automatic. "It was a celebration of baseball," O'Toole told a reporter in 2007. "It was what Cincinnati was all about."[2] Cincinnati residents knew that they may have had the smallest city in baseball, but for one day every year, the entire baseball world looked in their direction. "Whether you are a fan or a player, there is nothing like it," said O'Toole.[3]

As the crowd of fans proceeded up Findlay Avenue to Crosley Field on April 13, 1964, the familiar sights and sounds of major league baseball came

Anxious crowd lined up outside Crosley Field (Cincinnati Reds).

flooding back, as if they had never left. The smell of cigar smoke, peanuts and popcorn filled the air. Outside the gate, an elderly black man, dressed in a black coat with tails and a stove top hat, pushed his peanut cart to his familiar spot, which as far as anyone knew, he had been manning since the Wright brothers had been playing.

A crowd of 28,110 filed into Crosley Field, many carrying pocket transistor radios (available at Sears in a pre–Opening Day special for $5.95) to listen to Waite Hoyt call the game. Hoyt, a former New York Yankee pitcher, a teammate and good friend of Babe Ruth, was an institution on the Reds Radio Network. Fans loved the folksy way he called the game and the stories from his Yankee days. Some fans were upset in 1964 to find that the cost of hot dogs had risen from 25 to 30 cents for the new season. The next day in the newspapers the supervisor of concessions tried to placate them by explaining that the Reds still had one of the lowest prices in the league and that Reds dogs had one-third more beef than the similarly priced ones available downtown at the Cincinnati Gardens[4] (which fans munched while watching Oscar Robertson and his Cincinnati Royals play basketball).

New Reds batboy, 15-year-old Mike Holzinger, busily prepared for the game. Holzinger was a born Reds fan. He attended Cincinnati's Western Hills High School and played baseball for the same coach as had Pete Rose a few years earlier. Although the work was hard, this was the opportunity of a

Crosley Field crowd (Cincinnati Reds).

lifetime. "It paid five dollars a day," he recalls, "and it was usually a ten-hour day. We had to be there about two or three hours before the game to get the uniforms ready, clean spikes, put saddle soap on the shoes to keep them in good shape. Then we went out for batting practice and had to make sure we had all the bats out they wanted and then clean up everything off the field. After the game we had to clean the clubhouse and get ready for the next game. It was hard work but the Reds players treated us really well, like we were members of the team, and I got to meet Casey Stengel, Don Drysdale, Sandy Koufax, all those guys. I was lucky enough to realize how great it was at the time—how fortunate I was to get to do that."[5]

Sitting in the Reds' bullpen down the third base line, Billy McCool got his first player's view of Crosley Field and its charm. A 58-foot tall, 65-foot wide scoreboard in left field showed concurrent games in the two leagues along with the Reds' and visitor's lineups. This was topped by an 18-foot Longines clock. Ads ran along the left field wall under the scoreboard with Wiedemann Beer having the most prominent spot. A net above the fence protected cars in the parking lot beyond left-field. The parking lot had been created in the early sixties by bulldozing a laundry building which had previously been a favorite target for home run hitters. The new I-75 freeway ran behind the center field fence and a backdrop had been built over the fence to help prevent batters from being distracted by passing trucks. The only seats behind the outfield fence were in right. These bleacher seats made up what was called the moon deck for night games and the sundeck for day games.[6]

The most prominent feature of Crosley Field, which every former player recalls first, was the outfield terrace. Built in the days before warning tracks existed to warn outfielders of an impending collision with the fence, the terrace was a large slope in the terrain which rose perhaps 15 to 20 degrees toward the fence. Not infrequently visit-

Fifteen-year-old batboy Mike Holzinger. The opportunity of a lifetime (courtesy Mike Holzinger).

Crosley Field — before the laundry building behind the left field fence was removed in the early 1960s. Note the change in contour of the foul line in front of the left-field fence for the infamous terrace (Cincinnati Reds).

ing outfielders, especially first-timers, stumbled running up the terrace while looking back for the ball. This made for great amusement to the inhabitants of the Reds' bullpen. The most famous victim of the terrace had been none other than Babe Ruth. Playing in his next-to-last game with the Boston Braves on July 25, 1935, the Babe had tripped on the terrace chasing a fly ball, fallen on his face and stormed off the field.[7]

Fans and players shared the intimacy of Crosley Field. Fans in their seats were close to the game and could hear the players on the field. Players parked behind the home plate stands and walked through the gate to get to the field, mingling with fans along the way. Some players, especially Joe Nuxhall, Jim O'Toole and Pete Rose, were famously casual and talkative with fans as they entered the field.[8] The Reds' clubhouse was entered through stairs beyond the home team dugout down the third-base line. Players were clearly visible to fans, separated by bars as they trudged up to the clubhouse.

The optimistic Opening Day crowd was ready for the 1964 season. The fans believed the Reds were in position to challenge the Dodgers for the National League title. The mayor of Cincinnati, Walt Bachrach, threw the first pitch of the year to City Manager William Wichman. The batter, Ohio

Governor James A. Rhodes, took the pitch for a ball and the season was officially under way. Jim Maloney then took the mound for the Reds against the Houston Colt 45s. Fred Hutchinson was ready for the 1964 season also. He had worked hard to get back to this spot. He began his game day routine in the Reds' dugout: a mixture of nervous energy, worry and calculating analysis; a fingernail-biting, ice-chomping fury. In 1963, Dale Shaw had described Hutch's dugout behavior for readers of *Sport* magazine: "The Bear in his cage ... paced nervously from one end [of the dugout] to the other, hands in his hip pockets, shooting furious glances at his players in the field. Periodically he would crouch with one foot on the dugout steps, his huge chin in one hand and the other hand in his hip pocket. Motionless and scowling, he watched his pitcher, his infield and his outfield ... gnawing on his fingers .... later crouches solemnly behind the bat rack beside the bullpen telephone.... He stalked the watercooler at the far end of the dugout.... Finally he would pounce on the cooler and drink, turn, swizzle and spit.... In the dugout he behaved like a man who wanted to get into the game but couldn't."[9]

Frank Robinson was in the lineup for the Reds. There had been a scare at the end of spring training for Robinson as he had developed an infection "in his groin region" and was sent back to Cincinnati from Tampa and hospitalized at Christ Hospital. He had been released April 11 and was in good shape for the opening game. Jim Maloney was sharp early and the game was a scoreless duel through four innings. The Astros scored three in the fifth and got three more in the sixth off Maloney who left after the sixth inning. Only two of the runs were earned, however, as Maloney and Ruiz committed errors to help the Colts' cause. The Reds did not score until the ninth inning off ex–Red pitcher Ken Johnson and his knuckle ball, losing 6–3. Jim Wynn, a young Cincinnati native, was the star of the game for the Astros. In addition to hitting a home run, Wynn made a great diving catch in deep right-center to rob Mel Queen who had pinch-hit for Maloney. On the positive side for the Reds, young Sammy Ellis looked good pitching two scoreless innings.

The Reds had two days off before their next game in Los Angeles. Fred left for Seattle immediately after the opening game to check in with his doctors. The trip had been planned for the day off before the team's West Coast swing — a convenient time to visit Seattle — and announced to reporters on April 9. Upon leaving, Hutch told reporters "I'm hoping to rejoin the team in time for the exhibition game with San Diego Wednesday night."[10] The papers reported on April 15 that doctors at Swedish Hospital's Tumor Institute said they were very pleased with the results and no further exams would be needed until June.[11] Fred was able to catch up with the team in Los Angeles in time for the next game.

Jim O'Toole and Joey Jay won the next two games for the Reds, looking in midseason form. Jim Maloney took the mound for the third game of the series against the Dodgers' Sandy Koufax in a match-up of two of the most overpowering pitchers in the league. Before the 1963 season, the National League had enlarged the strike zone from the belt to the middle of the chest. This opening of the high strike zone was a license to kill for those pitchers whose velocity was sufficient to prevent hitters from reaching a high strike, particularly Koufax, Maloney, Don Drysdale and Bob Gibson.[12] Koufax had improved from 14–7 in 1962 to 25–5 with 306 strikeouts. Maloney had gone from 9–7 to 23–7 with 265 strikeouts in 1963, at one point tying a major league record by striking out eight consecutive batters. Not quite 24 years old in 1964, Maloney was recognized as a growing star. "Jim Maloney had the best arm in the National League," says Sammy Ellis. "There were a lot of guys back then who had good arms, but nobody had an arm like he did." Nobody? "Nobody had an arm like Maloney," he repeats.[13] Loose in the clubhouse, always joking and laughing, Maloney was also the team clown.

"Maloney was always pulling stuff in the clubhouse," says Bernie Stowe, the Reds' clubhouse man. "Setting shoe strings on fire, tying them together. Him and Nuxhall were always up to something."[14]

"Maloney was a crazy guy who would do stupid stuff in the clubhouse or on the plane," O'Toole said. "He'd do disgusting things that made you want to puke from watching him."[15] Maloney was always looking for something to give his teammates a laugh.

Batboy Mike Holzinger, now a retired postal worker still living in Cincinnati, remembers passing around a baseball to get autographed by the team for a young female friend. "When Maloney found out it was for a girl he wrote something extra on it and I had to throw the ball away. I couldn't give it to a girl after he wrote that. But that was fun; he made me feel welcome because he would joke with me."[16]

"Maloney still has some of my shirts," says Edwards. "We were roommates in the minors and when he got called up he took a bunch of my clothes with him. When I came up later, he had worn one of my shirts so much it was in such bad shape we had to burn it. But he was a good roommate. He was a lot of fun."[17]

There was no fun for batters when facing Maloney, however. His fastball had been timed at 99 miles per hour and had unbelievable movement. "When I first watched him warm up from up close I couldn't believe it," says Rick Hutchinson. "I had been hitting off college pitchers but Maloney was just incredible. I didn't think it was possible to hit off him."[18] If Maloney consistently got his curveball over, he was indeed unhittable. He would go on to throw five one-hitters and three no-hitters for the Reds in the sixties. Maloney was also an excellent hitter. He regularly led the pitchers in batting practice games. He hit .379 in 1961 and had 13 RBIs in only 73 at bats in 1964. He hit seven home runs in his career.

Facing the Dodgers on April 18, Maloney was getting his curveball over often enough and pitched a shutout. Koufax, his arm bothering him, allowed three runs and the Reds won. Koufax's arm would bother him all spring, putting a serious damper on the Dodger's hopes of repeating as National League champs.

On April 23, the Reds faced Houston in the final game of the first western road trip of the season with a record of 4–4. Ken Johnson of the Astros was the one who was unhittable that day, holding the Reds hitless over nine complete innings. Joe Nuxhall had scattered five hits without any runs for the Reds as both pitchers took shutouts into the ninth inning. Then Pete Rose showed why his manager's faith in him was justified. He led off the inning with a bunt in front of home plate. Pitcher Johnson quickly fielded the ball but rushed his throw trying to beat the charging Rose. The throw went past the first baseman and Rose went to second for a two-base error. Rose took third when Chico Ruiz grounded out. Vada Pinson then hit a routine grounder which second baseman Nellie Fox mishandled and Rose

All-Star catcher John Edwards (Cincinnati Reds).

scored — without the benefit of a base hit or a batted ball leaving the infield. Nuxhall finished off the Colts in the bottom of the inning and the Reds had a 1–0 win and Johnson became a footnote as one of the only pitchers in history to lose a game in which he threw a no-hitter.

Billy McCool made his major league debut the next night in Cincinnati, mopping up in a 13–6 loss to the Giants. The 19-year-old gave up one run in two innings but showed poise throwing to the powerful Giant hitters. "I was never intimidated by anyone," says McCool of pitching as a teenager to Mays, Cepeda and McCovey in his first game. "I knew what I could do."[19]

Over the next month, Fred Hutchinson would gain more confidence in McCool and Sammy Ellis, using them in key late inning situations. The two youngsters would prove to be much more valuable than anyone would have guessed before the season, eventually forming the best righty-lefty bullpen combination in the league in 1964. "Coming out of spring training I had been just happy to be on the team," says Sammy Ellis. "I was just thinking about getting a chance to pitch and helping the team win. I hadn't had experience in the bullpen, that was new for me, but McCool did well as a lefty and I did pretty well as a righty and we ended up making a good pair in the bullpen that year. I think I was so enamored of being in the big leagues that I wasn't worried about choking, I was just going to let it rip. It was fun knowing I only had to get four or five guys out. Me and McCool didn't have any knowledge in spring training that we would be able to do that."[20]

"You don't feel like you're a real member of the club until you know you can help," McCool said in 1965. "I didn't feel that way [early]. But I will say the veterans were great. They kept me from feeling like a total stranger." McCool definitely showed he could help as the season progressed. "I think it was good that Sammy Ellis and I developed together in the bullpen," he added. "We had more or less a friendly contest going on between us. I tried to outdo him and he tried to outdo me."[21]

The two young pitchers benefited from having an experienced, excellent defensive catcher to help them along. John Edwards was 26 years old in 1964, playing in his fourth season. He had come up to the Reds in the middle of the tense pennant race of 1961, helped solidify the team and led the Reds in hitting in the World Series. Tough and smart, Edwards had made the All-Star team in 1963 and was considered to be the best defensive catcher in the National League in the early sixties. "Both Ellis and McCool had very good stuff when they came up," Edwards says. "I would help them out going over the hitters, but they both were the type of pitchers that if you wanted the ball inside or outside, they could hit the spot."[22]

Edwards was also one of the smartest players in the league. Possessing an engineering degree from Ohio State, he worked with General Electric in the nuclear field in the off season. While conversation in most bullpens is limited to women in the stands, sneaking a nap or food and, occasionally, base-ball, Jim Brosnan wrote in *Pennant Race* of Edwards and pitcher Jay Hook, who had an engineering degree from Northwestern, in the bullpen discussing missiles and nose cones and solving "the problem of atmospheric re-entry."[23] Although he possessed great intellect, Edwards was not considered to be an intellectual, however, as he was definitely one of the guys off the field and a natural leader in the clubhouse.

The Reds closed out a mediocre April by losing two in a row to the Philadelphia Phillies, who had streaked to a 9–2 record. O'Toole and Nux-hall both pitched well, but lost 2–4 and 1–3 respectively. Lack of run support was becoming a common theme in the early season. The second loss put the Reds at 6–7 for the first month of the season.

14

May: Blind Ryne, Nuxie, Tootie and the Two Chicos

IN EARLY MAY, Fred Hutchinson was feeling good and his main worry was how to keep the Reds from falling behind in the standings. He seemed more concerned about the health of good friend Birdie Tebbetts than his own. Tebbetts, his golfing partner, had recently stepped down from managing the Indians due to a heart attack. Fred spoke to reporters during an early May trip to New York. "I feel fine," he told them. "The check I had made just after the start of the season was quite favorable and the doctors are pleased. I've cut down on my weight a bit.... But never mind about me. I'm all right. I'd rather talk about my ball club — we could have a good year — if. That's our trouble. We have ifs."[1]

One of the ifs was extra pitching. Fred knew that in major league baseball you can never have enough pitching. The Reds were soon able to pick up not only another good pitcher, but a classic character to add to their clubhouse. Ryne Duren, 35, was already a legend when the Reds purchased him from the Phillies on May 13. His reputation preceded him to Cincinnati. When first discovered in the tiny Wisconsin town of Cazenovia, his fastball exceeded 100 miles per hour. He was said by most baseball men of the time to be faster than anyone other than Bob Feller. The problem was that no one, especially Ryne, knew where the ball would go when he turned it loose. It was reported that he had not been allowed to pitch in high school after breaking a batter's ribs. Later, another problem was found: he couldn't see. His vision was measured at 20/70 and 20/200 — almost legally blind. He was rumored to have once hit a man in the on-deck circle.

When he finally made it to the big leagues, Ryne was smart enough to use these stories to his advantage. His warm-up routine when he came into a game from the bullpen classically started with a nasty heater flung up against the backstop. He squinted in at the plate through coke bottle thick, darkly tinted glasses. Strong men had to battle their better judgment before stepping into the batter's box against Rinold Duren. "Part of that was an act," Duren says with a chuckle. "It started in New York. I was a pretty good drinking buddy of some of the New York writers and they told me, 'Hey, throw one up at the stands.' They needed something to write about. Of course, it didn't hurt me when the batters didn't want to dig in."[2]

The story about hitting a guy in the on-deck circle was partially true. "It was Jimmy Piersall in Boston," Duren remembers warmly. "Ted Williams used to come up from the on-deck circle and watch you pitch when you warmed up, to get a closer look at the timing. Sometimes he would take a practice swing as the ball crossed the plate. But he was Ted Williams, what are you going to do? Then one day, I'll be damned if Piersall didn't come over and do that. Well, he was no Ted Williams. So I threw a ball in his direction. I didn't get too close, it was just to get his attention. He shouted, 'What the hell's the matter with you?' I said, 'What the hell's the matter with you. You've got yourself confused with a hitter.' That's probably where the story got started."[3]

Reds catcher Johnny Edwards remembers a similar incident against the Pirates in which the unfortunate Pirate batter actually got hit. "Ryne nailed him right in the side — put him on the ground. Ryne said, 'That's too close.' He could be a tough competitor."[4]

Edwards is not so sure about the vision either. "His first game with us was in Chicago and when he came in the game I went out to talk to him to ask him if he could see the signs okay, because we had all heard about his vision. He said, 'No problem, no problem.' He only had two pitches, a one or a two. I get back there and get ready to give the sign and hell, he's already winding up — I haven't even given the sign yet. After the pitch I called time and I told him, 'You give the sign then.' And he would call it by what position his glove was because he couldn't even see the signs and I didn't want to get killed not knowing what was coming."[5]

Ryne Duren was soon found to be a guy who also liked to have fun, which allowed him to fit in with the Reds quickly. "The Reds were about the rowdiest team I ever played on," he says.[6] And he had played on the Angels and Yankees of the early sixties — teams known for their enjoyment of off-field activities.

"We had a bunch of guys who had a lot of fun together," says Edwards. "Deron Johnson, Maloney, O'Toole, Nuxhall. Ryne joined in. We goofed around a little bit. Ryne Duren thought the telephone was the greatest invention there ever was. He would call all around the world. He called Princess Grace in Monaco. He called President Johnson at the White House — I think he almost got in trouble over that one."[7]

"One night we were in the hotel in Johnson's room, and Ryne got on the phone. I think he was trying to call Mauch, the Phillies manager," says Edwards.

"We had a little beer that night," Duren adds in his version of the story.

"Well, Deron said, 'Damn it Ryne, you're in my room, you're going to follow my rules,'" continues Edwards.

"I think I threw a pitcher of beer on somebody," says Duren.

"It was a tub of beer," says O'Toole, "and he threw it against the wall and some of it hit Deron on the head."

"The next thing I knew," says Edwards, "Deron's got him held out the window by his feet." Duren's entire upper body was suspended outside the window as Johnson held his lower legs and feet inside the window sill.

"And they were probably twenty stories up," remembers Billy McCool.

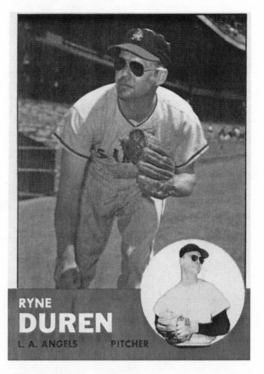

RYNE
DUREN
L. A. ANGELS   PITCHER

Batters did not get comfortable in the box with Ryne Duren pitching. Card is from 1963 (Topps Company, Inc.).

"I started to take off out the door," says Edwards, "then I stopped and said, 'I can't leave now.' I could hear Ryne Duren yelling, 'Go ahead, you haven't got the guts to drop me.' So then I'm hanging out there with him holding on to Ryne trying to get him back in the damn room."

"Nux and Edwards and I pulled him in," says O'Toole.[8]

Another time, in Houston, Duren and other rabble rousers ended up skinny-dipping in the closed hotel pool after hours. "We got down to the pool late at night," says Duren. "Somebody said something to somebody and got pushed in the pool. The next thing you know we're all in the pool ripping each other's clothes off."[9]

Earl Lawson later wrote that, around midnight, he heard a lot of laughing and looked out his hotel window to see a half dozen major league baseball players splashing in the pool in various degrees of dress. A siren was heard and, thinking someone had called the police, the players fumbled out of the pool, grabbing for any cover they could find, and hid in some bushes around the pool. When they realized the siren was from an ambulance at a nearby hospital, they returned to their fun.[10] The hotel manager was reportedly not happy about the incident. "We had a fun team," adds Duren.[11]

Bat boy Mike Holzinger recalls an incident in which Duren answered the phone in the Crosley Field bullpen before a game. "It was Mrs. DeWitt, she was looking for one of the coaches or something," says Holzinger. Unfortunately for the owner's wife, Ryne Duren did not just use a phone for communication but used it for fun as well. "He started giving her a real hard time, talking back, laughing and refusing to help her. Finally I heard her shout over the phone, 'Who is this?' Ryne answered, 'Gordy Coleman' and hung up."[12]

There was a dark side to the Ryne Duren story, however. He was an alcoholic. In an era when most players drank, Ryne seemed to drink differently. Teammates on other teams had noted that he had trouble knowing when to stop. Many times he woke up with no memory of the preceding night — only broken doors and furniture and a black eye to give him hints. "One time in New York, Whitey Ford and Mickey Mantle told me I shouldn't drink," says Duren of those two noted Yankee milkshake drinkers. "They said I was a different type of drinker."

"I was so addicted to alcohol that it was part of my makeup and personality," Duren continues. "I think I was probably irreversibly addicted from a very early age. Alcohol is a drug and if you don't understand it as such it's pretty dangerous." Duren lost more than one baseball job during his career because of off-field, alcohol-fueled incidents. That was the reason the Yankees had dumped him, the Angels had let him go and the Phillies had sold him to the Reds. In the early sixties, the term "alcoholic" was rarely used and never used in association with baseball. Many players during those years ruined their careers and lives without ever getting treatment. "I knew a lot of guys who drunk themselves to death," says Duren.[13]

Fred Hutchinson was familiar with Duren's baseball talents, having managed him briefly in Seattle. "In 1955, I went to spring training with the Orioles but they didn't keep me with the big league club," says Duren. "Paul Richards, the manager, told me, 'I want you to go out and play for Freddie Hutchinson. He's a good friend of mine and I'm sure he can help you with your control.' Of course, control was the issue with me. I went out there but they later had to send me down to San Antonio. Hutch did that with his usual sense of humor. He threw batting practice to the pitchers that day and I hit two out of the park off him. I don't know if I ever hit a ball out of the park in practice before, but I hit two that day. So when he called me in to tell me I was being sent out he said, 'Kid, I'm sorry, you just hit me too good today.' I really liked Hutch and I was happy to be going to the Reds later. I think he had remembered me."[14]

Fred knew what kind of arm Duren had, but, more importantly, he knew that he possessed the kind of competitive fire that Hutch loved in players. Duren had played a key role in the bullpen for several pennant-winning Yankee teams in the late fifties. He had been a winner and knew what it took. He demanded a lot of himself on the baseball field. After he delayed covering first base on a routine grounder and then muffed the late throw letting a run score, costing the Reds a midseason game against the Mets, Duren went into Hutch's office and handed him a check for $100. "This club is fighting for the pennant and I goofed. I deserved to be fined that much," Duren said.

"I didn't take it," Hutch told reporters. "He has been around long enough to know what he did was wrong. Taking his money wouldn't prove anything."[15]

Duren was a smart baseball player and also knew a few tricks to help his team. He was not above dipping into Ivory flakes to give his pitches an extra jump,[16] and he told Earl Lawson early in the year that, as a batter, a pitcher should be able to get on base any time he wanted: "All you have to do is get hit with the pitch."[17]

The Reds would need all the competitive fire and tricks they could get to climb back into the pennant race. On May 23, they lost to Chicago, their fourth straight loss, putting them two games under .500. They were not getting any hitting. Rose, Robinson and Pinson especially were all slumping badly.

While the hitting was struggling, the Reds were getting great pitching. Bob Purkey had gradually worked back into shape and was throwing well now. The Reds had the luxury of six quality potential starters: Maloney, O'Toole, Jay, Nuxhall, Purkey and John Tsitouris were all seeing regular time in the rotation. Sammy Ellis had also filled in admirably, starting in spots, and was now doing great out of the bullpen. Four of these seven would win twenty games or more in a season at least once between 1961 and 1965, and O'Toole won 19 in 1961.

Jim O'Toole was the most consistent member of the staff. Twenty-seven years old, he was now a veteran of five seasons and one of the acknowledged leaders of the team. He was also the most proliferative of the Reds. By 1964, he and wife Betty already had four children. They would go on to have 11 kids between 1961 and 1973, nearly one a year, sometimes two. "In 1967 and 1970, we did not have a child," Betty later told a reporter. "Jim told people he had pneumonia those years."[18] The majority of O'Toole's $30,000 salary evaporated in the grocery line each week. Reds players recall with laughter Betty telling of padlocking the pantry.[19] O'Toole had an endorsement deal with a local dairy which brought him 15 gallons of milk a week to help feed the hoard.[20]

"O'Toole was really nice to us bat boys," says Holzinger. "Whenever the Reds had a picnic or team event, he always took care of us; because what was one more kid when you had that many. He had a good personality, liked to laugh. You always knew when he was around."[21]

O'Toole had won 19 games for the pennant-winning 1961 team and won more than 15 games for four consecutive years. He had been the starting pitcher for the National League in the 1963 All-Star game. A series of freak injuries had haunted him since arriving in Cincinnati, costing him a few more wins each year. In 1959, he had been injured in a car accident and later missed a start when he cut a finger on his pitching hand putting a suitcase in his car. A few years later he had an accident at a team picnic. He was sitting on a wagon with his two-year-old son in one arm and holding the reins in the other when the horses pulled the wrong way. O'Toole fell off and got kicked in the ankle.[22] He missed a few weeks another season after suffering a knife cut on the thigh in an off-field brawl (the media was told he had been sidelined by a hamstring pull).[23] In June of 1963, O'Toole was 13 and 3, but he missed some starts when he tripped over a chain in the parking lot of a San Francisco hotel. "This year I'm thinking of sending a body guard home with him," Fred Hutchinson told reporters early in 1964, "just to make sure nothing happens."[24]

Reds coach Dick Sisler would long remember his first meeting with O'Toole's father, who was known to all back in Chicago as Happy. Sisler was the manager of the Nashville farm team in 1958 when Jim O'Toole had a rare poor outing. As Sisler went to the mound to remove O'Toole, he was showered with verbal abuse by a particularly loud, obnoxious, flush-faced, leather-lunged fan seated behind the dugout. After the game, Sisler was met by O'Toole outside the ballpark. "Hey skip," said O'Toole, "I want you to meet my father." Sisler was surprised to find that Happy O'Toole had been the loud fan from behind the dugout.[25]

While he was a joker who enjoyed a good laugh in the clubhouse, O'Toole was the most hard-nosed, combative competitor on the pitching staff, a man who would back down from no one. He had grown up as a tough south-side-of-Chicago-Irish-cop's kid. He had been a good Golden Gloves boxer in his teens and was not averse to putting this old skill to use. He ferociously defended his teammates when necessary. During that era if someone, say Willie Mays, slid into second base with his spikes a little too high and cut the second baseman, the pitcher was expected to subtly remind Mays the next time up that, "We would prefer, Mr. Mays, if it's not too much trouble, that you please keep your spikes out of our second baseman's legs if possible." The accepted way to deliver this polite message was a baseball aimed about two feet off the inside corner of the plate. O'Toole had no problem sending these messages to the opposition. "The game was more cut throat back then compared to today," says Edwards. "We knocked people down, hell we'd hit people if they were going real good. We'd tell them, 'You're going too good, you're going to get hit.' That was the way the game was played. You expected it from the other team and you had to be able to respond."[26] O'Toole was definitely able to respond. He was a favorite of Fred Hutchinson's because of his competitiveness.

Joe Nuxhall beat Sandy Koufax and the Dodgers 1–0 on May 27 for his third shutout in two months. It was a great comeback for Nuxhall. It couldn't have happened to a nicer guy. Joe Nuxhall was one of the most universally liked players in Cincinnati. Always smiling, always joking, he got along with everyone. "He loved his practical jokes," says Eddie Kasko. "Hot foots, putting shaving lotion in peoples' hats, anything for a laugh."[27]

"He treated everyone the same," says Dan Neville. "It was hard to forget him because he never forgot you. He remembered everybody's name no matter how important or unimportant they were. He didn't act like he was above the younger guys just because he had been there so long. He didn't talk down to you."[28]

Joe was very active in the community and a fan favorite. "That was just part of the whole package with Nuxhall," says Ellis. "Everyone in town loved him because of the way he acted: always willing to help, always great with the fans, never too busy to talk to people or sign autographs."[29] Nuxie's mug regularly showed up on advertisements around town. It was sometimes said, tongue in cheek, that he was a better pitchman than pitcher. He was always available to the press for a comment and always available to help with a good cause. Being from the nearby town of Hamilton, he was considered one of Cincinnati's own.

On the field, however, Nuxhall was an intense competitor, given to rage and destruction in the clubhouse after a poor outing. "One of the most tenacious pitchers I ever saw and one of the most competitive guys I ever played with," is how Pete Rose later described him.[30]

"You never met a bigger competitor," says Billy McCool. "He hated to lose. But the only one he got mad at was himself. Once he walked into the San Francisco clubhouse after a bad game. Joe had gotten beat on a late home run. He came in and saw the table with the spread of food. He was so mad, he went to kick the table but his spikes slipped on the concrete and he went flying on his keester. Food went everywhere. I'm at my locker hiding my face, doing everything I can to keep from laughing because he was still so mad."[31]

Nuxhall was also famous for his appetite. Once he got knocked out of a game early in Houston and angrily stomped into the clubhouse. The Houston clubhouse postgame spread was famous for deviled eggs. "Hutch loved those things," Rose later said. Nuxhall soothed his anger by eating every one of the eggs—fifty according to Rose. "Man was Hutch [ticked]," said

Tough lefty Jim O'Toole won at least 16 games each season from 1961 to 1964
(Cincinnati Reds).

Rose. "But (Nuxhall) paid the price for it, both in his stomach and the [garbage] he got from Hutch. From that time on you weren't allowed to touch the food until the game was over."[32]

Joe Nuxhall still holds the distinction of being the youngest player ever to appear in a major league baseball game. In 1944, when a large number of able-bodied baseball players were in the military, Joe, a promising high school pitcher from nearby Hamilton, appeared in a game for the Reds against the St. Louis Cardinals at the age of 15 years and 10 months. Lasting all of two-thirds of an inning, he gave up five runs on two hits and five walks. He returned to high school after that and eventually plowed through seven years in the minors before returning to the Reds in 1952. Thereafter, he was consistently one of the Reds' best pitchers throughout the fifties, twice making the All-Star team. Possessing excellent control, he rarely walked batters. And his natural competitiveness on the mound reminded his manager of a certain former Tigers pitcher.

In 1960, however, Nuxhall suddenly lost his effectiveness, stumbled to a 1–8 record and was booed mercilessly in appearances at Crosley Field. He was dealt to the Kansas City A's where he continued to struggle. He started 1962 with the Angels but was released early in the year. Refusing to give up on his career, he returned to the minors, caught on with San Diego, and diligently worked his way back to Cincinnati for the 1963 season. There he had one of the best years of his career, going 15–8 with a 2.61 ERA. "That fellow deserves a lot of credit the way he battled his way back from the minors," pitching coach Jim Turner told reporters in spring training in 1964. "And he's such a great guy, you're happy for him."[33]

While several of the Reds' stars struggled at the plate, the most consistent hitter for the Reds during the first two months of the 1964 season was shortstop Leo Cardenas, who had been over .320 all season. Known to most of the league as Chico, Leo Cardenas was 26 years old in 1964. He had been born in Matanzas, Cuba, the sixth of fifteen children. From a crowded, poor family, he had originally come to the United States to play baseball in 1956 as an 18-year-old without much formal education. He was one of the early forerunners of the Latin revolution at the shortstop position. In the forties and fifties, most major league shortstops were short, often light-hitting players, generally regarded as intelligent spark plugs and team leaders. Guys like Pee Wee Reese, Phil Rizzuto, Leo Durocher, Al Dark, and the Reds' Roy McMillan were often coaches on the field. They knew the ins and outs of baseball and used their knowledge of opposing batters to position themselves to overcome any lack of natural speed. They were expected to provide a settling influence on the entire infield. While Chico Carrasquel and Luis Aparicio from Venezuela in the fifties gave American Leaguers a view of the future, showing the type of infielders who could be found south

Joe Nuxhall — the old lefthander (Cincinnati Reds).

of the border, Chico was the first outstanding Latino shortstop in the National League.

The five-foot, ten-inch Cardenas was extremely athletic. The tight skin wrapped around the bones of his face and the cord-like straps of muscles on his arms gave the impression that he had zero percent body fat. Sometimes called the spider because of his resemblance to a spider monkey with his long thin limbs, he was amazingly quick, could jump high and possessed an unbelievable arm which he could uncork from any position. It was immediately apparent when the Reds brought him up in 1960 that they had an extraordinary shortstop on their hands. "You could see he had ability and he was going to be the shortstop of the future," says Kasko. "I knew that I was going to be moved eventually."[34]

Teammates all appreciated his skill in the field. "There wasn't anyone who could play shortstop like Chico could," says McCool.[35] Chico Cardenas was also a very good hitter. He hit .293 in 1962 and had surprising pop in his bat for a skinny guy. He would hit more than ten home runs in a season six times in his career — pretty good numbers for a shortstop in the pre-steroid era. He would make the All-Star team four times in the sixties.

Fred Hutchinson proclaimed Cardenas the best shortstop in the National League in the spring of 1964; better than the Maury Wills of the Dodgers or Dick Groat of the Cardinals. "Chico has wider range in covering either side and can throw from more positions with accuracy and speed," said Hutch. "As opposed to Wills, I would have to say Chico has considerably more zing in his play now. Wills has slowed down a bit since setting a record for stolen bases in 1962, although there's no doubt he is still pretty good. But Cardenas is getting better every day. And whatta pair of hands, they look like Kentucky hams."[36]

But Chico would never be referred to as a leader or one of the smartest guys on the field or a settling influence. Some teammates questioned his intelligence. He could barely speak English. His lack of understanding of the language could have been mistaken as a lack of intelligence. Many Latinos worked hard at English and soon learned enough to get by; however, Chico did not. He almost exclusively preferred the company of the other Latinos and coach Regie Otero, who was described as a "big brother to all the Latins."[37] Frank Robinson wrote that many times Cardenas would be misunderstood simply because of the language barrier. He would not show up where he was supposed to because he had not understood, but it would be charged to a bad attitude.[38]

As a dark-skinned Latino, Chico had experienced culture shock in the minor leagues. He had been one of only two "colored" players on the team in Savannah along with Curt Flood. The experience with racism in the Carolina League led a bitter Flood to later call it the "Peckerwood League."[39]

By state law, Cardenas and Flood could not even dress with their team-mates. They had to dress in a separate cubicle in the locker room. The memories of being a terrified teenager, unable to speak the language, forced to live separately and endure taunts from spectators probably did not help Chico's attitude about this foreign country once he reached Cincinnati.

Chico was moody and his American teammates sometimes had trouble figuring him out. "He was of a different breed, a different culture, very emotional," says one Red.[40] Many teammates would go the entire season and never have a conversation with him.

Fred Hutchinson was adept at handling Chico's mood swings and keeping him focused on the game, however. In addition to Otero, Fred assigned Frank Robinson to help watch over Cardenas. He also dealt with Chico with a firm hand when the sulking episodes occurred. "Once in the early sixties, Cardenas was in a bad slump," O'Toole later recalled. "He told Hutch 'I want to fly home, I quit.' Hutch told him 'If you're not in uniform and on the bench in 15 minutes you'll be out of here today. And we won't be paying [for the plane fare home].' In ten minutes he was in uniform and on the bench."[41]

Cardenas responded best to that type of treatment. "Cardenas would sulk all through his career," says O'Toole. "Hutch knew how to get to him. You just had to be right in his face and put the fear of God in him. You couldn't let him sulk."[42] No one could deny that Chico had good years playing for Fred Hutchinson.

Hutch also was, perhaps, a bit understanding of some of the other problems Cardenas faced. Bill Ford of the *Cincinnati Enquirer* related the story of the time Cardenas missed a team flight for St. Louis. He later caught a commercial flight for which he paid his own way. After arriving at the ballpark, Cardenas was hit with a fine. A few days later, when the team returned to Cincinnati, Chico's worried young wife, holding their baby in her arms, met the flight. According to Ford, "Hutch saw the frightened woman, spoke reassuringly to her, though her knowledge of English was negligible, and begged to hug the infant. Later Hutch reimbursed the tardy shortstop's plane fare."[43]

When 25-year-old Hiraldo Sablon Ruiz, known to all as Chico, joined the club in spring 1964, some teammates began calling Cardenas and Ruiz Chico One and Chico Two. Like Cardenas, Ruiz was from Cuba. He grew up in Santo Domingo, Cuba, where his father operated a cigar factory. Chico and teammate Tony Perez were part of the last of the wave of great players to come from Cuba before Fidel Castro shut down the pipeline. In the fifties the Reds had a great thing going in Cuba. Reds general manager Gabe Paul was good friends with the owner of the Havana club and the Reds actually made Havana a Triple-A team for a few years. Baseball had

been introduced to Cuba in the early 1900s and the island had a great baseball tradition, more than any other Caribbean country at the time. Ruiz told
reporters in early 1964, "Where I live in Cuba, if baby is boy, his first gift
is always a bat."[44] The Reds occasionally took spring training trips to Havana
in the fifties. The Reds got first shot at a large number of great players
thanks to their relationships on the island. In addition to Ruiz, Cardenas
and Perez, other players such as Mike Cuellar, Tony Gonzalez and Cookie
Rojas—players who had long successful careers in the majors—were
brought in and traded. Unfortunately, soon after taking power Castro
decided to favor the Communist Reds over the Reds from Cincinnati, and
he put an end to baseball players leaving the island for the major leagues.
The early days of the Castro uprising had centered in Ruiz's native area of
Santo Domingo and had closed the secondary school he was attending.
Ruiz's father had opposed Chico signing a baseball contract which would
take him to the United States. His father's fears were confirmed as, once
the Castro government had been established, Chico, like other Cubans playing major league baseball, could not visit his home because of the uncertainty of being allowed to leave to return to the United States.[45] It would
be years before Chico saw some members of his family again.

Although they shared a first name, Chico One and Chico Two were
very different. While Cardenas was moody, Ruiz was always smiling, bub-
bly—a happy-go-lucky kind of guy. He was proud of the control he had
gained of the English language through hard work, without any educational
assistance, and he mixed well with his teammates. "Everybody liked Chico,"
says Ellis of Chico Two.[46]

"Chico Ruiz was extremely funny," says Mel Queen. "He was always
joking."[47] One of the characters on the team, he kept teammates laughing.
One season he spent his idle time in the dugout making a huge ball of bub-
ble gum wrappers. He became renowned for the alligator shoes he bought
and fit with spikes.[48] "When we were going to be on the Saturday Game of
the Week on TV," adds Queen, "Chico would wear his alligator shoes and
sit in the front part of the dugout with his feet up so everybody on TV could
see them."[49]

Ruiz was once spotted on the bench with his own personal cushion and
a battery-operated portable fan. "If you're going to sit on the bench, why
not be comfortable?" he said.[50] He loved practical jokes, once slicing a teammate's sports jacket into shreds and then sewing it back together loosely so
that it fell apart as soon as it was put on.

While Ruiz had blazing speed, he was not near the all-around player
Cardenas was. Although the switch hitter had a good batting average in the
minors, he was never able to hit much more than .250 in the majors. But
he was a very valuable player to have on a team because of his disposition

and because he could play, better than adequately, every position on the field except pitcher and catcher. He started at third base early in 1964, but Steve Boros won the job after the first few weeks. Starting or not, Chico's attitude was the same. Later in his career, as a utility infield-lifer, he was forced by injuries to others to be in the starting lineup for several weeks in a row. He came into the dugout after a game, slammed his glove on the bench, complained that playing every day was killing him and jokingly yelled the immortal phrase, "Bench me or trade me."[51]

Late in spring training, Earl Lawson had run a column discussing the great speed of Chico Ruiz, who had led the league in stolen bases every year in the minors from 1959 through 1963. Three times in his career, he had gotten doubles on bunts and once had reportedly gotten a triple on an infield popup. "God give me speed," Chico told Lawson, "I got to use it."[52]

Lawson quoted coach Regie Otero as saying, "If Chico make team, we be the terrors of the National League ... we drive pitchers crazy."[53] Lawson and Otero did not know at the time that six months later their words would seem like prophecy.

15

June:
Pinson and Robinson

ON JUNE 2 the Reds defeated the Braves 7–5 in Milwaukee. Billy McCool, now being called Cool Billy in the papers but McGoo by his teammates, got his first major league victory. Nuxhall had started for the Reds and gave up five runs before leaving for a pinch hitter in the fifth. "I sure kept that Indian warm while I was in there," he quipped to reporters after the game, referring to the Braves' mascot who did a war dance after each Brave home run, accompanied by smoke signals rising out of his teepee. "If I'd stayed around longer they would have run out of smoke, too."[1]

McCool had entered and held the Braves scoreless on two hits while the Reds rallied for four runs in the eighth inning off Braves' ace Warren Spahn. Rose led off the eighth with a single to center and went to third on Tommy Harper's double down the left-field line. Vada Pinson followed with a triple, then scored on Deron Johnson's infield grounder. Frank Robinson and John Edwards both doubled and the score was tied.

The Braves threatened to take back the lead off McCool in their half of the eighth. Hank Aaron hit a one-out double (McCool apparently had ignored Maloney's advice about finding a way to keep Aaron out of the lineup) and Joe Torre followed with a walk. Hutch stuck with McCool and he got the next two batters out. After the Reds scored two more in the top of the ninth, Ryne Duren shut down the Braves in order to preserve McCool's win and pick up the save. "We haven't won a game like this in a long time," said the Reds' happy manager after the game. He continued to brag on McCool: "He's not doing anything I didn't expect. He's got a good arm and he's not afraid of a hitter."[2]

Nuxhall loudly disagreed with the last statement. He laughingly told everyone that when Billy entered the clubhouse after coming out of the game he told Joe, "Boy, that Joe Torre scared the hell out of me when he came to the plate. I'll bet he hasn't shaved in two weeks."[3]

The win pushed the Reds' record to 23–21 and kicked off a streak in which they would win nine of the next 12 games. They would not be close to .500 again, but they still had a long way to go to get back into contention. The Dodgers and Cardinals were with the Reds in the middle of the pack as the Giants and Phillies were slowly pulling away from the rest of the league.

The Reds left for Los Angeles the night of June 7 to begin a ten-game western road trip that would go through San Francisco and Houston. On June 8, the sports page of *Cincinnati Post* carried the headline, "Hutch is Back in Hospital for Treatment."[4] Fred had accompanied the club to L.A. but continued on to Seattle. The paper explained that he had decided to return to Seattle for treatment after consultation over the weekend in Cincinnati with Dr. George Ballou, the Reds' team physician. Hitting coach Dick Sisler would take over the team in Hutch's absence.

Bill DeWitt was quoted as saying, "Hutch has been having severe pain in his back and over his left eye. He also has lost a lot of weight. I have no idea when he will be able to return to duty."[5] The paper said Hutch would be gone indefinitely. The news surprised a lot of the Reds. Hutch had been quietly going about the business of running the team without any complaint. On the outside, he looked good. Few of the players suspected things were not going well.

But behind the façade of good spirits, Fred had been quietly experiencing tremendous pain. Ritter Collett later wrote that in late May in Pittsburgh "at least one writer and several of his players saw him fumble and then drop his jacket trying to hang it up in the visitors' dugout. Later that night, Hutch called Bob Prince, the Pittsburgh broadcaster, and asked him for a favor. 'Find me a doctor who'll keep his mouth shut and give me something to kill the pain.'"[6]

The Reds lost to the Dodgers and Sandy Koufax 2–1 on June 8, dropping Jim Maloney's record to 3–7 even though he had an ERA of 2.73. Maloney could have consulted a lawyer to sue his teammates for nonsupport. The Reds had only scored 26 runs for Maloney in his 11 starts. Koufax, his arm feeling much better, was coming off a no-hitter against the Phillies and allowed the Reds only four hits, one of which was a Deron Johnson home run.

The headline in the next day's sports page, however, was, "Hutch Rejoins Reds Today." Fred would be returning to the Reds after missing only one game. Owner DeWitt announced to the press that he had been advised by Dr. William Hutchinson "that the checkup had been completed and that tests taken indicated there was no need of treatment at this time."[7] Although Fred had been released quickly, this had been a definite setback. It was readily apparent now to those close to the situation that the season was going to be a struggle — an endless series of ups and downs. Fred had been telling everyone that he was fine, that he was only worried about the team, but the pain and weight loss were real. And now there was "no need of treatment" because there was, in fact, no treatment available which had any chance of reversing the process. The only treatment doctors could offer him was palliative — pain control. He had endured the radiation, the only hope — but now the relentless progression of the cancer was beginning to show. The clock was ticking.

As the weather heated up in June, the Reds hoped their bats would also. Pete Rose entered June with a .214 batting average and reporters were beginning to talk more about the sophomore jinx. Gordy Coleman told Earl Lawson he believed Rose would soon snap out of it. "I'm a worrier by nature," said Coleman, "Pete's not. That's why it should be easier for him to perk up."[8] If not worried, Rose was certainly concerned about his low batting average, as was his manager.

The greatest hitting concern, however, was that the Reds' two biggest stars were still battling slumps. Vada Pinson and Frank Robinson were both performing well below their normal levels. After hitting .366 in April, Pinson had plunged into the worst slump of his career, hitting .217 for the month of May and, at one point, going 2 for 33. He was battling a torn thigh muscle and other nagging injuries. The Reds could scarcely hope to remain in contention without production from the two men who had carried so much of the offensive burden the past five years.

Frank Robinson was 29 years old in 1964, a veteran of eight seasons. He had been the youngest of ten children growing up. His father had deserted the family when Frank was four. As a young child he had found refuge in baseball; he later said that he played some form of the game from dawn to dusk every day.[9] Signed out of high school by the Reds for a $4000 bonus, he had quickly worked his way up to Cincinnati after only two seasons in the minors. While the Reds had been the ninth team in major league baseball to play a black player in 1954 when both Chuck Harmon and Nino Escalera appeared in the same game, they had not had a black star before Robinson arrived in 1956. It would take some adjustments by both the city and Robinson over the years for both to become comfortable with his status.

Though only 20 years old as a rookie in 1956, Robinson was immediately recognized as a great player. He set the National League record for home runs by a rookie with 38. Off the field, Robinson struggled with loneliness on a team of much older players. "Frank was like a lost soul," general manager Gabe Paul later said about Robinson's early years with the Reds. "He had no companionship. No guidance."[10] At the time, Cincinnati and St. Louis were the southernmost cities in the National League and both cities were still largely segregated. The combination of age and race differences made for a difficult time adjusting to life in the big leagues.

"One thing was that there was no one my age on the ball club," Robinson wrote in his 1968 autobiography. "I was the youngest and since I was a

loner anyway, a fellow who doesn't make friends easy, it was doubly hard....
I lived at the Manse Hotel in Cincinnati, which was a hotel for Negroes. All
the Negro players on the Reds stayed there — Brooks Lawrence, George Crowe,
Bob Thurman and Pat Scantlebury. Because we were Negroes we did have
mutual interests but they were all older fellows and I just never felt that I
belonged.... I used to tag along with Brooks Lawrence and Bob Thurman after
the game, not because it was fun but because I didn't have anything else to
do. They liked to go to nightclubs, and I just wasn't in with that type of a
crowd and I didn't drink. I just sat there in a corner in a booth looking at
my watch and hoping they would get tired and we could go back to the
hotel."[11]

"It was worse when we were playing at home," he told *Sports Illustrated*
in 1963. "I hated to stay in my room by myself. I just hated to. Before I'd go
to bed at night I'd check the papers to see what time the movies started next
day. If there was one in the morning I'd make it. And the afternoon show,
too."[12]

Robinson spent the first few years of his career quietly piling up huge
numbers at the plate and establishing a reputation for particularly hard-nosed
play. He also acquired the reputation for moodiness and being temperamen-
tal. Some of this reputation may have been the result of youth and loneliness.
Some of it was earned with a series of incidents and misunderstandings with
management.

Things changed drastically for Robinson with the arrival of Vada Pinson. They had attended the same high school, McClymonds High School in
Oakland. McClymonds produced an incredible amount of athletic talent during that period with Cardinal All-Star Curt Flood and basketball immortal
Bill Russell also attending in those years (Robinson played on the basketball
team with Russell and they won quite a few games). Pinson was three years
behind Robinson and they had barely known each other while in high
school — only occasionally seeing each other through games or mutual friends.
Once they were both with the Reds, however, Robinson and Pinson became
great friends. "I finally had someone to talk to, someone who spoke my language, who liked to do the things I liked to do — taking in movies, watching
TV, just sleeping," Robinson later wrote.[13] The two were roommates on the
road and were soon inseparable.

Though they shared similar tastes and friendship, Robinson and Pinson
had very different personalities. Pinson was easygoing and much quieter than
Robinson. He had been so quiet that in his first spring training in 1958, coach
Jimmy Dykes spoke to him in broken Spanish for two weeks, assuming he
was Cuban because of the unusual first name and the fact that he didn't seem
to speak English. Pinson finally gathered the courage to tell the startled coach,
"I'm from California. I speak English you know."[14]

The greatest difference between Robinson and Pinson was in their approach to the game of baseball. Whereas Robinson had grown up thinking of nothing other than baseball, obsessed and determined in his pursuit of a career in professional baseball, Pinson sometimes seemed ambivalent toward the game. The story was told that he had been an accomplished trumpet player and reportedly had considered making music his career. He only turned his full attention to baseball his senior year in high school.[15]

Several inches shorter and much less muscular than Robinson, Pinson was nevertheless an exceptional athlete. He was as fast as anyone in baseball — he seemed to glide across the field, his feet barely touching the ground. He was graceful in the outfield and possessed surprising power at the plate. Baseball seemed to come easy for him. He hit a grand slam in his second major league game. He was proclaimed a "sure-thing Hall of Famer" as a 21 year old. Pinson played in every single Reds game his first five seasons. He led the league in hits in 1961 with 208 and 1963 with 204. Over his first five seasons, Vada Pinson had 985 hits, more than Musial (975), Mays (954), Aaron (917) or Rose (899) had in their first five seasons. There was a downside to all this production, however. Pinson was perhaps cursed with too much "natural" appearing athletic ability. Perhaps he set the bar so high with his great early seasons that he could never live up to the expectations of the fans and media. He performed magnificent feats so easily that they almost appeared, well, effortless. Fans and reporters were left to think, "Why can't he do that every time?" The term "effortless" would haunt him his entire career as people, especially in the front office and press, would come to question his effort. People mistook his quietness for a lack of competitive desire. The Dodgers' Clem Labine voiced the thought shared by many around the league in 1960 when he said, "What's wrong with Pinson? The day he becomes aggressive he will be better than Willie Mays."[16]

Some of this was nonsense. Professional baseball is not an easy game — a person cannot hit .309, and average 202 hits, 20 homeruns and 89 RBIs a year as Pinson did his first five seasons without a great competitive desire and effort. Vada Pinson directed his competitive desire internally rather than by throwing bats and helmets. His numbers could hardly have been better had he acted differently, could they? Maybe, maybe not. It is unfortunate that Pinson battled this reputation his entire career. Even among teammates who liked him there was always a slight, hesitant, "What if?" How great could he have been if he had a more aggressive, competitive personality? "Vada Pinson was a great, great ballplayer. People were already saying (in 1959) he was going to be a Hall of Fame player," O'Toole later said, then added the opinion which was the millstone around Pinson's neck: "His trouble was that he was too laidback. I think if he had more heart, he could have been the best player in baseball."[17]

Vada Pinson, one of the best centerfielders in baseball in the early 1960s (Cincinnati Reds).

Another factor which perpetuated this question was certainly the side-by-side comparison with his close friend and teammate Frank Robinson. There was never a question regarding Robinson's desire or competitiveness—except perhaps that it was too excessive. He viewed every game as a war with the other team. There was no room for friendship on the field of battle. "Once, before a game, the other club was still taking batting practice and we were down the line in the outfield," says Queen. "I was talking to one of the opposing players who I had known back in California. Frank walked up to me and said, 'What does it say on the front of your uniform?'

"I said, 'Cincinnati.'"

"And he said, 'What does it say on the front of that other guy's uniform?'"

"And I said, 'Cubs.'"

"He said, 'When we are on the field, you don't talk to them, you don't socialize with them, they are the enemy. After the game, out of uniform, you can do whatever you want, but on the field, they're the enemy.'"

"Later in the early seventies," Queen continues, "when Frank was with Baltimore and I was with the Angels, I was walking down the line after BP and Frank came up behind me and said, kind of low, 'Hey Queenie, how're you doing?'

"And I said, 'Hey Frank, how are you?' And we kept walking. If you were watching from the stands you wouldn't have known we said anything."[18]

Frank Robinson was not well liked by opponents, many of whom considered him to be a dirty player. He was called a "black Ty Cobb"[19] by some. He had maimed Braves shortstop Johnny Logan with his spikes while breaking up a double play in 1957, putting Logan out for six weeks. In a memorable fight with the Braves' Eddie Mathews in the first game of a doubleheader in 1960, Robinson crashed into Mathews at third base while being tagged out on a close play. Mathews dove on Robinson and Robinson received a bloody nose, a jammed thumb and a swollen purple eye. Robinson stayed in and finished both games—leading the Reds to victories with a home run and a double and making a spectacular catch of a deep Mathews fly. Afterwards Robinson told teammates, "I won the fight." When they laughed at his swollen face, he said, "We won the game, so I won the fight."[20]

"I'm not out there to win friends," Robinson told *Sports Illustrated* in 1963, "just ball games, and I'll do that any way that I can."[21]

"Robinson was as tough a competitor as you will ever see," says Kasko.[22] Most men who played baseball in the National League in the early sixties agree that Frank Robinson was one of the most competitive players they ever faced. He would lean over the plate, his head bent down, with his left arm (unprotected by body armor in those days) virtually in the strike zone, daring pitchers to hit him. Some pitchers gladly did. However, there was a price to pay for throwing at Frank Robinson.

"Gene Mauch had a rule when I was in Philadelphia: 'You don't throw at Robinson,'" says Duren. "He didn't want you to wake him up. Whenever the pitchers threw at him, he would get up and hit the ball hard somewhere."[23] Robinson had an uncanny ability to motivate himself to inflict damage on teams with his bat after they threw at him.

Robinson had some memorable confrontations with Don Drysdale who professed legal title to the real estate comprising the inside half of home plate in all National League parks. Robinson often led the league in being hit by pitches and Drysdale often led the league in hitting Robinson with pitches. Drysdale seemed to enjoy throwing at Robinson, regardless of the consequences—two tough gladiators squaring off against each other. "Once we were beating the Dodgers pretty good," says Kasko. "The game was already out of hand and you could tell Drysdale was really mad. When Frank came up, Drysdale threw three straight brushback pitches, each one further inside. The umpire came out and gave Drysdale a warning. With the next pitch, Drysdale drilled Frank right in the ribs and then just walked off the field."[24]

Robinson, who had viewed his first manager Birdie Tebbetts as a priceless mentor, did not immediately hit it off with Fred Hutchinson. "It took me a long while to understand Fred Hutchinson," Robinson later wrote. "My first impression of Hutch wasn't a good one.... You could have a great day and you knew that if he was happy he might come up and say, 'Nice going,' but it wasn't what you would call a warm, spontaneous thing. But that's the way he was.

"And, at first, I didn't understand him, and maybe he didn't understand me. He was a real firm type of manager. He always had the respect of the team but it was hard for the players to really get close to him.... We had our misunderstandings, but (by 1964) I had come to respect him greatly as a manager."[25]

Their mutual misunderstanding started in spring training of 1960. Robinson was a notoriously slow starter and, because of a chronic nagging injury to his throwing arm which always troubled him in the spring, he usually eased into spring practice. The new manager saw this as loafing. "I think Fred Hutchinson, who was new to the club as far as spring training went, resented my way of getting into shape, though he never said anything to me," Robinson wrote. According to Robinson, Fred "blasted" him in a column in a Cincinnati paper for not hustling. This caused hurt feelings in the very proud Robinson. The two did not talk over their differences but silently steamed at each other.[26]

Coach Regie Otero acted as a go-between and helping the two headstrong men come to a better understanding. He told Robinson, "When Hutch chews you out, he's doing it for your own good. Not because he dislikes you. Hutch never had your great natural ability. Few players do. He hates to see you waste it."[27]

A later incident caused similar hard feelings. "Hutch didn't like players who got to the park late or wouldn't play hurt," says O'Toole. "He did have a little trouble with Robinson early because of this. Once Frank was hurt and out of the lineup and Hutch expected Frank to come to him to tell him when

Frank Robinson takes a vicious cut in front of a Crosley Field crowd (Cincinnati Reds).

he was ready to play. He thought a player, especially the star of the team, should be so anxious and foaming at the mouth to get back in the lineup that he would tell the manager he wanted to play."[28] Robinson wrote that he did not know he was expected to go to the manager to get back in the lineup. He expected the manager to come to him and ask. So Robinson sat out a few more games and the two quietly grew angrier at one another, each expecting the other to make the first move.[29]

Over time, they came to a better understanding and mutual respect. Robinson appreciated the fact that Fred firmly stood in his corner after he was arrested on a concealed weapon charge in Cincinnati before the 1961 season. The incident, which arose over an argument at a diner and resulted in Robinson pleading guilty and being fined $250 by the judge, threatened to erupt into a major scandal in the press and could have been allowed to damage Robinson's reputation and affect the team. According to Robinson, rather than blow up or condemn Robinson, the only thing Fred said to him in their first meeting in spring training was, "That was a stupid thing to do." Robinson wrote that he admitted it and promised to learn from it and the matter was dropped.[30]

In another version of their conversation, Al Hirshberg wrote in 1962: "Hutch said to him, 'Frank, you know you did a silly thing, and it'll be a long time before you hear the last of it. They'll ride the hell out of you all over the league and you're going to have to take it. No matter what happens, you'll stay in there. I don't care if you hit two hundred."[31]

Regardless of the exact dialogue, the point was that coach and player acknowledged that it would never happen again and Fred was not going to allow this to hurt either Robinson or the team. Robinson went on to have his best season to that point and the Reds won the pennant. Robinson wrote that this incident was "a turning point in my life" and that he matured as a result.[32]

Fred certainly came to admire the hard-nosed manner in which Robinson played the game. He especially appreciated the way Robinson battled, broke up double plays and refused to back down when he was the favorite target of opposing pitchers. Noting his speed, power, batting average and fielding ability, Fred told *Sports Illustrated* in 1963, "He's the most complete ballplayer in the game."[33]

Fred later told another reporter that Robinson showed the kind of leadership Joe DiMaggio had. That is, he led by example on the field and not with his mouth. Robinson appreciated the compliment.[34] "Frank Robinson was one of my father's favorite players," says Rick Hutchinson.[35]

"Fred really liked Frank Robinson," says Patsy Hutchinson. "He thought the world of Frank."[36]

While Pinson never had any major public run-ins with his manager other than complaints of not hitting the cutoff man, he had some memorable troubles with the press. Pinson was sensitive to criticism in print and was especially angered by an inflammatory article by Lawson in 1962. Pinson confronted Lawson in the clubhouse and an argument ensued, Pinson yelling, "What made you an expert, what the hell did you ever hit in the majors?"[37]

Lawson fired back choice words and challenged Pinson. "I thought Lawson had a lot of guts," said Jim Brosnan later. "He was a little bitty guy.... When Vada said, 'I ought to punch you right in the face,' little Earl said, 'Well, just try it.'"[38] The argument ended with Pinson punching Lawson right in the face.

The next day, Lawson wrote about the fight and concluded with "When I write that he's squandering much of his God-gifted talent, I'm expressing an honest opinion, one I share with many, including, if the truth were known, many of his teammates."[39] The incident faded rather quickly and quietly, however, sore feelings persisted.

As the team underperformed in 1963, Lawson again railed about Pinson's mistakes and effort and later became fixated with the thought that Pinson should bunt more to use his speed rather than try for home runs. Teammates teased Pinson about Lawson's articles and, as it often does when the team is not doing well, the teasing began to open a nasty wound. Pinson became more frustrated. On September 4, after a column entitled "Bunts Could Make Champ of Pinson," Pinson again confronted Lawson. Lawson wrote that Pinson blocked his path in the clubhouse and, following a "steady stream of profanity," grabbed him by the wrist, then grabbed his shirt collar and ripped it.[40]

Lawson immediately went to Fred Hutchinson's office and called the police and later went to the police station and signed a warrant for Pinson's arrest. Three weeks later DeWitt intervened and met with Lawson to try to get him to drop the charges against Pinson which he feared would result in poor relations in the Cincinnati community. Lawson demanded a public reprimand of Pinson by the team. When DeWitt refused Lawson's demand, a legal hearing was held and the issue went to trial in December. Fred Hutchinson was called to Cincinnati from Florida to be interviewed by the Reds' attorneys who wanted him to testify in Pinson's (and the team's) defense. When asked what he would say if called to the stand, Hutch said, "If they ask me if Pinson had any provocation at all for what he did, my answer will be 'No.'" The club's attorneys decided not to put him on the stand. Lawson later wrote, "Hutch knew going against DeWitt could have cost him his job. But he still wouldn't lie."[41] Lawson, believing the suit had served its purpose, soon dropped the charges. He never did get an apology, however.

Regardless of the thoughts of the press, Pinson was popular with his teammates. They all agree that he was a great player and a great teammate. Pete Rose, in two of his autobiographies, tells the story of being locked out of his room one night on the road as a rookie when his roommate had "company." He was sitting in the hotel lobby late at night with nowhere to go when Pinson came through, saw the problem and invited Pete to spend the night in the extra bed in his room.[42] Apparently, Pinson made a habit of providing sanctuary for teammates displaced by amorous roommates as Dan Neville tells a nearly identical story: "Once in spring training we were playing some games in Mexico City. My roommate had a girl and asked if I would vacate the premises. So I was sitting in the lobby about midnight and Pinson came in and saw me. He said, 'I've got a spare bed in my room.' The older guys got private rooms. We talked a long time that night. He was a very nice and interesting guy. I'll never forget that because I was just a rookie trying to make the team and he was one of the stars."[43]

Batboy Mike Holzinger also appreciated Pinson. "He used to give me a lot of his used equipment. We were both left-handers so he would give me gloves and stuff. He was really a nice guy. But boy, did he get a bum rap by the press."[44]

Pinson had the reputation around the league as someone who could be softened up by being brushed back at the plate. Whereas Robinson would get back up breathing fire and make the other team pay, Pinson merely got back in the box and stoically awaited the next pitch. Often Robinson, like a protective big brother, would shout at the pitcher from the on deck circle after Pinson was knocked down. "He would yell at them and call them every name in the book while he was walking up to the plate next," says Eddie Kasko.[45]

"I remember once in San Francisco, Ron Herbel threw at Pinson," says Mel Queen, "and Frank hollered from the on deck circle, 'I'm up next, do that to me. Then he got in the batter's box and hollered, 'Come on, do that to me.'"[46] It takes a special kind of guts to intentionally provoke a man capable of throwing an object 90 miles an hour when the man is holding that object only 60 feet away.

Because of their race and the times in which they lived, Robinson and Pinson had been through experiences which their teammates could never appreciate and this contributed to their ambiguous status in the clubhouse. Although in a predominantly black neighborhood, McClymond High School had been integrated and was relatively free of racial strife for the time. Robinson later admitted that he was shocked and angered upon arriving at his first minor league stop, Ogden, Utah, when he was refused admittance to the town's only movie theater. The ticket girl told him, "We don't patronize Negroes."[47] In Ogden, Robinson could not use the hotels or restaurants his teammates did. The following year in Columbia, South Carolina, he was in for much more of a shock. Later with the Reds, spring training always amplified the difference in status between black and white teammates. Black players were not allowed to stay in the team hotel. They either had to stay in local "Negro hotels," boarding houses or with private families. In 1961, for instance, Pinson and Robinson stayed at the house of a black doctor during spring training.[48]

Patsy Hutchinson recalls that one year in the early sixties, Pinson brought his wife with him to spring training. "His wife was a lovely person," she says. "I met her at the field one day and told her I was glad she came to spring training and she said, 'This is just an experiment. We want to see how it is.' Spring training was difficult for the blacks. It's hard to believe now that it was that way."[49]

Although there were no written segregation laws in Cincinnati as there were in Florida, things were still difficult. African Americans were not allowed into the large swimming pool at Cincinnati's Coney Island until 1961. Nearly all the neighborhoods in Cincinnati were still segregated in 1964. The first Reds of color to break the segregated housing system were Tony Perez and Chico Ruiz in 1967.[50] So it must have been frustrating for Pinson and Robinson to realize that no matter how many home runs they hit, no matter how high their batting average was, there were still places they could not swim or live in Cincinnati. They did not speak out publicly about this, however. As a young player Robinson was asked to join the NAACP. He told them he would under the condition that he not be called on to make appearances. His belief was: "I don't think baseball should be a fight for anything but baseball."[51]

While many of their teammates did not seem to notice or care what they were going through, others noticed but felt there was nothing they could do to help. At the time, attitudes and cultures were different and many players may not have taken the time to consider things from their standpoint. Some feel a little regret with time, however. "It's unfortunate they had to put up with that shit," says one former player succinctly.[52]

Robinson had a very poor relationship with Bill DeWitt, who he later referred to as "Bill CheapWitt."[53] Robinson wrote that hard feelings between the two began almost immediately.[54] DeWitt was notoriously cheap and miserly in contract talks and each year he and Robinson had a difficult time reaching an agreement. Robinson, the best player on the team, was the highest paid as well. He made $60,000 for 1963, the most in franchise history. DeWitt may have resented so much of his precious money going to one player. Personal things were said in meetings and to the press while the two haggled and no doubt this led to even more hard feelings. After his subpar 1963 season, Robinson was forced to take a $5000 pay cut after particularly nasty negotiations. He joked with reporters, "I got cut so deep, I'm going to have to go to the clubhouse to be sewn up."[55] But there was an edge to his joke.

Robinson wrote in 2008 that his reputation as anti-management was also caused by the fact that he had become somewhat of a team spokesman by his later years with the Reds. "Most of the time, it wasn't my problems that I was speaking out; it was a teammate's problem. They would come to me. 'Frank, you're the big guy on the club, you know, you could go talk to them and they're not doing this, I'm unhappy with this or that.' And I would always take the problems of my teammates to management as my own problem.... When you would speak up or speak out against management, they would classify you as a troublemaker. And this is what I became, a troublemaker. I was also bad for the young players."[56]

The hard feelings between Robinson and DeWitt would eventually result in the infamous Frank Robinson for Milt Pappas trade in 1966, generally considered one of the worst trades in baseball history. Robinson would respond by leading the Orioles to the World Series in 1966 while winning the American League Triple Crown — all after DeWitt told everyone he dumped Robinson because he was an "old thirty."

The poor relationship with DeWitt coupled with DeWitt's close ties to the press may have been the cause of the rumors and innuendos in the press about Robinson and Pinson. In the 1964 baseball preseason edition, *Sports*

Illustrated said, "Robinson was involved in another Cincinnati problem, one that did the team no good at all. Robinson and his good friend Vada Pinson are unquestionably the stars of the team, but many Cincinnati players resented them because they too often acted like the stars of the team, taking fielding practice if they were in the mood, often skipping it."[57]

Mark Kram wrote in *Sports Illustrated* later in 1964, "It is no secret that Hutchinson has been silently infuriated by Pinson on and off for a long time (due to his attitude and lack of competitive zeal).... Robinson and Pinson, who are close friends were accused of acting like stars (last year) ... and would take fielding practice only when the spirit moved them."[58]

The term "clique" popped up several places from unnamed sources. In his *1964 Major League Baseball Handbook*, Dave Anderson wrote, "It was whispered ... that Robinson and Vada Pinson had formed a clique which was sabotaging team morale."[59]

Robinson wrote in 1968, "The truth is, there was no clique on that team, no more than there is a clique on any team in baseball. On every ball club you have fellows who have a lot in common and who like to do things together. Under the unwritten rules of baseball in those days (it's not as bad now) the Negro players and the white players were friends on the field, but once the game was over, went their separate way ... no one on the ball club ever said anything directly to me about a clique — not the management, the manager, or the players.... The clique thing was just nonsense."[60]

Robinson, Pinson and Tommy Harper were the only black members of the Reds in 1963. While Rose did hang around them some, he was more often off on his own pursuits after games and could not be called part of their clique. It is ridiculous to suggest that three players could be called a clique that is damaging team morale. Fred Hutchinson, in the same *1964 Major League Baseball Handbook*, was quoted by Dave Anderson saying he thought the clique rumors were exaggerated. "When everything goes well nobody pays attention to such stuff. But when things go bad, people have to put the blame somewhere."[61]

By 1964 there was no more talk of cliques. Robinson and Pinson were acknowledged as the two best players on the team. Robinson went into the 1964 season with a lifetime .303 batting average. He had averaged 30 home runs and 100 RBIs a year in his career. By 1964 he was unquestionably the Reds leader on the field. If there had been a "clique" the previous year, there was no sign of one now. None of the players who were new to the team in 1964 mentions any knowledge of a clique or noticed any problem with the team's atmosphere. All acknowledge Robinson as the leader.

"Robinson was the leader on the team, he led by his action," says Sammy Ellis. "He went out and played hard every day. I remember him helping Gordy Coleman and Deron Johnson with their hitting, talking about the theoretical approach to hitting."[62]

The Reds had a large number of first or second-year players in 1964 and Robinson, as a leader, helped them as well. "Frank Robinson was just a great guy, he took a lot of us young guys under his wing," remembers Billy McCool. "When we went to San Francisco the first time, it was a big deal because I was from a small town. Frank called us and said, 'Come up to my room.' Me and Sammy Ellis and Mel Queen and a few other guys went in and Frank had called room service and had about 25 hamburgers sent up to the room. We sat there and talked baseball for hours.... He was the team leader."[63]

This sentiment is echoed by rookies Bobby Klaus and Dan Neville. "Everybody looked up to him (Robinson), he was a good leader," says Neville.[64]

As the Reds closed out June, some of the hitters were starting to come around. Deron Johnson took over the first-base job with a strong month. John Edwards was hitting .300. Pete Rose, however, continued to struggle. At this point in time, the baseball future of Pete Rose was still somewhat in doubt. Sure, he played hard and looked like he could hit, but many players fade after a good first year. Pitchers find a hole in the swing. Word spreads. The batting average tumbles. Would this be the fate of Pete Rose? As he had when Rose was a rookie, Hutch felt that Rose was pressing too much because he was slumping and wanted to sit him out a short time to allow for extra batting practice to get his stroke and confidence back. Pete drove to Dayton to visit his uncle, Reds scout Buddy Bloebaum, and get advice. Bloebaum told him to lower his hands at the plate and stop swinging defensively.[65]

While not in the starting lineup, Rose still contributed when he could. On June 20, the Reds were battling Don Drysdale and the Dodgers when Pete pinch hit for Klaus in the bottom of the seventh inning. Vada Pinson had tied the score at four the previous inning with his second home run of the game. With one out and Cardenas on third, Rose laid down a squeeze bunt off Drysdale that scored what proved to be the winning run.

But the inactivity of not starting was almost more than Rose could stand. He was determined to use all means necessary to quickly get back into the lineup. "I used to shag flies in the outfield before games with Pete Rose," says Rick Hutchinson. "He wasn't too much older than me. When my father sat him out a few games when he was in a slump it almost killed him. He was so anxious to get back in the lineup he was driving everyone crazy. He came up to me and said, 'You've really got to get me back in the lineup. Say something to your father.'"

"I said, 'I'm not sure that would help. Knowing my father, if I did that he may keep you out just to spite me. But if I get a chance I'll put in a good word for you.' That night, I was in my father's office and he was filling out the lineup card and he paused. I asked him what was the matter and he said, 'I'm trying to decide whether or not to put Pete back in yet. I told him, 'Pete

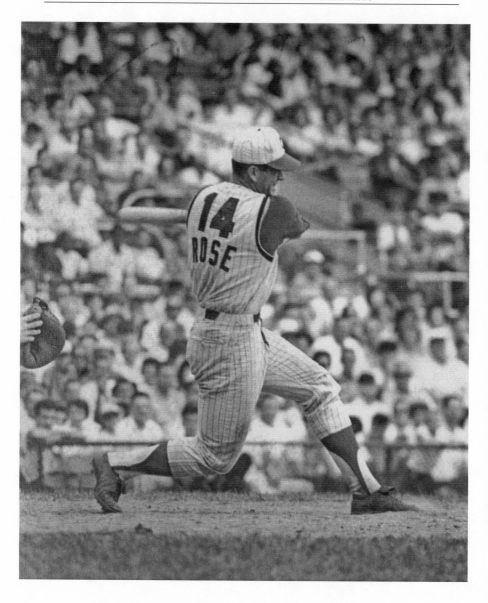

Pete Rose swings from the right side (Cincinnati Reds).

is so anxious to get back in the lineup it's killing him. He even tried to get me to talk you into putting him back in.' My father laughed and said, 'I guess it's time to get him back in there then.'"[66] Soon after, Pete found his stroke and went on a 17 for 32 tear, getting his average above .250 by July 4.

On June 30, Rose got the only hit for the Reds off Larry Jackson of the

Cubs. Rose led off the seventh inning with a single to break up the no-hitter and prevent the Reds the indignity of being no-hit twice in the span of two months. The loss dropped the Reds record to 39–34.

While in Chicago, Dick Sisler was called to Fred's hotel room. As he took a seat in the room, Sisler was not prepared for what his friend was about to say. "He told me he had terminal cancer, just like that," Sisler said in 1965. "Just like you might say 'I'm going to have my hair cut.' I was so shocked I don't know whether I heard the rest of what he had to say." Up to that point, the only thing Sisler and the other coaches really knew about Fred's condition had been what they had read in the papers. They knew he had been diagnosed and treated and had gone to Seattle for checkups, but that was it. Fred had not discussed the situation with any of the coaches and his public face remained one of determination and optimism. Sisler was shaken up at hearing the news straight out. "It jars you when the victim tells you himself," he continued. "He said he didn't know how long he had to live. Maybe one month, maybe two."[67] This was the first time anyone other than Fred's immediate family had been told the full extent of his condition and what lay ahead. It was also the first time Fred admitted to anyone that he knew he was not going to make it. Sisler began to realize what the rest of the season was going to be like. For the players, still focused on playing baseball every day, the realization would come soon.

16

July: "It's what he wants to do"

THE REDS SLOWLY BEGAN to play better and moved further over .500. On July 1, the Reds were six and a half games behind the leading Giants and Phillies. Steve Boros had played well defensively at third base and set a Reds record with over 45 straight errorless games at third base, his first error in almost two months coming July 2. Boros was injured soon after, however, and Chico Ruiz took over at third. The Reds were living on good starting pitching and cold-blooded late-inning relief work from Ellis and McCool. The July 4 home game against the Cardinals was typical of this. The Reds took a 3–1 lead into the 9th with Jim O'Toole on the mound. After Ken Boyer led off with a double, McCool came in and promptly struck out the first two batters he faced. Boyer scored on an error by Cardenas on what should have been a game-ending ground ball. With the tying run on base and the fans on their feet, McCool — just ten days short of his twentieth birthday — remained true to his name and struck out Tim McCarver to end the game and get the save.

As midseason approached, the Reds could no longer ignore the fact that there was something very wrong with their manager. His weight loss, initially gradual, was becoming alarming. His uniform and clothes hung loosely on his once massive frame. His famous lumbering gait was becoming more and more labored. He was visibly uncomfortable just sitting on the bench. Sitting through a complete game was becoming a major ordeal. Rookie Mel Queen, observing the games from the bench, had a chance to watch Fred closer than most players. "The first I really noticed was that he would be sitting on the bench with one of those thick rubber hot water bottles and they would keep changing those," says Queen. "I thought 'Something's wrong, he's worse than we thought.' You could tell he was in a lot of pain but he wouldn't say anything to anybody about it. He just kept managing the team."[1]

An interesting phenomenon developed among writers. The early battle cry to circle the wagons around Hutch in January had given way to expressions of admiration in March and April as he appeared to have licked it and kept his promise to show up in time for spring training. Jack Hand of the Associated Press had summed up the general feeling in late March by stating: "The best story of the spring training season is Fred Hutchinson ... fighting a courageous battle against cancer," in an article entitled "How Can You Beat a Man Like Hutch."[2] In April and May, the theme was how good Hutch looked and felt and his determination to continue. By July, the tone was much different. The home town writers, out of respect, did not elaborate on

Nineteen-year-old Billy McCool became one of the best relief pitchers in the National League in 1964 (Cincinnati Reds).

Fred's condition publicly now. Visiting writers, however, could not help but notice the changes in Fred's appearance and the fact that pitching coach Jim Turner was going to the mound instead of Fred to make pitching changes. No one suggested that this was the best story of the year anymore. As Fred's condition progressed, writers shifted to a kind of respect bordering on awe, inspired by the way he was taking the whole thing. Refusing to complain or indulge in pity, he doggedly showed up for work every day, answered all questions optimistically and concerned himself with how to help his team get back in the pennant race. One reporter wrote, "I thought I would feel sorry for Hutch, instead I feel — I don't know — proud. I feel proud to be a human being because Hutchinson is one. I mean, he has cancer but instead of letting me feel sorry for him he makes me feel good just because I know him. What a man he is."[3]

The All-Star game was held in New York's new Shea Stadium in 1964. Chico Cardenas and John Edwards were the only two Reds players selected to the National League team. Fred Hutchinson was picked to be one of the coaches by National League manager Walter Alston. Members of the National League All-Star team, seeing Fred up close for the first time all season, were surprised at the changes. Arthur Daley of the *New York Times* later wrote,

"His face had become gaunt and he walked slowly, much like an old man. Fearless Fred, the unyielding fighter, was losing his battle even though he stalwartly refused to admit it."[4] Although in obvious pain to observers, Fred kept busy at the game, hitting fungoes to outfielders in pregame drills and coaching third base all nine innings. He joked with fans and American League players and appeared to truly enjoy himself. The game was a close one. In the ninth inning the score was tied 4–4 with a man on second and first base open and John Edwards at the plate. The American League elected to intentionally walk Edwards. Philly Johnny Callison then hit a game-winning walk-off home run to give the National League a 7–4 victory. Hutch gleefully pounded on Edwards and Callison as they rounded third.

In the meantime, a rumor swirled that Fred was going to announce his retirement at the All-Star game. Upon questioning, Bill DeWitt said, "This is news to me. Fred is doing fine and he's our manager until he says otherwise. I wouldn't think of replacing him."[5]

Patsy, who had accompanied Fred to New York, told reporters, "Fred feels fine. I just don't know how such things come up."[6]

Fred put the official lid on the rumor: "I'll quit only if they fire me or if the man upstairs tells me."[7]

Back in Cincinnati after the All-Star break, the Reds players seemed buoyed by Fred's reassurance and won seven of nine games. The two losses came on July 12 in a doubleheader to the Mets in New York, with the Reds scoring only one run the whole day off the lowly Mets pitching staff. Fred hated dropping games to the Mets, it provoked one more appearance by the Bear of old. "We went into the clubhouse after the game and all the players were sitting at their locker," remembers Queen. "I was a stupid, naïve rookie. There was a spread of food on a table for after the game. I went up and started making myself a plate.

"I'll quit only if the man upstairs tells me" (Cincinnati Reds).

Fred came in, kind of looked at me, then walked by into his office. So I finished making my plate and went over to my locker, not noticing that no one else was eating. He came back out and cleared the whole spread with one swipe of his big arm. 'I don't want anybody in here eating,' he said. 'There better not be a player in this clubhouse when I come out of my office after I shower.' All of the sudden you've got guys like Pinson, Robinson and Rose flying through their lockers getting out of there. Nobody wanted to take a chance on being caught when he came out. He had seen me and knew I was a rookie and didn't know any better. So instead of saying something there to embarrass me in front of the whole club, he walked on by and let me get back to my locker, then came back out and had his tirade. I really respected him for that because he could have embarrassed me greatly but he chose not to, knowing I was a rookie."[8]

The Reds bounced back to sweep a doubleheader from the Colt 45s at home on July 14 to move to within five and one-half games of first. Billy McCool, pitching on his twentieth birthday, threw two perfect innings to get the win in the opener. Afterwards, he told reporters, "I'll take a victory over a birthday cake any day."[9]

The second game of the doubleheader was notable for the first major league home run off the bat of Mel Queen. The seventh-inning home run put the Reds in front 10–3 and loosened up the Reds bench. When Queen came back to the dugout he witnessed Marty Keough stretched out on his back, apparently fainted from shock. Backup catcher Hal Smith was fanning him with a towel while Joe Nuxhall was administering mouth-to-mouth resuscitation. "We just had to acknowledge the first one," a laughing Keough told reporters after the game.[10]

"Queenie was so excited the second time he went to the plate that he was going to use the lead bat we use for warm-up swings in the on-deck circle," Pete Rose joked.[11]

Soon afterwards Frank Robinson began to return to his old form. He told reporters the change had occurred after watching some old movies of himself hitting; he had discovered a flaw and it had been corrected.[12] He went on a 15-for-27 tear with three home runs and inched his average back up to .300. Catcher John Edwards hurt his arm in late July and Don Pavletich came up from San Diego to help out the catching. The muscular Pavletich, a strong hitter but not quite the defensive ace that Edwards was, hit three home runs in four days to help the Reds at the plate. But it was the pitching which continued to hold up the team. Billy McCool had a stretch of ten relief appearances in July without giving up a run.

Tony Perez made his major league debut on July 26. He had been having a great year at San Diego. Cincinnati papers had periodically carried reports of the damage Perez was inflicting on Triple-A pitching through the summer. "That guy doesn't belong in this league," a San Francisco Giant scout had remarked after watching Perez hit his 19th home run in less than half the season on June 11.[13] It was hoped that Perez could provide some extra punch in the lineup.

Tony Perez grew up in the city of Camaguey, Cuba. He had been working in a sugar cane factory when signed by the Reds. His signing bonus from the Reds consisted of a plane ticket and $2.50 for a visa. Time would prove the $2.50 to be money well spent. When Perez arrived in Geneva, New York, in 1960, he could not speak any English. He later recalled sitting in restaurants and pointing to items on the menu. One time a waitress brought him apple pie by mistake. Unable to speak enough English to correct the mistake, Perez had apple pie for dinner that night.[14]

Perez's agreeable personality and hard work trying to learn English allowed him to mix with non–Hispanic players well, getting along with everyone. "He was a very nice guy," remembers Mel Queen. "Hardly ever lost his temper, very funny. He worked at trying to master the English language and sometimes he would butcher it. But he would make fun of himself when he did."[15]

Although he struggled with the glove early, there was never any doubt about his bat. "He was so scrawny when he first got here," says Dave Bristol who managed Perez at two stops in the minors, "but he always had amazing power. He worked hard and got better every year. And I've said it a thousand times, if you played a game long enough, Tony Perez would find a way to win it for you. Even as a youngster he had that attitude that you wanted him at the plate in big situations. He had the perfect temperament for a baseball player. He loved to hit with men on base."[16]

Although Perez would later play third base for the Reds from 1967–70, he was better suited for first base and in 1964 he was definitely not ready for third base in the major leagues. With Johnson and Coleman already at first, there was not a spot for Perez in the lineup. After a few starts in which he failed to produce, he was relegated to pinch-hitting the rest of the season — a difficult chore for a rookie. He would end the season with only two hits in 25 at bats. Tony Perez would go on to drive in more than 1600 RBIs in a 23-year Hall of Fame career but only one came in 1964.

In mid– to late–July, Fred Hutchinson seriously began to lose ground. He could no longer hide the fact that he was in big trouble. His condition was there for all to see each day but no one talked about it. No one mentioned the elephant in the room. "We all know Hutch's condition but we don't talk about it," Bob Purkey told a reporter in late July.[17]

"I hadn't known he was sick when I joined the team in May," says Ryne Duren. "I found out later when he had to miss some games. It wasn't the type of thing you would talk about as a player. You might be standing in the outfield with one other guy and mention it to him but for some reason you wouldn't talk about it in a group of guys. We all knew it by July, you could see it, but we just didn't talk about it. But I just felt so sick when I realized how bad he was. Here was this great guy literally dying in front of us."[18]

"I never heard any of the players or coaches talk about it," says bat boy Mike Holzinger, who had the run of the clubhouse and field. "We could tell that he was losing a lot of weight but everyone kind of went about their business. I don't know if it was conscious or unconscious but nobody seemed to talk about it."[19]

"Major league baseball is a hard game," says McCool. "You try to keep your mind focused on playing the game day to day. But it was impossible not to notice what was happening."[20]

"He would joke about it though," says Duren. "He was very honest about the thing toward the end. I remember him leaning over to me on the bench one day, he was losing so much weight and he said, 'You know what the worst thing about this is? Just sitting here without any flesh on my ass. It hurts sitting.' And he laughed as he said it, kind of jokingly. I thought from a guy who knew he was dying of cancer he was kind of lighthearted, but that's the kind of guy he was."[21]

"It got to where he had a hard time just getting up off the bench," says Edwards. "But he would not let anyone help him. He didn't want to bog us down with his problems. I used to get to the ballpark early and every day when I would get there he would be in the whirlpool trying to get enough strength to get through the ball game. He just went on managing the club. Once you knew about it, you started watching his actions and you knew he was in pain but he didn't want you feeling sorry for him. It was one of the saddest times I remember. His youngest son was only about nine, a redhead and full of life. It was really sad to see him running around the field and clubhouse knowing how bad Hutch was getting."[22]

"One sight I'll never forget," says Don Pavletich, "is Hutch trying to walk down to the end of the dugout to get a drink. The dugout at Crosley Field had poles spaced out supporting the front of the roof and he had to hold on to each pole as he walked to make it down to the end of the dugout. He went from pole to pole. But he wouldn't let anyone help him."[23]

Fred's family began to realize that he was not going to get better. This was one battle no amount of determination and grit could win. Bill visited Fred in Cincinnati in July to check on him. Bill understood what the weight loss meant and was greatly saddened by the change in Fred's appearance since he had last seen him. When Patsy drove Bill to the airport, she said, "We'll see you again when the season is over."

"You may see me before that," Bill ominously replied.[24]

Fred's oldest son was both amazed and perplexed that he kept managing the team. "I was hoping he would just quit and go home where he could be comfortable, to be in a situation where he didn't have to go through any stress," says Rick Hutchinson. "I really wanted him to stop. I didn't see the point in it. Mayo Smith, who was a friend of my father's, was in town for a game with the team he was coaching and he came over and talked to me one day. I asked him if it made any sense to keep going. I said, 'Why doesn't he just quit?'"

"And he said, 'It's what he wants to do. It's what he loves. Your father's only got so much time and this is what he enjoys, this is his wish. You should just go along with it.'"[25]

"It was something to see the way this big, strong guy hung on," Pete Rose later wrote. "It was sad but it was inspiring. We saw Hutch go from 220 pounds to 140 pounds with the cancer and he never once complained.... He had this cough and he was getting skinnier every day, but Hutch was a fighter. He'd come into the clubhouse to conduct the meetings and after a while looking at Hutch was like looking at a skeleton. But I'll tell you this, that skeleton was in charge. I was a kid, I'd never seen cancer before. Never seen courage like Hutch's either. We all knew he was sick. You couldn't not know he was sick. But he ran the meetings the way he always had. He didn't want sympathy.... We would have walked through walls for Hutch."[26]

The Houston Colt 45s came to Crosley Field for a mid–July series. Eddie Kasko, a Hutchinson favorite from the 1961 pennant winner, was now the Colt shortstop. He was saddened by the appearance of his former manager. Kasko talked to Hutch on the field before the game, remembering the good times. "The weight loss was the big thing you noticed," he recalls. "He was making a courageous stand trying to last the season. He said that was the way he was going to go. He tried to sound optimistic."[27]

Fred refused to admit defeat or dwell on his condition even though visiting reporters constantly brought it up. "I am not worrying," he told them on July 20. "Others have the same problems I have and I am satisfied with my condition. I think I am doing all right and I am looking forward to winning the pennant and then I am going to my home in Florida."[28]

On July 27, as the Reds prepared to leave for a road trip, they learned Fred Hutchinson would not be coming with them. "He felt so bad about not being able to make that trip," says Rick, "but he got to the point where he was just physically unable to do it. I was going to go with him on the trip to help him and he really tried but he just couldn't do it. It bothered him so much to have to stay home. It really was devastating to him to not be able to go with the team."[29] The decision to stay home was made at the last minute.

Though trying valiantly, Hutch finally realized that he couldn't make it and called DeWitt. Sisler told reporters the first he knew Hutch was staying home was when DeWitt called him at the airport and said, "Hutch isn't making the trip, you're in charge."

"When Hutch went to Seattle and I was left in charge (in June) I was left instructions. This time, though, I didn't have time to get any instructions,"[30] said Sisler, illustrating the haste in which the decision to stay home was made.

Fred checked into Cincinnati's Christ Hospital for treatment and rest. He called Sisler after every game and listened to the games on the radio. Sisler noted to reporters that he consulted Hutch by telephone about the lineup. On July 28, about an hour before the Reds took the field in Milwaukee, a telegram arrived in their clubhouse. It read, "Spent most enjoyable relaxing night after 10 P.M. Keep it up."[31] It was signed Fred Hutchinson. Shortly before 10 the night before, the Reds had scored five runs to blow open the game and win 11–2.

By the end of July, Pete Rose was hitting the way his manager knew he could and had raised his average more than 50 points in less than a month. Bobby Klaus, dropped from the roster when Tony Perez was recalled from San Diego, was claimed by the Mets for the $20,000 waiver price on July 28. Klaus would get the chance to play every day in New York but it was somewhat sad leaving his first big league team. He had appreciated the compassion Hutch had shown earlier in the season when he had allowed him to leave the team to travel to Chicago to visit his mother who had developed meningitis.[32]

The departure of Klaus had most likely been hastened by the sudden rebound of Rose. Pete had made the most of his return to the lineup with several big games. On July 1, Rose hit a two-out home run in the bottom of the tenth inning to beat the Cubs 6–5. The next day Rose continued his hot hitting, going 3 for 4. On July 18, after getting another three hits the day before, Rose drove in 6 runs, going 4 for 4 with a walk and his first career grand slam.

The reliable Reds pitching was beginning to show signs of faltering however. Joey Jay had never been able to put together a consistent streak all year and was only 5–8 by the end of July. Purkey had not returned to his pre-injury form. After the fast start, Nuxhall appeared to be running out of steam, as his 35-year-old arm was giving him trouble. When he lost to the Braves 6–2 on July 29, his record dipped to 8–6. The Reds finished July struggling to win on the road without their manager and with no idea if they would see him in the dugout again.

17

August: Leave of Absence

WHEN THE REDS returned to Cincinnati in early August, Fred was back on the bench. The team officials had left it up to Fred to return when he wanted — and he wanted to return as soon as possible. The *Cincinnati Post* announced to the citizens of Cincinnati on August 4 that Hutch would rejoin the team that night for a doubleheader against the Braves.[1] The Reds players and newsmen welcomed him back when he arrived at Crosley Field. Fred was in uniform and managed the Reds the first seven innings of the first game, then changed to street clothes and watched the rest of the doubleheader from Bill DeWitt's private box alongside the press box on the roof of Crosley Field. The Reds did their best to make him happy by sweeping the doubleheader 5–2 and 4–2. It was obvious that the games were much more of a struggle for Fred now. Clubhouse man Bernie Stowe recalls that Fred had trouble making it through complete games in early August. "There was a cot in the clubhouse and he would go back and lay down for an inning at a time, then go back out and try to finish the game."[2]

Fred published an article in the August edition of *True Magazine* entitled "How I Live with Cancer."[3] He donated the $1000 fee he received for writing the article to cancer research. The article, written with the assistance of writer Al Hirshberg, detailed his fight from the time the cancer was diagnosed until the present. He explained his treatment and his feelings toward the disease. Although it had been reported that he originally had lung cancer, he noted in the article that doctors had eventually decided that he had a malignant thymoma which had spread to the lung. The article was obviously written in May or June, when he still felt good and had not begun to lose weight. Fred remained remarkably in character and optimistic throughout the article and concluded with: "Whatever happens, I'm grateful for everybody's good wishes. Cancer is a tough foe and not easy for anyone to whip.

158

But with luck, I expect to be around as long as most people my age [45 in August], malignant thymoma or no malignant thymoma."[4] Unfortunately for Fred Hutchinson, by the time the magazine hit the newsstands, it was apparent to all those around him that he would need much more than luck.

Former players heard about how Fred was doing and had difficulty believing he was getting so bad. "I was with the Washington Senators by then," said Don Blasingame in 1991. "Everyone in baseball knew he was dying and I was real glad I wasn't there to see him waste away. I wrote him a letter, reminding him that he used to tell us we can beat anything if we tried hard enough. You know he somehow managed to answer my letter with a hand-written one of his own."[5]

For the players who were in Cincinnati watching Fred every day, emotions were difficult to sort out: sad, determined, inspired — it was becoming hard to concentrate on baseball when a human drama of much more significance was playing out in front of them. The unspoken tragedy had the effect of a shared secret, a silent bond between the players on the team. Most players were unable or unwilling to voice the sentiment they were feeling, but it united them nonetheless. "I think the players are closer because of Hutch's illness," an unnamed Reds player told *Sports Illustrated* in early August. "They are pulling together a lot harder. They don't try to make it obvious, but you can sense the feeling."[6]

The players desperately wanted to win for Hutch, but baseball is a game best played when loose. The emotion took its toll. Frank Robinson later wrote: "Fred Hutchinson was ill, very ill with cancer, and this had a profound effect on the ball club ... when he came back [in August] you could look at the man and tell he was real sick. You could see it in his face, in the movement of his body, in his stiffness as he walked. Everybody tried to ignore the fact and not talk about it too much, but it was in all our minds. In fact we might have been just a little tense, a little too tight because of his illness. I think we were more conscious of making mistakes, that if we did make a mistake on the field we would intensify his pain, his agony. And we might have tried a little too hard to win for Hutch."[7]

"It was an inspiration for us," Joe Nuxhall later said, "to try to win it for Hutch."[8] *To win it for Hutch* — an unspoken desire on the part of all the players. But real life is not like the movies. It is hard to win for someone when the other teams are trying just the same to beat you. As Robinson said, this desire *to win it for Hutch* may have had a negative effect on the team's play, especially at first.

To his family, Fred's decline was a cause of both great anguish and wonder at how he was dealing with it. "You could see the effect it took with the weight loss and in his eyes," says Rick Hutchinson. "The cancer was just eating him up. It was tough. But boy, he sure didn't whine about it. During this time, I asked my mother 'Did he ever complain or say anything about it to you? Because he never complained to me about anything.' And she said 'All he ever said was 'I never thought I'd go this way. I always thought it'd be something quick.' And he never really gave in and conceded defeat. He always fought it. He kept saying 'I'll beat this thing' and he would talk and say 'When I get better from this,' and talk about next season. And you would think 'Excuse me? Next season?'"[9]

"The whole time he was sick I never heard him complain," says Patsy Hutchinson. "I never heard any 'Why me?' or anything. He just didn't say anything. He was the kind of person that if that's the way it was, that's the way it was and he would take it."[10]

When Fred talked to reporters, he appeared more interested in the team and its fortunes. "Hutchinson still thinks his Reds can win the pennant" wrote *Sports Illustrated*'s Mark Kram after an interview in early August. When Fred complained to him about the Reds losing six games to the lowly Mets, Kram wrote, "It is to Hutchinson's credit that he can get upset over losing to the Mets or that he can manage at all, for that matter.... Always a man who exuded indestructibility, both physically and mentally, Hutch is just a fragment of what he once was. His uniform hangs loosely on him. His face is pallid, his eyes are weak and tired and his left eye is partially closed."[11]

In early August, when the Reds were in San Francisco, Charlotte Hutchinson went to visit her uncle. "I went by the hotel to pick up the tickets and talked to him and he was very serious," she says. "He said, 'You know, I don't think we're going to see each other again.'"

"It broke my heart," she continues, remembering the *gorgeous big guy* she had idolized and who had been so important to her teen years. "We sat right behind the dugout and when the game was over, he gave me a little salute and walked off the field and that was the last time I saw him."[12]

On August 12, the Reds held a birthday celebration for Fred at Crosley Field before their scheduled game with the Dodgers. Jack Hutchinson was given the day off from the Cedar Rapids team and flew in to be present for his father's birthday. He had not seen his father since spring training. He was shocked at his appearance. "I had been working hard at playing in the minor leagues and they hadn't really told me how the treatments were going," says Jack. "Maybe they didn't want me to worry. In the minors, you played and practiced every day, there was very little free time to worry about things. So I didn't know the extent of his illness until I saw him that day. That was the first time I realized how bad his condition was. He had just changed so drastically. It was shocking. You just don't expect that, you don't know what to think when you are a teenager. But when I saw him August 12, I knew from looking at him that he was in very bad shape and things were not going to go well."[13]

"Hutch just looked terrible on his birthday," says Jim O'Toole. "His eye was swollen shut with a tumor, he could barely walk. One sight I'll never forget is when he was walking around the field before the game, he was walking with his youngest son, who was only about nine. Hutch was hunched over a bit, shuffling his feet, walking slow because he was so frail and his son was walking exactly like his dad. Everything the dad did, he did. It really choked you up to watch it."[14]

Bill DeWitt was the master of ceremonies on the field for the pregame festivities. DeWitt presented Fred with a five-hundred pound cake "on the behalf of everyone." The cake was so big that reportedly the bakery had to remove a window to get it out after making it. There were numerous gifts and presentations: a personal check from DeWitt, a color TV from the Reds players, a clock-barometer from the Dodger players, an engraved sterling silver pitcher from the TV-radio broadcasters and a Brunswick pool table from the local chapter of baseball writers.[15] DeWitt had initially planned a low-key tribute and had not solicited input from the other sources. As word got out, however, it snowballed with the public, writers, broadcasters and even the Dodgers begging to do something.[16] The ceremony concluded with Hutch standing at homeplate, while the crowd of 18,000 was led in a chorus of "Happy Birthday" by a choral group, the Village Voices, and local singer Cindy Grogg who seemed to choke up toward the end of the song. DeWitt, standing behind her, began to weep as if he had seen one of his nickels roll into a drain. When she concluded, she walked over and kissed Fred on the cheek. Fred uneasily said into the microphone, "How lucky can you get?"[17] The crowd was visibly moved as were Fred's wife and children who watched from a box near the Reds' dugout.

More than a clock-barometer, what Fred really wanted from the Dodgers was a win, but they started Sandy Koufax who had been red hot. The Reds battled hard, wanting to win for the special occasion. Emotions were difficult to keep in check. In the third inning Jim O'Toole brushed back Dodgers hitter Tommy Davis. On the next pitch, Davis swung and missed and permitted his bat to fly toward the mound. O'Toole came in off the mound and Davis started toward him. The umpire got between them as they exchanged words. "If the bat had come closer to me I'd picked it up and thrown it back at him," the combative O'Toole told reporters after the game, "and I wouldn't have missed."[18] Unfortunately the Reds' batters missed too many of Koufax's pitches, getting only five hits and only scoring on a Deron Johnson home run, and the Dodgers won 4–1.

The Reds prepared to leave the next day for a road trip starting in Houston, however, they discovered that their manager would not be going with them. It was announced that Fred Hutchinson was being given "a leave of absence for the duration of the present road trip."[19] Dick Sisler was named

Bill DeWitt addresses the Crosley Field crowd as Fred and the players watch, August 12, 1964, during Fred's birthday celebration (Cincinnati Reds).

the acting manager, the first time all year he had been given that title while Fred was out. Only DeWitt had known this before the game, perhaps contributing to the tough executive's tears during the proceedings. The *Cincinnati Post* reported that Hutch had made the request "because of illness." Fred made the announcement to the press himself. "I intend to take a short vacation and spend it with my family here in Cincinnati," he said. He told reporters he had no plans for hospital treatment at the present time and hoped to return to the team. "I'll see how I feel when the team gets back. Possibly by the time of the next road trip I will be feeling better." Bill DeWitt said that Hutch was still the manager of the team. The paper noted that this was the "third time this season that Hutch has passed up a trip."[20] No one knew it at the time, but Fred Hutchinson had managed his last major league baseball game.

Fred was admitted to Christ Hospital on August 14 and was treated for back pain and given further diagnostic tests. He was still in the hospital August 25 when a hospital spokesperson told reporters that he was in good spirits and doing well. The hospital spokesperson would not comment any further

A thin Fred Hutchinson receives well wishes (Cincinnati Reds).

on his physical condition. Bill DeWitt visited Fred in the hospital several times, telling everyone he was doing well.

The Reds had been going through the motions on the field in August — barely staying within striking distance. After starting at third base several stretches, Chico Ruiz had once again been replaced by Steve Boros. Ruiz played second base a little when Pete Rose was slumping but soon slumped himself and was eventually sent down to San Diego. He returned to the Reds after a few weeks and immediately made his presence felt. He eventually took third base back from the ailing Boros and would finish the season as the everyday third baseman. On August 18, when Jim O'Toole shut out the Giants to improve his record to 13 and 5, Ruiz scored the only run of the game on a force play. The next day Ruiz had four hits. On August 21, Ruiz plated pitcher Jim Maloney with what proved to be the winning run with a third-inning bunt single in a 3–2 win over the Dodgers.

In the win against the Dodgers on August 21, Maloney had driven in the other two runs himself. Maloney was finally getting some run support in addition to his own bat and was pitching very well. He had won six of seven decisions in July and August, however he was showing signs of the frailty which would haunt him throughout his career. On July 23, Maloney had nine strikeouts in six innings against the Mets, but had to leave the game early with a strained muscle in his back. On August 8, Maloney had twelve strikeouts in six innings against the Giants, but left early due to his arm tightening up. The following day teammates jokingly put get well cards up in the clubhouse for Maloney.[21] In the August 21 game, Maloney had left after the third inning due to a sore muscle in his pitching arm. The enormous stress Maloney placed on his arm to throw a baseball with such violence exacted a toll. Throughout the sixties Maloney was as good as any pitcher in baseball, compiling a 134–84 record before his career was essentially ended by a horrific Achilles tendon injury in the spring of 1970. But he was only able to top 225 innings in a season once in the years from 1963 to 1970, being limited by an assortment of minor ailments each year. This tendency toward fragility would play an important role in the decision-making process of acting manager Sisler later in the season.

Fortunately for the Reds, McCool and Ellis were picking up the slack and more from the bullpen. Time and again the youngsters were inserted in tight late-game situations. Time and again they worked out of jams.

Vada Pinson was still playing inconsistently. He had several two-home run games but struggled to get his average above .260. Frank Robinson, however, rebounded in a big way and carried the team through August, winning the National League's Player of the Month award. During August, Robinson hit an even .400 (40 for 100) with 8 home runs and 24 RBIs in 27 games.

Nerves were frayed and tempers flared for the Reds as the dog days settled in. On August 28, coaches Regie Otero and Johnny Temple were involved in a vicious brawl in the Reds clubhouse at Crosley Field just before a game against the Colts. Temple suffered a black eye and cut cheek and Otero was bleeding from the mouth when players separated them.[22] The fight between Otero and Temple brought Temple's bizarre tenure with the 1964 Reds to an end.

A tough, hard-nosed All-Star second baseman for the Reds in the fifties, Temple had been popular with the fans before being traded in the winter of 1959. He made several commercials on local television and had a ghost-written column in the *Cincinnati Post* and *Times Star*. Incidentally, his ghost writer was Earl Lawson, with whom Temple had a fist fight in the clubhouse after a game in 1957. Temple had been signed by the Reds as a player-coach before the 1964 season. Temple's exact role with the team was hard to define by players and his hiring reportedly caused some problems with the other coaches who acted coldly toward him. Different accounts have been given over the years regarding the purpose of bringing him in. One of his major roles apparently had been to act as a tutor for Pete Rose. Hutch had wanted him to help teach Rose the finer points of second-base play, particularly how to turn double plays more efficiently (i.e., how not to get killed on the pivot). It was also rumored that he had been brought in to teach the young Rose the finer points of life in general and possibly provide more appropriate companionship — to keep him away from Pinson and Robinson, whom management felt may have been a bad influence on young Pete's attitude. Fred later told Earl Lawson about Temple: "I'd want him to go out to dinner with Pete on the road ... polish him up a little."[23]

Another player put it more bluntly, stating that Temple's job was to "make sure Rose learned how to use a fork when he ate."[24]

While Temple may have helped Rose with fielding tips, it is unlikely that he helped him with anything else. Also, Temple quickly proved to be out of shape and only played in a few games. Temple had been dropped from the active roster on July 15. On August 28, with his chief ally on a leave of absence and the great "Rose social experiment" a failure, Temple was informed by the Reds' management that he was being let go all together.

"Temple was taken on as a free agent last December at the insistence of manager Hutchinson," Bill DeWitt told reporters the day after the fight. "Hutch felt at the time that he could help us as both a player and adviser to Pete Rose. We signed him as a coach because we didn't have room on our playing roster at the time. But we wanted him chiefly as a player and we were disappointed when we learned he wasn't in condition to play."[25] Temple arrived at the Reds' clubhouse on August 28 to clean out his locker, reportedly after having several drinks to ease the pain of rejection. Otero, not exactly a friend, was unaware of the fact that Temple had just been let go and slapped him on the back and asked how he was doing. Temple felt Otero was being sarcastic and answered by taking a swing at Otero who immediately swung back and landed a punch to his eye. The bitter Temple left the Reds, never to return. He gave the *Cincinnati Post*'s Lawson the following quote as he left: "I came to Cincinnati as a nobody, became a star, admired and respected by the fans, now I'm leaving as a bum, battered and bruised."[26]

The game on August 28 was postponed by rain and the Reds held a clubhouse meeting to clear the air. Hutch had come to watch the game and stayed for the meeting. "The Reds apparently ironed out their problems and agreed to stick together and try to win a pennant as a matter of pride in their own abilities," William Leggett reported in *Sports Illustrated*.[27] The Reds limped to the end of August as a team on the edge of disarray. Their leader in and out of the hospital, the emotional toll of the season causing internal strife; things did not look good for the final month of the season.

18

September: Nine in a Row

BY EARLY SEPTEMBER rookie Mel Queen was beginning to feel like he belonged in the majors. After struggling for much of the year with his average below .200, Queen began to get key hits to help the team. On August 1, his seventh-inning pinch-hit three-run home run off Bob Gibson had led the Reds back from a 3–1 deficit. On September 2, Queen's twelfth-inning pinch-hit single drove in Keough from second base with the only run of the game against the Cubs.

Interim manager Sisler was also struggling to feel like he belonged. He had been thrust into a very difficult situation. Sisler, 43 years old, was the son of Hall of Famer George Sisler, who hit over .400 for the St. Louis Browns in 1920 and 1922. Dick had been a fair major league hitter but never came close to his father's level. He did have one shining moment, however, when he hit one of the most dramatic home runs in baseball history. On the last day of the 1950 season, Dick hit a tenth-inning home run to beat the Brooklyn Dodgers and give the Phillies the pennant. He was temporarily world famous. Ernest Hemingway even mentioned him in the novel *The Old Man and the Sea.* Unfortunately, the next year Bobby Thomson hit his "shot heard 'round the world"— displacing Dick Sisler's home run of the previous year from the collective consciousness of all but the most die-hard baseball fans.

Dick Sisler had been with the Reds as their hitting coach since 1961 and considered Fred Hutchinson to be a good friend. He and his wife spent many evenings at the Hutchinson's house socializing and playing cards. Although he had been greatly saddened by the loss of health of his friend, he was determined to do the job which he had inherited. "I felt this guy [Hutch] has done all he can and I can do something now to help him," Sisler told reporters in September. He told them that they talked on the phone often and discussed the club. "I tell him what went on and I tell him the condition of the ball club, the moves I've made. Only one time did he ask, 'Why did you do that?' and then he agreed and said, 'That's what I would have done too.'"[1]

While Sisler was a capable baseball man, he did not have the presence and force of personality which Fred possessed. It was difficult to rally the team and keep them focused on the task at hand while the other drama was playing out. He was aware that the team's heart still lay with Fred. Sisler was careful to tell anyone who listened that this was still Fred's team. "I was told to take over the team," he said, "but it's Hutch's club.... I knew that I put both my job as a coach and my future as a manager on the line when I took over. If Hutch should not come back — well, they might get someone else to run the club, and the new man wouldn't want me around as a coach knowing that I had been the manager."[2]

Once, when Sisler told Fred that he hated the condition under which he had gotten the job, Hutch told him, "Don't worry about that. Just give 'em hell."[3]

The Reds played out the string in September, staying within viewing distance of the front-running Phillies whose lead remained between six and eight games. On September 19, the Reds split a doubleheader with the Cardinals. Frank Robinson won the first game with a dramatic two-out, three-run home run in the bottom of the ninth inning. The win gave the Reds a short streak of three wins in a row. In the night cap, however, the Reds suffered another frustrating loss. Billy McCool made his first major league start and pitched great, but lost 2–0. The only two runs scored on backup catcher Don Pavletich's wild throw attempting to head off a double steal in the second inning. The season was rapidly slipping away. The Reds appeared ready to put the entire season of stress and heartbreak behind them. On September 20, as the Reds prepared to play the final game of the three-game series against the Cardinals in Cincinnati, they found it difficult to motivate themselves for the game. They had no idea they were on the brink of a monumental turnaround.

The Cardinals jumped on Joe Nuxhall early and led 6–0 in the fourth inning after knocking him out of the box. Ryne Duren relieved for the Reds. With the Reds trailing by so much he was not going to be lifted for a pinch hitter as usual and was scheduled to bat in the fifth. "I looked around the dugout and everyone was really down; just sitting on their dead asses like it's over," says Duren. "I got mad and said to everyone on the bench, 'Why don't we just go in the damn clubhouse, take off our damn uniforms and concede the damn game. If you don't want to compete, let's just go home. But if you're out here, let's have a little life.' I balled everyone out for being deadasses on the bench. So they hollered back at me, 'Well why don't you go up there and do something; you think you're so damn good, go up and get a hit.' So I made up my mind I would take one for the team, which I did."[4]

As Cardinal pitcher Gordie Richardson threw, Duren stepped forward and leaned across home plate, taking the pitch in the upper thigh. "Duren walked right into the pitch," says Holzinger. "I never saw anything like that. The Cardinal bench was going crazy complaining but the umpire ignored them."[5] The half-blind pitcher with a career .050 batting average triumphantly trotted down to first base.

"I'll never forget that crazy damn Ryne Duren with those thick glasses taking one off the knee just to get on base," says Ellis. "He didn't even try to get out of the way. And there's no way he would have gotten a hit. He couldn't even see."[6]

The play seemed to spark the ashes of the Reds' frustration. The inspired Reds began hitting. When Duren scored moments later everyone was on their feet in the dugout to greet him. The whole atmosphere had changed. The Reds scored three in the inning and were back in the game. Duren shut the Cardinals down for four innings before giving way to Ellis who pitched the last inning and two-thirds. The Reds clawed back, scoring three in the bottom of the eighth and won 9–6.

"Frank Robinson always gave me credit for waking the club up," says Duren. "Coming from him that was a lot because, as you know, he was a bear-down son of a bitch."[7] The triumphant Reds stormed into the clubhouse. That night, they packed their bags and headed to Philadelphia for a date with the first-place Phillies.

On the afternoon of September 21, 1964, the Philadelphia Phillies gathered in their dugout and looked out across the field at Connie Mack Stadium and watched the Cincinnati Reds taking their positions. The Phillies were in first place by six and a half games with only twelve left to play. They were starting a seven-game home stretch in which they hoped to clinch the pennant. Battle-tested and tough, they had supreme confidence in the strategic genius of their leader. They did not realize at that moment, however, that events were soon to occur which would render this moment the high-water mark for their 1964 pennant hopes. After that day's game, the Phillies would experience an irreversible decline.

The Phillies had not been given much chance in the preseason of 1964. It had been a long time since the Phillies had been serious contenders. At the start of the 1960 season, manager Eddie Sawyer, looking over the hopeless, miserable prospects abruptly resigned saying, "I'm 49 years old and I want to live to be 50."[8] Sawyer was replaced by Gene Mauch. At 34 years old, Mauch was the youngest manager in the majors, but he had seemingly been born ready to manage major league baseball. Although a seldom used, light-hitting major league shortstop when he came up through the Dodger system in the late 1940s, he had been an avid student of the game and a fervent disciple of Leo Durocher. He had learned his lessons well.

Often considered to be one of the most intelligent managers in baseball, Mauch was known for his innovative moves and strategy during games. "He was far ahead of everyone and knew the rules better than anyone, and used that to his advantage,"[9] said Dallas Green who pitched for Mauch and later became a major league manager and executive. Mauch was also known for his temper. In the late fifties, as a player-manager at Minneapolis in the minors, he had reportedly gotten so mad at himself for his own poor playing during a prolonged slump that he nailed his cleats to the clubhouse wall after a game to prevent the temptation to put them on and play again, thereby forcing himself into full-time managing.[10] Like Leo the Lip Durocher, he was merciless in his bench jockeying and umpire baiting. While some managers can perform these tasks without incurring lasting hatred, Mauch sometimes crossed the line, particularly with his comments from the bench directed at opposing players. Nothing was off-limits in an attempt to gain an edge. Opposing players often remembered these comments to use as motivation later.[11]

Mauch was a proponent of "small ball," playing for one run at a time, and was a fanatic about fundamentals and details. While he was often quoted as saying, "Most one run games are lost not won,"[12] he loved nothing more himself than stealing a game with an unorthodox move. Mauch was felt by some to be the manager-of-the-future, but others felt that he tended to over-manage. Mauch's style certainly earned him many enemies on other teams and it could wear on his own team as well. When things went according to plan, everyone was happy. When things didn't go the way they should, the stress could become contagious.

Mauch had endured a disastrous 1961 season with the Phillies in which they had lost a league-worst 107 games, including a major league record 23 in a row. Combative, tough and abrasive, he had slowly driven the club up — to seventh place in 1962 and fourth in 1963. By 1964, Mauch had gained some powerful weapons to help his team.

Richie Allen was signed by the Phillies in 1960 for a reported bonus of $65,000. At the time it was, in the culturally sensitive words of the *Cincinnati Post*'s Earl Lawson, "the highest bonus ever paid to a Negro."[13] As a 22-year-old rookie in 1964, Allen was astonishingly strong. He swung an enormous hunk of lumber at the plate: a bat weighing 44 ounces. Most players use bats of 32 to 34 ounces—any heavier and the bat becomes difficult to swing with enough control and speed to catch up with a major league fastball. Allen swung his telephone pole with ease and success. Allen's career would include over 330 home runs and the 1972 American League MVP award but the Hall of Fame potential was derailed by alcohol and repeated run-ins with management. Years later, Gene Mauch would say of Allen, "He could handle a high fastball, it was the fast highball that gave him trouble."[14] In

1964, Allen didn't have trouble with much of anything. He was on his way to being named Rookie-of-the-Year and would finish the season with 29 home runs, a league-leading 125 runs, 91 RBIs, 13 triples and a batting average of .318.

The best player on the Phillies in 1964, however, was rightfielder Johnny Callison. An extraordinary athlete, Callison was what baseball men would later refer to as a five-tool player: he could hit for average, hit for power, run, throw and field. Callison was having his best year in 1964 with 31 home runs and 104 RBIs and would finish second in the voting for MVP. Callison had a cannon for an arm; a hose; a howitzer; a rifle. In other words, he could throw very well. When baseball men discussed great arms from the outfield in the sixties, there were three men who were far above everyone else: Roberto Clemente, Rocky Colavito and Johnny Callison. Callison led the National League in assists from the outfield each year from 1962 through 1965 until runners wised up and quit challenging him.

The Phillies pitching staff was led by Chris Short and Jim Bunning. A future baseball Hall of Famer and a future Republican senator from Kentucky, Bunning had been acquired from the Tigers before the season. On June 21, 1964, he pitched a perfect game against the Mets, becoming the first man in major league history to throw no-hitters in both leagues. Short and Bunning were both nearing twenty wins for the 1964 season.

As the 1964 season progressed, the Reds and Phillies had not developed any friendships. In the last inning of an early season game, Frank Robinson had been on first base. Robinson was generally regarded as one of the hardest sliders in the game when breaking up double plays at second. Robinson, running on the pitch, heard the batter connect. Ahead of him, he saw Phillies second baseman Tony Taylor quickly bend over as if to field a ground ball. Shortstop Bobby Wine covered second and frantically yelled, "Give it to me quick" as he prepared to make the pivot for the double play. Robinson barreled into second. Only then did he realize that neither Taylor nor Wine had the ball. The ball was actually hit in a soft fly to right. Callison made the catch and threw to first to easily double up Robinson. "What an act. If I could hit, I'd be worth a million dollars," Wine crowed to reporters after the game.[15] It is an old trick which works occasionally on either a very stupid runner or a very aggressive runner and it makes the runner look very bad. Robinson was not stupid. He would not forget.

It had been the kind of year for the Phillies where every trick play seemed to work. Every move Mauch made was the right move. It seemed as though every pinch hitter came through, every relief pitcher slammed the door. With essentially only two regular players, Allen and Callison, Mauch juggled a lineup of platoon positions to perfection. The Phillies entered the September 21 game with a six and a half game lead over the Reds, seven over the Cardinals. They appeared to be in the driver's seat, cruising for their first pennant since the Whiz Kids of 1950. Art Mahaffey took the mound for the Phillies against John Tsitouris.

Tsitouris was only starting because Joey Jay had a sore foot and Maloney was recuperating from a virus attack. One of the quieter players on the Reds, Tsitouris had been a pleasant surprise in 1963, winning twelve games for the Reds. "John Tsitouris was one of my father's favorite players because he got so much out of his ability," says Rick Hutchinson. "I remember watching him warm up one day and telling my father, 'I could hit off John Tsitouris,' because it didn't look like he had that much. But he really was a battler."[16] Tsitouris had struggled much of 1964, not quite able to recapture the magic of 1963, and entered the game with a 7–11 record.

The game turned out to be a pitcher's duel. Tsitouris, rising to the moment, pitched the game of his career. As the innings passed and neither team could mount a threat, tension slowly built. In the top of the sixth inning, Chico Ruiz reached first on a single with one out. Pinson followed with a line shot which bounced off Mahaffey and rolled past Taylor into right centerfield. Ruiz cruised into third but Pinson was gunned down trying for second by a perfect throw from Callison.

Frank Robinson stepped into the batter's box. After a great month of August, Robinson had remained hot in September, his batting average now over .300. Robinson menacingly took his familiar stance, head bent, elbow leaning over the plate, daring the pitcher to give him anything close. Mahaffey peered in for the sign. He knew he would have to be careful with Robinson. With first base open, there was no need to give him a good pitch, but the next batter, Deron Johnson, had also been hitting well and so Mahaffey didn't want to intentionally put Robinson on. The right-handed Mahaffey slowly went into his windup and fired a fastball which Robinson took a vicious swing at and missed.

Leading off third, Chico Ruiz watched the windup and pitch. Had Mahaffey checked him or was he focusing only on the dangerous batter at the plate? Ruiz looked at Mahaffey, then looked at homeplate, then back at Mahaffey. As the pitcher lifted his left foot to bring it back to start his windup, Ruiz ... took off!

Out of the periphery of his vision, Mahaffey detected movement in a place where his brain quickly registered no movement should be. Having already committed to his windup, Mahaffey could not break off and simply throw the ball home for fear of committing a balk. Was it a bluff, a steal or a squeeze bunt? Why would they squeeze with two outs? Why would they steal or squeeze with Robinson at the plate? With two outs?! Mahaffey's brain quickly tried to process the information in a fraction of a second while completing his windup as 20,000 screaming fans, along with the players and coaches from both teams reached the astonishing conclusion at the same time: he's trying to steal home!!

Robinson also noticed movement out of the corner of his eye and sort of half turned as if to bunt and stuck his bat out. "I did what I could to protect him," he later told reporters.[17] A pitcher's normal response to a squeeze or steal of home is to throw the pitch either at the batter to force him to get out of the way or to throw it outside where it can't be reached with a bunt attempt. Perhaps Mahaffey's brain quickly ruled out throwing inside due to the standing order from Mauch not to ever throw inside to Robinson. Perhaps he just threw it as fast as he could. The ball reached home in time to get the streaking Ruiz, but it sailed too high and outside. Catcher Clay Dalrymple jumped but couldn't reach it. Ruiz scored.

A steal of home is one of the rarest plays in baseball. Most are part of a double steal with a man on first and third. A straight steal from third is an almost impossible task off a major league pitcher. The baserunner is betting he can sprint almost ninety feet faster than the pitcher can throw a ball sixty feet. Most managers tend to discourage taking such chances. Ruiz had taken this chance entirely on his own. Indeed, perhaps the most surprised person in the park to see him running was acting manager Dick Sisler. When Ruiz broke for home, Sisler jumped up screaming, "No, No!"[18] To take a chance like that, in that situation, at that stage of the season was mind-boggling. And for a rookie to risk laying there at homeplate, being tagged with the third out and looking up at the unhappy face of Frank Robinson, standing there holding a baseball bat, defies comprehension. After witnessing this, one of his Spanish-speaking teammates may have been moved to tell Ruiz, "*Senor, tu tienes agallas*," which roughly translated means, "mister, you've got guts."

"Chico Ruiz was a smart player who wasn't afraid to take a chance," says Billy McCool. "Of course, if Frank had gotten a good pitch and turned on it, Chico would have died a whole lot sooner."[19]

"If he had been out they would have shot him," says Ellis.[20]

"It was about the dumbest play I've ever seen," Rose said years later, "except that it worked."[21]

Tsitouris blanked the Phillies the rest of the way, striking out the final batter with a man on third, and the Reds won, 1–0. After the game in the Reds clubhouse, a jubilant Ruiz told reporters, "I was hoping I would be safe because I didn't want to hear what the manager would say if I was out."

"On the first pitch to Robby, Mahaffey only look at me once and then went into a slow windup," Ruiz explained. "He did the same thing on the second pitch and I run." Ruiz admitted that he had stolen home a few times in the minors but had never attempted it in the majors. "I don't think I try again," he laughed, "I keep my record perfect."[22]

"I didn't give Ruiz the steal sign," Sisler told reporters. Then, stating the obvious, added "with Robby up there at the plate, I'd rather gamble on him hitting than Ruiz stealing."[23]

"When I saw Ruiz start running I just went blank," said third base coach Regie Otero. "I couldn't say anything."[24]

Gene Mauch certainly could say something. In the Phillies clubhouse he was beside himself. "Who the f--- is Chico Ruiz?" he screamed to no one in particular. "If he had been thrown out he would be sent back to the minors where he belongs." The play had defied logic. It was an affront to all that Mauch believed in. To lose a game on a play like that, by an unknown player like that, was more than he could stand.

"Chico F---ing Ruiz! Chico F---ing Ruiz!" he screamed over and over at his demoralized team. "I can't believe it. You guys let Chico F---ing Ruiz beat you."[25] The Phillies had reached their highwater mark. They would never recover.

When the two teams met the next day, the change in momentum was palpable. The Reds were now loose, having fun and full of confidence. The Phillies, still seething over the loss of the previous day, were beginning to feel the weight of the entire season bearing down on them. Jim O'Toole took the mound for the Reds looking for his sixteenth win of the season against Chris Short.

O'Toole had little trouble while Short only lasted four and two-thirds innings. Mauch spent much of the game screaming from the bench at Robinson, Ruiz and the rest of the Reds. Robinson answered him the usual way, with a home run. Deron Johnson added a two-run, bases loaded single to help break the game open. As the Reds cruised to a 9–2 win, the Phillies' frustration and near-panic was beginning to show. Chico Ruiz led off the eighth inning and was nailed in the back by Phillies relief pitcher Ed Roebuck, obviously in retaliation for the events of the previous night. Ruiz responded by immediately stealing second. As Roebuck headed off the field at the end of the Reds' half of the eighth he had harsh words for Ruiz who remained silent. After returning to the dugout, Roebuck threw a baseball over Ruiz's head as he stood at his third-base position. Ruiz responded by yelling into the Phillies' dugout.

After the game, Sisler explained to reporters, "I want the Phillies to know that, ordinarily, with an eight run lead, he (Chico) wouldn't try to steal. But he was mad about getting hit and he had a right to be."[26]

"I didn't say anything to Ed Roebuck," Ruiz said, "not until he threw the ball at me. Then I called him a gutless so and so."[27] Chico's command of the English language was surely good enough to come up with a better word for Roebuck, but most likely his decorum with reporters prevented him from telling them what he really yelled.

The so and so's of Philadelphia were definitely showing the strain and the Reds were beginning to believe they had a shot at the pennant. The Reds looked at the schedule and saw one more game in Philadelphia followed by a five-game series with the Mets in New York, while the Phillies traveled to Milwaukee and then St. Louis. The two teams would meet in Cincinnati for the final two games of the season. A pennant suddenly looked possible for the Reds players and they talked openly to reporters about it. "The Phils have two real good pitchers in Jim Bunning and Chris Short," O'Toole told them, "but we've got the depth and this is the time of year when pitchers get a little weary."[28]

"We've been battling for fourth. I don't think anybody in Cincinnati has been thinking pennant," Pete Rose said. But now things were suddenly different. "We've got the steam up now. Listen. You can tell. This is a pretty lively clubhouse, right? I think we've got the best club in the league — I really do. It would be real nice for Hutch if we win. It would help him out a lot."[29]

"Hutch? Yeah," added Sisler. "That has something to do with the way we've come back. They're thinking of Hutch and they're thinking of themselves. They smell that money now."[30]

The Reds finished the sweep of the Phillies the next day with a 6–4 win. Vada Pinson hit two homers and (no doubt to the delight of Lawson) beat out a bunt for another hit. Ruiz continued to be the subject of Gene Mauch's nightmares with a home run of his own, the second of his career. Billy McCool got the win. Sammy Ellis came on in the seventh inning and got the first man out. "All of a sudden I couldn't find the strike zone and I walked the bases loaded," recalls Ellis. "Johnny Callison is the batter and he was having an MVP year, a great year." Callison had beaten the Reds a month earlier with a 3-run ninth-inning home run. "I look down to the bullpen and Sisler's got Nuxhall warming up," continues Ellis. "Sisler comes out to the mound. I'm expecting him to take me out. But he looks at me and says, 'Look, you've been doing the job all year, get this guy out.' And so I struck the son of a bitch out and then struck out the next guy too."[31]

Ellis' description belies the true tension of the moment. With the Phillies trying to hang on to their season, the tying run on first and no place to put the batter, Ellis, the man who had said in spring training that he had to fight to control his temper when things started going bad, ran the count full. He later admitted to reporters, "I've never been so scared in my life. My knees were shaking and my hands were perspiring."[32] He then threw a perfect pitch and caught Callison looking at strike three on the outside corner. Ellis finished the last two innings quickly for his 11th save of the year and the Phillies lead over the Reds was down to three and a half.

The Reds' clubhouse after the game was riotous. Chico Ruiz was dancing around waving a clipping from a Philadelphia newspaper that read, "Phils Unworried by Red Surge."[33]

Sammy Ellis: "Clench your fists and wish somehow there was something you could do" (Cincinnati Reds).

"Take it over to Gene Mauch," said Nuxhall, "and ask the Little General what he has to do now."[34] Nuxhall pushed a make-believe button on the wall of the clubhouse. "The panic button," he said, "The Little General will begin to push the button."[35] The Reds headed to New York, as Pete Rose said, full of steam.

As the Reds took the field for the first game of a doubleheader with the Mets after a travel day, the lead was down to three because the Phillies had lost the previous day to Milwaukee. Pete Rose immediately got the Reds on top in the first inning by walking, taking second on a Ruiz bunt and then scoring on a single by Pinson. That was all the Reds would need as Jim Maloney was simply overpowering. The Mets could manage only a second-inning single and the Reds won 3–0. Robinson and Marty Keough hit homers to help Bob Purkey win the second game 4–1, with Ellis getting another save. After the game, the Reds hurried to the clubhouse to hear how the Phillies were making out in extra innings against the Braves. As the game could not be picked up on live radio, Sisler called the sports department of United Press International and relayed the reports to the players who were gathered and hanging on every word. "The Braves scored two in the top of the twelfth," he announced. Then he shouted, "Braves win!" and the clubhouse erupted.[36] The lead was now one and a half.

"'We're not worried,' those will be Gene Mauch's famous last words," said Bob Purkey.[37]

That afternoon the Reds brought up six players from San Diego for the traditional "cup of coffee" with the big league club at the end of the season. Among those called up was Dan Neville, who was coming off a good year in Triple-A. He would be a witness to the drama of one of the classic pennant race finishes in baseball history.

The next day the Reds won again. John Edwards had three hits. Marty Keough, now playing left field regularly, continued his hot hitting with three RBIs and John Tsitouris got the win, 6–1. McCool came on in relief with one out in the seventh, two runners on and the Reds holding a 3–1 lead. With the fans on their feet, McCool struck out the first batter on three pitches, then got a soft fly to right to end the inning. In finishing the last two and two-thirds innings of the game, McCool faced the minimum eight batters and struck out five of them.

The Reds were flying high. "We felt like we were going to win every single day during the streak," says O'Toole.[38] Their ailing manager was never far from their thoughts.

"Wherever we go as a team this year," Sammy Ellis told *Sports Illustrated*, "Hutch is somehow there. His name will come up over dinner. You're sitting there and somebody says, 'Hear anything about Hutch?' There is a kind of quiet that comes over everybody. It makes you put your hands under the table and clench your fists and wish somehow there was something you could do.... Sure, we want to win the pennant for ourselves and get the series money. But a ballplayer wants a World Series ring more than anything else, and we want to put a ring on Hutch's finger."[39]

Clench your fists and wish somehow there was something you could do.

Most of the players were in their twenties or early thirties and had not even been touched by the death of a parent yet. For players— young and supremely athletic — sickness usually meant a cold or maybe a hangover. Death was not something they had ever been faced with —certainly not in someone with whom they played or worked. And now they were being forced to watch it unfold, not suddenly as in an accident, but slowly in an agonizing unstoppable process. It was frustrating for men who had spent their lives overcoming physical challenges to witness this and realize there was nothing they could do.

On September 27, the Reds swept another doubleheader from the Mets. O'Toole handcuffed the Mets in the first game and won 4–1, with Ellis getting the save. Robinson used his legs to get the Reds going in the fourth inning when he singled, stole second, took third on a wild throw and then scored on a Johnson sacrifice fly. In the eighth inning he did it with his muscles with a two-run homer. The streaking Reds wasted no time in the second game as four of the first five batters got hits and three scored. Pinson, the third batter of the game, hit a two-run triple to give the Reds all the runs they would need. Joey Jay went the distance and won 3–1. In the ninth inning, as Jay was preparing to pitch, he heard some shouts from his infielders and turned to look at the scoreboard. The score of the Phillies loss to the Braves in Milwaukee had just been posted. Jay smiled, rubbed the ball, then finished off the Mets and the Reds took over first place.

Cincinnati pitching had been fantastic, giving up only four runs in 45 innings in the five game series against the Mets. After the game, Sisler called Hutch from the clubhouse to share the good news. "I'm not saying for sure yet we're going to win," he said, "but I'll guarantee you this club won't choke."[40]

The Reds prepared for the flight home that night. The Reds had now won 12 of 13 games at the most important time of the season. They had left Cincinnati a week ago trailing by 6 and a half games, but now they were returning in first place.

19

The Final Home Stand

THE IMPROBABLE TWO WEEK stretch had catapulted the Reds into first place. They returned to Cincinnati as conquering heroes. When the Reds' chartered flight arrived at the Greater Cincinnati Airport late that night they were met by a delirious crowd estimated at 10,000. It reminded the older players of the scene from 1961. "It's like something you see in the movies," Robinson said.[1] The fans packed into the field and pressed their way onto the ramp, making it impossible for the team to deplane. A second ramp was placed at the cabin door on the opposite side and the team got off the plane. The crowd was so boisterous that Mayor Walton Bachrach's planned welcome-home speech was cancelled.

Among the crowd of 10,000 was one particularly familiar face. Fred Hutchinson was there to greet his returning players. "He looked terrible," says Jim O'Toole. "His eye was sagging, you could tell he was having a hard time just walking, he was in a lot of pain. That's one sight I'll never forget. Here it is two in the morning and this guy who can barely walk or see is at the airport congratulating us, giving us all hugs. That's how much he loved the fact that this was his team. I thought 'God, we've got to win this thing for Hutch.'"[2]

The Reds opened the home stand on September 29 against the Pirates. There were five games left in the season. For the first time since 1940, four teams still had a mathematical chance at the pennant in the final week of the season with the Phillies, Cardinals and Giants all still alive. The Reds management, feeling confident, had begun taking orders for World Series tickets and had ordered a rush supply of a chemical spray to turn the Autumn-baked blotchy, scuffed up turf of Crosley Field back to a more pleasant green to look good on national television for the World Series.[3]

"The Pirates saved their aces for us," says O'Toole. "They threw rookies against the Cardinals the series before and saved their aces, Veale and Friend, for us."[4] The Reds players were all disappointed when they took the field and saw the sparse crowd. The official attendance would later be announced as 10,858 but to the players, it seemed more like only the 858.

"We couldn't believe it," says Duren. "There were more people at the airport when we came back than there were in the stands for the game."[5]

"That's one thing that has stuck in my craw all my life," says Ellis. "How bad is that? Here we were with a nine-game winning streak, in first place, and no one came to the game. That disappointed the guys. I never have figured out why more people didn't come to that first game."[6]

"Barry Goldwater [1964 presidential candidate] was in town having a rally that night and he outdrew us," says McCool. "He drew more than 10,000."[7]

"I think it kind of got our daubers down when we saw the crowd" says Duren.[8]

Whether due to downed-daubers or good pitching the Reds could not get a run against Bob Friend that night. Billy McCool started on the mound for the Reds and, despite the stakes, showed few nerves. Pitching like a seasoned veteran, he did not allow a base runner until one out in the fifth inning. In the sixth inning, the Pirates loaded the bases but McCool worked out of the jam. The game was still a scoreless tie going into the ninth. With one out and one on, Roberto Clemente doubled off the center-field wall. After an intentional walk loaded the bases, McCool got the next batter to foul out. With two outs, Bill Mazeroski singled to center to bring in two runs. The Reds got two runners on base in their half of the ninth but Chico Ruiz grounded out to second base to end the game. The Cardinals, suddenly very hot, had beaten the Phillies in St. Louis and they were now tied with the Reds for first place.

The next night, the Cincinnati crowd was even smaller: 8,188. *New York Journal-American* writer Jimmy Cannon was in town to cover the series and the light attendance provoked him to blast the city of Cincinnati in his column the next day: "Seldom has a ball club demeaned with such disinterest. This town doesn't deserve a big league team. There were 5,000 at the airport to meet them when they came home as winners. You don't have to pay to get into airports. And they gave away tickets for Goldwater's rally. Maybe that's the reason there were so many empty seats in Crosley Field. This has to be a city of freeloaders."[9]

"Cincinnati is a great baseball town," says O'Toole in defense of his adopted hometown, "but it was a night game and the kids were back in school. I think that kept the crowd down. But it was certainly disappointing."[10]

Those few fans who bought tickets the night of September 30 were certainly given their money's worth — especially those who appreciated a good old-fashioned pitching duel. The Reds sent Jim Maloney to the mound to face Bob Veale. A six-foot six-inches tall flame thrower, Veale was on his way to leading the National League in strikeouts for the 1964 season. Maloney and Veale traded smoke for smoke throughout the night and neither team could score. Veale struck out 16 Reds over 12⅓ innings. Maloney went 11 innings, striking out 13 and giving up only two hits and two walks. After Maloney left for a pinch hitter in the bottom of the 11th inning, Sammy Ellis came on and struck out four in two innings. By the end of the game there would be 36 strikeouts, setting a record for two teams in an extra-inning game. The Reds, continually got runners on second and third in the late innings but could not push across a run. They stranded an incredible 18 base runners while being shut out — three in the 11th, 13th and 14th innings and two in the 6th, 9th and 10th. The frustration of Reds players and fans was unbearable as six times in the game the Reds had a runner on third base and could not score him. Finally, in the top of the 16th inning, the Pirates got a double from Donn Clendenon off John Tsitouris. Mazeroski sacrificed him to third. Rookie catcher Jerry May, called up only two weeks before the series, then plated the run with a squeeze bunt down the third-base line. The Reds could not answer and lost 1–0.

The 16-inning loss to the Pirates was devastating to the players. It took away all the momentum they had from the winning streak. Now the team was desperately trying to hold on. The Reds managed to respond with a 5–4 win the next night with Joe Nuxhall getting the win to make his record 9–8. Recently picked up reserve catcher Jim Coker, filling in for the injured John Edwards, had a big game with three hits, including a home run off the left-field screen. The Reds got the winning run in the seventh inning when Robinson doubled home Pinson who had tripled. Sammy Ellis pitched two perfect innings to notch his sixth save in a little over two weeks.

Fred Hutchinson watched the games against the Pirates from DeWitt's private box atop the roof at Crosley Field. He left the games early — unable to take the constant pain. He talked to the players individually but did not address the team as a whole, careful to avoid stepping on the toes of acting manager Sisler. He realized what a difficult situation Sisler had been placed in and told anyone who asked that it was Sisler's team now. He took pains to avoid any appearance of second-guessing Sisler. "The thing that struck me though," says Neville, "is that it was obvious that he was in a lot of discomfort and felt really bad but he was still taking an interest in the team."[11]

On September 30, Fred came to Crosley Field as the team gathered for the official team picture. It would be the last time he put on a Reds uniform. He appeared cheerful as he moved through the players. After the pictures, he chatted with the many writers who were visiting to cover the pennant race. The Reds turned their attention to the Phillies for the final two games of the season.

It was a much different Phillies team that came into Cincinnati October 2. They had been swept in St. Louis and had now lost ten straight games. Everything had gone wrong. In a 15 game span, Philly runners had been thrown out ten times trying for an extra base.[12] The pitching staff had imploded. Sore arms and lost confidence had forced Mauch into believing that he had to pitch Bunning and Short as often as possible. Six times in the final month Bunning and Short had started on two days rest — the Phillies had lost all six games. An endless trail of relief pitchers paraded to and from the mound, all with the same miserable results. "Mauch runs, doesn't walk, to the mound in a crisis," the *New York Times* stated.[13]

Later Mauch would tell reporters that when he went to the mound to talk to his pitchers during the streak he could "see the fear in their eyes."[14]

The Phillies players were visibly pressing, shaken by their horrendous slump. "You've got to feel sorry for them," Braves catcher Joe Torre told reporters on September 27. "They'd come up to the plate speaking slowly, groping for the right words ... usually you talk to hitters. You kid around with them a little bit. But these guys ... I didn't know what to say to them. I mean it's hard to believe what happened to them."[15]

Just two weeks earlier, the Philadelphia front office had been taking World Series ticket requests. That seemed like a lifetime ago now. The Phillies had endured what would come to be known as the most monumental late-season collapse in major league history. More than ten years later, Mauch was asked by a reporter what he remembered of the September 1964 losing streak. He lowered his head and slowly said, "Only every pitch."[16]

The Reds started the day 92–68, the Phillies were 90–70, the Cardinals were 92–67 and facing the New York Mets. "The Phillies were dead," says Billy McCool, "they had nothing to play for nor the will to fight because they had lost the seven-game lead. They just wanted the season to be over."[17]

More than 25,000 fans showed up for this game. Rose led off the Reds' first inning with a walk and scored on Robinson's double to give the Reds an early lead. O'Toole breezed through the frustrated Philly lineup, allowing only three hits over the first seven innings. The Reds lost a chance to blow the game open in the fourth when Philly outfielder Alex Johnson made a tremendous over-the-shoulder running catch off a long Deron Johnson fly. Pinson and Robinson, certain the ball would be over Johnson's head, had been running hard. Johnson threw to second to get Pinson and the relay to first beat Robinson to complete the triple play.

The Reds were leading 3–0 in the seventh inning, with the game seemingly in the bag, when Leo Cardenas came to the plate with one out and Deron Johnson on second base.[18] Moments earlier the scoreboard had flashed the news that the Cardinals had been beaten by the Mets 1–0, putting the Reds into position to take over first place. Gene Mauch called time and went to the mound for a conference with pitcher Chris Short and three members of

his infield. After Mauch returned to the bench, Short's first pitch hit Cardenas in the back. From the bench, the incredulous Reds watched the 5'10", 160-
pound enraged Cardenas, with bat in hand, head for the mound challenging
the 6'3", 215-pound Short who walked forward to meet him. "The Phillies
had been ready to go home. Why would you want to wake up a dead team?"
O'Toole asks. "Cardenas acted like they had hit him on purpose. Like they
would want to purposely hit the number eight guy in the lineup who's hitting .250."[19]

"Mauch later told me he had Short throw at Cardenas,"[20] says Duren who
was on good terms with his former Philly manager.

The furious Cardenas was intercepted from behind by the catcher and
players streamed onto the field from both benches. No punches were thrown
as the Reds players quickly tried to pull Cardenas away, wanting merely to
finish the game. There was a little pushing and shoving with the Phillies but
most of the Reds were congregated around Cardenas and did not mix with
the Phillies. Robinson and Jim Coker took Chico's bat away from him.

"We tried to stop him and make him calm down," says Duren. "We told
him, 'We've got too much going to lose it, let's just finish the game.' But I don't
think he seemed to understand what we were saying. He had very poor English."[21]

"He didn't speak good English, but he understood," says O'Toole.[22]

Cardenas visibly sulked on the bench. He seemed to think the Reds had
not backed him up. "Guys in the dugout were telling him to keep his head
in the game, to cool it," says Neville.[23]

When the Reds took the field in the top of the eighth, Cardenas, standing with his arms crossed, would not take the ball when it was thrown around
the infield. "He looked like he was still sulking when he went back out to
shortstop," says Duren.[24]

With one out, O'Toole sawed off Frank Thomas, breaking his bat. The
ball blooped in a shallow fly to the edge of the grass behind shortstop — a
routine play, except Cardenas didn't move. "He just stood there with his hands
on his knees," says O'Toole.[25]

Controversy exists over the effort of Leo Cardenas on the play. Several
players are still mad about it. "Cardenas didn't even go after it," says one.
"He acted like he wasn't even in the game."[26]

"He absolutely didn't go for it," says another.[27]

Earl Lawson later wrote, "A still pouting Cardenas made only a half-
hearted attempt to catch the ball."[28]

Ritter Collett later wrote, "Cardenas, seemingly sulking, made no move
to catch the ball and Rose, playing second, couldn't."[29]

Robinson wrote in 1968 that both Rose and Cardenas "started after the
ball and neither one of them called for it. They both stopped and the ball
dropped in."[30]

Pete Rose ran from his second-base position and tried for the ball but it fell in for a hit. After the game, Sisler told reporters that he believed the incident the previous inning affected the play of Cardenas. "He took it out to his position," Sisler said. "Thomas' ball should have been caught. There was confusion out there (between Cardenas and Rose)." Sisler repeated to reporters that Cardenas should have had the ball.[31]

On the mound, O'Toole was furious. "I wanted to go after him right there," he says of Cardenas.[32] O'Toole walked the next batter, then gave up another hit. Suddenly the Phillies had come back from the dead. Billy McCool was summoned from the bullpen and struck out Johnny Callison. "Then, Sisler should have taken him out and brought in Ellis," says O'Toole. "Ellis had been unhittable the past few weeks. He was right-handed. He should have come in to face Allen."[33] McCool stayed in and the right-handed Richie Allen blasted a triple to right field, tying the game. Alex Johnson followed with a single and the Reds trailed 4–3. That was the final score of the game.

After the game, O'Toole charged at Cardenas in the clubhouse. They exchanged angry words and O'Toole grabbed Cardenas and threw him up against the wall. The ex-gold glove boxer "wanted to pound his head a few times."[34] Reds players pulled the two apart, however Cardenas picked up an ice pick and came back at O'Toole.

"You say I miss ball, I get you," Cardenas yelled according to Robinson.[35]

"He came after me with an ice pick, saying, 'I keel you!'" O'Toole later said.[36]

Joey Jay grabbed Cardenas from behind saying, "If there's gonna be any fighting, it's not going to be with an ice pick."[37] With Robinson, Purkey and Nuxhall acting as peacekeepers, O'Toole and Cardenas were separated and tempers were finally calmed down.

"We made up later," [38] says O'Toole. The game and the fight had an unsettling effect on the team and was the culmination of the stress of the entire season.

"It was kind of ugly," Joe Nuxhall later said.[39]

"I think it was just two highly competitive people under a lot of stress and it turned into something ugly," says Ellis.[40]

In the newspapers the next day, reporters wrote that they heard "violent arguing" coming from the players' dressing quarters, however the door was locked, barring newsmen. Sisler was interrupted from talking to reporters in his office by Regie Otero and ran into the dressing room. When reporters were allowed in a few minutes later, "there was no evidence of even a smoldering quarrel.... If [any serious blows were landed] the players weren't talking.... [Sisler] refused to disclose the nature of the dispute."[41]

In the culture of "what happens here, stays here," no player or coach discussed the fight with outsiders other than Sisler. "Fight, what fight?" said

Robinson to reporters after they were let in. "Was there a fight? I was back there in the shower. I didn't hear anything."[42]

Sisler tried to downplay the incident. "It was nothing. Just forget it," he told reporters. "In the heat of a pennant race like this, they say things before they think.... Of course they took it (the loss) tough. Tempers go up a little. Guys blame each other.... It is a thing that has happened before elsewhere and will happen again. I went out and quieted the boys. We're a happy team, and I think we still can win."[43]

The Reds were definitely not a happy team at the moment. Years later, Reds players are still split on Cardenas' actions and intentions. A few claim not to have seen the play clearly, one claims not to remember it at all, a few don't want to speculate on what was going through his mind, but a few are fairly certain of what they saw and what they felt and still hold hard feelings. Perhaps it's best to leave it with Robinson's later attempt to put it in perspective from everyone's point of view, when he diplomatically stated, "It was an unfortunate incident, a classic case of misunderstanding. Both were at fault. But you have to remember, this game meant so much to us and the tension was very high and tempers just flared.... We all lost the ball game. Not just Cardenas and not just O'Toole. We had come that far as a ball club ... no one individual should be blamed for any loss."[44]

On Saturday, the Reds and Phillies had a day off. The Mets beat the Cardinals in New York, 15–5, and so the entire season came down to one day — the previous 161 games had settled nothing. Reporters scrambled to sort out the playoff possibilities of the last day of the season. If the Reds won and the Cardinals lost, the Reds would be champs. If the Reds lost and the Cardinals won, the Cards would be champs. If the Phillies won and the Cards lost, there would be a three-way tie, unprecedented in major league history. A complicated three-way miniseries was announced by the commissioner's office to deal with the prospect.

Sisler held a workout for the players at 11 A.M. on the off day. At the workout, "Leo Cardenas moved among his teammates, but not with them," reported Frank Deford in *Sports Illustrated*. "He sat in the shade of the dugout, staring and mute, until his turn came to hit. Pete Rose tried to pick him up.... Cardenas went through the motions and then he went back and sat by himself in the dugout again."[45]

Dick Sisler spoke to reporters once again about Friday night's clubhouse disturbance. He stated that he did not feel it would have any effect on the performance of the team in the final game. "We got that all squared away at a meeting this morning," he said. "It was unfortunate, but that can happen in as hectic a race as this. No hard feelings. They know they've got a job to do."[46] The Phillies would be pitching their ace, Jim Bunning. Everyone was waiting for Sisler to announce who the Reds starter would be for the one game with the pennant on the line. The Reds players wanted Jim Maloney to pitch. Maloney had pitched brilliantly the past three months, going 9–2. Although he had three days rest after facing the Pirates in the duel with Veale, Maloney had thrown well over a hundred pitches in striking out 13 in 11 innings. Sisler decided to start John Tsitouris.

Fred Hutchinson showed up at Crosley Field in street clothes on Sunday, October 4, to watch the end of the 1964 season. He planned to watch the game from Bill DeWitt's box, but first he went by the Phillies clubhouse to talk to his friend and rival Gene Mauch, who had shared much anguish the final month. Phillies trainer Joe Liscio later recalled the scene: "It's 9 A.M. on the Sunday morning of the last day of the season. Gene and I are sitting in the dugout at Crosley Field, our whole world is crashing down around us. We hear this shuffling coming down the tunnel and it was Fred Hutchinson. 'Just wanted to wish you guys good luck ... not to worry, everything will be okay, no matter what happens.' Then he went back up the tunnel. Gene looked at me and said, 'Here we are worrying about what's going to happen this afternoon and they say Fred might not make Christmas.'"[47]

A capacity crowd of more than 29,000 eagerly awaited the start. The Reds began their game one hour before the Cardinals started in St. Louis in the Central Standard Time zone. Many fans had their transistor radios set to the Cardinal game and gave periodic updates to neighboring fans. With the crowd cheering on every pitch, Tsitouris started out well, holding the Phillies scoreless the first two innings. Then, with one out in the third, the wheels came off. A walk followed by a Richie Allen double off the center-field wall scored the first Philly run. Sisler ordered Callison to be walked intentionally. The strategy backfired as the next batter singled to right to drive in Allen. Sisler returned to the mound and replaced Tsitouris with Joe Nuxhall who struck out the first batter he faced. Before Nuxhall could get out of the inning, however, Tony Taylor followed with a single and the Phillies led 3–0.

Billy McCool came in for the Reds in the fourth inning and retired the side in order. When Richie Allen, McCool's nemesis from two days earlier, greeted him leading off the fifth with a home run to center field, Joey Jay was called in from the bullpen. McCool was so mad after coming out that he shattered the dugout water cooler and maintenance workers had to be summoned to stop the flow of water which flooded the dugout.[48] Meanwhile, Philly runs flooded the field. Jay was unable to get out of the sixth inning, giving up five runs, being chased by a three-run homer by Richie Allen. Jay was followed by Henry, Purkey and finally Ellis as Sisler used a total of seven pitchers in the game.

The Reds could do nothing with Bunning, getting only six singles and no runs. The carnage was complete. The Reds lost 10–0. The shell-shocked Reds retreated to the clubhouse to listen to the end of the Cardinals-Mets game and hope for a miracle, but there would be no more miracles for the 1964 Cincinnati Reds. The Cardinals defeated the Mets and won the pennant.

In the clubhouse after the game, Sisler defended his choice of pitchers. "Maloney puts a tremendous stress on his arm. He normally takes more than three days rest between starts.... Percentages favored Tsitouris. John has pitched very well for us.... He has always been real effective against the Phils.... He shut out the Phillies the last time he faced them to start the streak."[49] Maloney had pitched on three days rest four times in 1964, with a record of 3–1 in those games, striking out 27 in 27 innings and giving up 9 runs (an ERA of 3.00).

When asked about his arm, Maloney told reporters, "I could have pitched but I don't think I could have thrown a shut out."[50]

The dejected Reds slumped in the clubhouse — staggered by the incredible roller coaster of emotions they had endured the past month. Disconsolate losing pitcher John Tsitouris sat on a stool in front of his dressing cubicle, his head sunk in his hands. As Sisler walked by he stopped, patted Tsitouris on the back and whispered into his ear. But no words could ease the pain of frustration the players felt. Robinson later wrote, "I sat there by my locker, head down, unable to move. So close, so close, I said to myself. So close and we come up empty. It was a long time before I could pick myself up, shower, get into my street clothes and leave that dressing room and the long 1964 season behind me."[51]

The players struggled to come up with an explanation for the game, to put things into perspective. "Sure it's tougher this way," Rose told a Philadelphia reporter. "We lost two games we shouldn't have lost. It was ours, I thought we were going to win it when we got into first place.... I think the fellas tried too hard."[52]

"If you're gonna go down," Purkey told Lawson, "then that's the way to do it. There's nothing to look back at."[53]

Fred Hutchinson walked into the Reds clubhouse after the game. "It must have taken a monumental effort for him to make it up those stairs to the clubhouse after that last game," says McCool. "But he wanted to see everybody one last time."[54] He entered the hot, sweaty room which had been the site of some of his biggest triumphs, his most memorable professional moments. He loved baseball: the camaraderie, the challenge, the competition. *It's been good to me.* This would be the last time he would ever be in a major league clubhouse with a team he could call his own. Fred Hutchinson was a frail, thin shell of his former self.

"He had on a sport coat," says Ellis, "obviously one of his sport coats, but now it hung on him like a tent. He had lost so much weight."[55]

Fred sat quietly while Sisler replayed the game and season to reporters.

"The boys and myself," concluded Sisler, gesturing toward Fred, "are sorry we couldn't win it for that gentleman over there."

Fred quickly added, "I'm sorry they didn't win it for themselves."[56]

"It was really sad in the clubhouse after the last game," says O'Toole. "You don't know how hard we wanted to win it for Hutch. We came so close."[57]

Fred slowly made his way around the clubhouse, quietly talking to his players and shaking their hands. He had held out against all odds to make it this far, now the struggle was over. Strong men, athletes in the prime of their life, choked back sobs. Hutch thanked O'Toole, Purkey, Robinson and Pinson — the only four men to play for him all six of his seasons in Cincinnati. There were Jay and Coleman who had done so much for the pennant-winning season of 1961. He shook hands with Edwards, the dependable rock behind the plate, and Maloney, the man with the unbelievable arm. He talked to Rose who he was certain would become a major star. He thanked the youngsters, particularly Ellis and McCool, who had played such a big role in 1964.

"He had fined me fifty dollars back in May for not covering first base on a ball hit to the right side," says Ellis. "I had written him a check for it. He came up to me in the clubhouse after the last game and gave me that check which had never been cashed. He said, 'Tear this up. You became a helluva pitcher this year, congratulations. You're going to have a nice career.' And then the thing that really tore me up, he said, 'I'll see you next spring.'"[58]

"You just knew to look at him that we weren't going to see him next spring," says McCool.[59]

The season was over for the Reds. They had waged a brilliant comeback but had fallen just short. The emotional struggle, trying to continue playing baseball as they watched their manager slowly dying in front of them was finally over. Bill Ford in the *Cincinnati Enquirer* summed it up: "Thus ended a gallant crusade to which the Reds had been dedicated: win for Hutch."[60]

Epilogue

AFTER THE 1964 SEASON, Fred Hutchinson went home with his family to Anna Maria Island. His health rapidly deteriorated. On October 11, he wrote a letter of resignation to Bill DeWitt: "I do not believe the condition of my health will permit me to continue to perform the duties as manager of the Reds. I, therefore, request that I be relieved of these duties and also relieved from my contract."[1] The famously thrifty owner DeWitt kept Fred on the payroll and made sure his insurance rights and pension were covered.

In what was probably his last interview, Fred told a reporter, "It is just one of those things that come along.... I thought for a while it could be stopped but my condition has worsened. The only thing I want now is to spend some time with my family."[2]

Fred Hutchinson died on November 11 at Manatee Memorial Hospital in Bradenton with his wife and sons at his side. Many baseball personalities and writers attended the memorial service on Anna Maria Island on November 14. Among the first to arrive were Bill DeWitt, John Edwards and Jim O'Toole, who told reporters, "He was like a father to me. I had more respect for him than any other man I've met in baseball."[3] Fred was buried in Seattle on November 16 next to his parents in Renton's Mount Olivet Cemetery.

Fred was named Man of the Year by *Sport* magazine for 1964. "Sometimes the world of games is a setting for an act of courage which glitters with meaning when measured by any yardstick," the article read. "And such an act of courage was evident in 1964."[4]

The Reds announced in the spring of 1965 that they would wear black armbands during the season as a tribute to Fred Hutchinson. The Reds officially retired his number one in 1965 — the first number to be retired in team history.

Pete Rose finished the 1964 season with a .269 batting average. He would go on to hit over .300 in 14 of the next 15 seasons. He finished his career in 1986 with 4,256 hits, the most in history. He later said of his first major league

189

manager: "I owe the most to Hutchinson, because he gave me the chance to play."[5] Also, "The [award] I cherish most is the Fred Hutchinson Award."[6] Pete Rose is currently banned from baseball due to gambling, preventing consideration for the Hall of Fame.

Frank Robinson finished his 21-year career in 1976 with 586 home runs, fourth on the All-Time list at the time behind Hank Aaron, Babe Ruth and Willie Mays. In 1975, he became the first African American manager in major league baseball history. He was elected to the Hall of Fame in 1982. Inexplicably, there was no official response from the Reds organization upon his induction even though his tenure in Cincinnati was much longer than in any other city. Over the years, the team made amends by retiring his number in 1998 and inviting him back for many events. In 2009, he was the Grand Marshall of Cincinnati's Opening Day Parade.

Vada Pinson experienced a rapid decline in his career due to a series of injuries beginning in 1968. He retired from baseball in 1975 and spent many years as a major league coach. He remained a close friend of Frank Robinson until he died in 1995 at the age of 57 due to complications of a stroke.[7] As of 2000, he had more career hits (2757) than any other eligible player not in the Hall of Fame.

Chico Ruiz, happy-go-lucky Mr. Bench-me-or-trade-me, spent the rest of the sixties as a valuable utility player with the Reds. He never had more at bats than the 311 he had as a rookie in 1964 and he never stole home again in the major leagues. He was traded to the Angels in 1970 and was tragically killed in a car accident in California in 1972. He was 33 years old.

Sammy Ellis moved into the Reds' starting rotation in 1965 and won 22 games. "My wife and I had been looking forward to going to New York for the World Series in 1964," he says. "But after the season we figured it wasn't too bad because there would be a lot of other chances."[8] Unfortunately for Ellis, there would be no other chances to play in a World Series for him. After his playing days were over, he was a long-time major league pitching coach.

Billy McCool, the peach-fuzzed 19-year-old rookie who fearlessly stared down Hank Aaron and Willie Mays but was taken aback by the menacing five o'clock shadow of Joe Torre, was elected Rookie Pitcher of the Year for 1964. In 1965, he missed being National League Reliever of the Year by one point. In 1966, he made the All-Star team. The next year, he tore cartilage in his left knee when his spikes got hung up on the mound during a delivery. The injury forced him to alter his pitching mechanics which caused arm problems. He was out of baseball by 1970 at the age of 25. "Nowadays, I would have had surgery and been back to normal in one month," he says, "but that was just what happened a lot back then. You can't look back or complain."[9] After a long career in the steel industry in Cincinnati, he is now retired in Florida.

Mel Queen was never able to crack the powerful Reds outfield. In 1967, he did the unthinkable — he switched to pitching. He went 14–8 with a 2.76 ERA that year before hurting his arm toward the end of the season. While several players have changed from pitching to another position, Queen remains the only player in the past fifty years to switch from another position to pitcher while already in the major leagues. After retiring as a player, he spent many years as a pitching coach and roving instructor for the Blue Jays. His prized project came in 2001 when he revamped struggling young pitcher Roy Halladay. Halladay went on to make six All-Star teams and win the Cy Young award over the next nine years.

John Edwards was traded by the Reds in 1968 to make way for a hotshot rookie catcher the organization thought might turn out to be pretty good — a guy named Johnny Bench. Edwards finished his 14-year career with the Astros in 1974 and put his engineering degree to use, working as an engineer and operations manager for Cooper Oil Tool Industries in Houston. "Hutch had a greater influence than anyone else in my life in and out of baseball," he said in 1991. "Even today, I try to deal with people I supervise in my line of work the way he handled his players."[10] He is now comfortably retired near Houston.

Dan Neville, the self-admitted baseball fanatic who fought his way back onto the playing field after being a minor league clubhouse boy, spent two weeks on the bench for the Reds at the end of the 1964 season but did not get into a game. "It was such a tight pennant race, they didn't want to take a chance on a rookie making a mistake," he says now. "I wasn't too upset. I thought I would make it back to the major leagues soon." He never did. A series of arm problems derailed his career the next season and he was out of baseball a few years later. Now retired after a career with Proctor and Gamble in Cincinnati, he says, "I don't have any regrets, it was the best two weeks of my life."[11]

Jim O'Toole settled in Cincinnati after his baseball career was over, making many personal appearances, remaining a frequent spokesman for the team and keeping very available to fans and writers. He still lives in the house he bought using the bonus from the 1961 World Series as a down payment. He and his wife raised 11 children and currently have 35 grandchildren. The entire O'Toole clan annually gets together in a special box for Reds opening day games. "I still think about Hutch all the time," O'Toole says. "When he died it was like part of my career died."[12]

Chico Cardenas had very good 15 year major league career, finishing up with Minnesota and Texas. He moved back to Cincinnati and was sighted making spider-like plays from the left side of the infield on Cincinnati area softball diamonds for many years. Chico experienced difficulty adjusting to life after baseball, however, and was nearly deported when it was discovered in the 1990s that, in all the years in the United States, he had never properly filed the paper work for citizenship. He was jailed three months for felonious assault after breaking a man's arm with a bat in a fight over a woman in 1998 when he was 58 years old.[13] He lives in Cincinnati and makes appearances for the Reds, in which he is very gracious and friendly to fans.

Joe Nuxhall played for the Reds until 1967, then stepped into the radio broadcasting booth and became an icon. His postgame signoff of "this is the old left-hander rounding third and heading for home," will linger in the air over Cincinnati for years to come. When he died in 2007 he was perhaps the most beloved person in Cincinnati.

Ryne Duren went through several attempts at alcohol rehab before he was finally successful. He became one of the first to talk to organized baseball about alcoholism. He spent years as a counselor and speaker. Thanks to implants after cataract surgery, the man who could not see a catcher's signs from 60 feet can now drive without glasses. He has not had a drink in 41 years. He would not say how long it has been since he tried to call Princess Grace.[14]

Patsy Hutchinson remains active and divides her time between Anna Maria Island and Seattle. In 1975, she threw out the first ball for the World Series in Cincinnati, believed to be only the second female, after Babe Ruth's daughter, to have such an honor. She didn't have to brush anyone back and it was a good throw. "I was determined to throw that ball out there," she later said.[15]

Bill Hutchinson completed his dream of a major cancer research center. The center was opened in 1965 and named after his brother. "He wanted to do something very special for Fred's memory and the cancer center was the thing that presented itself," says his daughter Charlotte. "It's a tribute to the love of two brothers."[16] The Fred Hutchinson Cancer Center was initially established as a division of the Pacific Northwest Research Foundation, but Bill continued driving to get a totally independent center. He worked tirelessly over the next decade as money was raised through Congress, from the National Cancer Institute and from local sources. Groundbreaking took place for the new center in August 1973. In 1975, the Fred Hutchinson Cancer Research Center was opened as an independent entity. The dedication of the $12 million, seven-story research and treatment facility on September 5, 1975 was attended by luminaries such as President Gerald Ford, Senator Edward Kennedy and Joe DiMaggio. In 1991, the "Hutch" moved from what had become cramped quarters to an 11-acre, $300 million campus where it stands today. The center currently employs more than 2,800 faculty and staff and boasts three Nobel Prize winners. Today it is world renowned as one of the top ten cancer research centers in the world and a world leader in bone marrow transplants. It ranks first in National Institute of Health funding among all independent research institutions.[17] "That place has helped so many people and it's all because of Hutch and his brother," says O'Toole.[18]

Dr. William Hutchinson (middle) smiles as he breaks ground for the new independent Fred Hutchinson Cancer Research Center which opened in 1975. At left is ally Senator Warren Magnuson. At right is the senator's wife, Jermaine Magnuson (courtesy Fred Hutchinson Cancer Research Center).

Bill Hutchinson died at the age of 88 on October 26, 1997. A *Seattle Times* editorial stated: "His legacy was his battle plan for cancer: compassion, diligence and creativity, one patient, one study, one step at a time."[19]

Emmett Watson put it more succinctly: "He was a giant."[20]

In 1965, *Dayton Journal-Herald* sports editor Ritter Collett organized the creation of the Hutch Award along with long-time friends Bob Prince, broadcaster for the Pirates, and Jim Enright, a Chicago sportswriter. Many major league personalities, including Lou Boudreau, Joe Cronin, George Kell, Ralph Kiner, Harry Caray, Jack Buck and Mel Allen, donated to help fund the award. It is annually given to a major league baseball player who best exemplifies the honor, courage and dedication of Fred Hutchinson both on and off the field. The first five awards were given to, in order, Mickey Mantle, Sandy Koufax, Carl Yastrzemski, Pete Rose and Al Kaline. The award was initially

Top: With the majestic Mount Rainier looming in the background, the campus of the modern-day Fred Hutchinson Cancer Research Center encompasses all the buildings in the forefront of the photograph lining the lake. *Above:* Rick Hutchinson smiles as he presents Craig Biggio with the 2006 Hutch Award (both photographs courtesy Fred Hutchinson Cancer Research Center).

Fred Hutchinson, 1919–1964 (Topps Company, Inc.).

presented at a banquet in Pittsburgh, however, it was moved to Seattle in 1994 and is now managed by the Fred Hutchinson Cancer Research Center.

Charlotte Hutchinson Reed, wanting to do something to honor both her father and her uncle, started a benefit run along Lake Washington in Seattle in 1977. The event blossomed into a popular fundraising event. Now in its 33rd year, the Shore Run has raised more than $2.3 million dollars. Charlotte has served on the Hutch Award committee and the board of trustees of the Fred Hutchinson Cancer Research Center. "I'm very proud that we have taken a sad incident and turned it into a postitive thing," she said in 2006.[21]

In 1999, Fred Hutchinson was named Seattle's Athlete of the Century by the *Seattle Post-Intelligencer*,[22] beating out Ken Griffey, Jr. and Alex Rodriguez among others.

When Safeco Field opened in Seattle in 1999, the likeness of Fred Hutchinson was imprinted on the end of every row of seats in honor of his contribution to Seattle baseball. His grandson Joey was chosen to make the first run around the bases before the first game.[23]

What was it that inspired all these tributes for a man who never won a World Series as a player or manager? As a player, he won less than 100 major league games. As a manager, his career record was barely over .500. Fred Hutchinson's legacy was not made, and cannot be measured, by numbers. There was much more to the man than numbers. His legacy was forged with those who knew him by his personality, drive, competitiveness and ultimately, in his final season, by his grace and courage. Gene Mauch said it best: "Hutch taught us all to live, and when the time came, he taught us how to die."[24]

Notes

Chapter 1

1. Mark Kram, "Not Enough Talkative Bats in Cincy," *Sports Illustrated,* August 24, 1964.
2. Personal interview with Jim O'Toole, May 15, 2009.
3. Earl Lawson, *Cincinnati Seasons: My 34 Years with the Reds* (South Bend, IN: Diamond, 1987), 79.
4. Emmett Watson, "In Sunshine or In Shadow," *Sports Illustrated,* August 26, 1957.
5. Murray Olderman, "Reds Wipe That Scowl Off Hutch's Face," *The Sporting News,* August 2, 1961.
6. "Cincinnati Reds: The Pennant Is Up to the Doctors," *Sports Illustrated,* April 8, 1963.
7. Emmett Watson, "In Sunshine or In Shadow," *Sports Illustrated,* August 26, 1957.
8. Al Hirshberg, "Baseball's Angriest Man," *Climax,* September 1962.
9. Dale Shaw, "Fred Hutchinson: The Manager Down the Stretch," *Sport,* November 1963. As with many oft-repeated quotes, the origin and exact words have been lost over time. This quote was also attributed to "a Philadelphia sportswriter, Larry Merchant" in Earl Lawson, *Cincinnati Seasons: My 34 Years with the Reds* (South Bend, IN: Diamond, 1987), 78; and "a Philadelphia writer" in Bill Koch, "Hutch–Reds Manager Feared, Loved," *Cincinnati Post,* August 30, 1996.
10. Personal interview with Rick Hutchinson, May 10, 2009.
11. Personal interview with Jim Brosnan, May 5, 2009.
12. Personal interview with Jay Hook, April 27, 2009.
13. Jim Brosnan, *The Long Season* (New York: Harper, 1960), 204.
14. Al Hirshberg, "Baseball's Angriest Man," *Climax,* September 1962.
15. Earl Lawson, *Cincinnati Seasons: My 34 Years with the Reds* (South Bend, IN: Diamond, 1987), 75.
16. Al Hirshberg, "Baseball's Angriest Man." *Climax,* September 1962.
17. Dan Raley, "Athletes of the Century," *Seattle Post-Intelligencer,* December 24, 1999.
18. Personal interview with Rick Hutchinson, May 10, 2009.
19. Personal interview with Jim O'Toole, May 15, 2009.
20. Personal interviews with Patsy Hutchinson, May 11, 2009; Rick Hutchinson, May 10, 2009; and Jack Hutchinson, May 27, 2009; Fred Hutchinson with Al Hirshberg, "How I Live with Cancer," *True,* August 1964.

Chapter 2

1. Blaine Newnham, "Local Sports Came of Age With a Teen," *Seattle Times,* December 25, 1999.
2. Walt Crowley, "Vancouver Begins British Survey of Puget Sound on May 19, 1792" (Feb. 18, 2003), www.historylink.org; Walt Crowley, "Denny Party Scouts Arrive at Mount of Duwamish River in Future King County on September 25, 1851" (March 8, 2003), www. historylink.org.
3. www.historylink.org; www.wikipedia.org.
4. Frank Chelsley, "Hutchinson, Fred (1919– 1964): Baseball Legend" (November 12, 2007), www.historylink.org; Emmett Watson, "In Sunshine or In Shadow," *Sports Illustrated,* Au-

gust 26, 1957; Personal interview with Patsy Hutchinson, May 11, 2009.

5. Personal interview with Charlotte Hutchinson Reed, December 7, 2009.

6. Mickey Mantle and Robert Creamer, "Honest Hutch," in *The Quality of Courage* (Lincoln: University of Nebraska Press, 1999); Clay Eals, "The Thought of Losing was Just Abhorrent," in *Rain Check: Baseball in the Pacific Northwest*, ed. Mark Armour (Cleveland: Society for American Baseball Research, 2006); Personal interview with Rick Hutchinson, May 10, 2009.

7. Personal interview with Patsy Hutchinson, May 11, 2009.

8. Personal interview with Charlotte Hutchinson Reed, December 7, 2009.

9. Personal interview with Patsy Hutchinson, May 11, 2009.

10. Personal interview with Charlotte Hutchinson Reed, December 7, 2009.

11. Personal interview with Patsy Hutchinson, May 11, 2009.

12. Al Hirshberg, "Baseball's Angriest Man," *Climax*, September 1962.

13. Ibid.

14. Ibid.

15. Personal interviews with Rick Hutchinson, May 10, 2009; Jack Hutchinson, May 27, 2009.

16. Personal interview with Charlotte Hutchinson Reed, December 7, 2009.

17. Dale Shaw, "Fred Hutchinson: The Manager Down the Stretch," *Sport*, November 1963.

18. Emmett Watson, "'Hutch': His Days Were Full of Deeds," *Seattle Times*, November 4, 1997.

19. Judith Hjertstedt Crist, letter to the editor, *Seattle Times*, December 25, 1999.

20. Dan Raley, "J.B. Parker Caught 'Hutch' in Pitcher's Formative Years," *Seattle Post-Intelligencer*, October 5, 2005.

21. Personal interview with Charlotte Hutchinson Reed, December 7, 2009.

22. Al Hirshberg, "Baseball's Angriest Man," *Climax*, September 1962.

23. Emmett Watson, "In Sunshine or In Shadow," *Sports Illustrated*, August 26, 1957.

24. Dan Raley, "J.B. Parker Caught 'Hutch' in Pitcher's Formative Years," *Seattle Post-Intelligencer*, October 5, 2005.

25. Emmett Watson, "In Sunshine or In Shadow," *Sports Illustrated*, August 26, 1957.

26. Lisa Neff, "Lasting Legacy: A Ballplayer's Record, A Family, A Research Center," *The Islander* (Holmes Beach, FL), March 5, 2008.

27. Personal interview with Patsy Hutchinson, May 11, 2009.

28. Blaine Newnham, "Local Sports Came of Age With a Teen," *Seattle Times*, December 25, 1999; Emmett Watson, "In Sunshine or In Shadow," *Sports Illustrated*, August 26, 1957; Personal interview with Patsy Hutchinson, May 11, 2009.

29. Lenny Anderson, "The Doctor is In," *Seattle Post-Intelligencer*, April 20, 1995.

30. Personal interview with Patsy Hutchinson, May 11, 2009.

31. *San Jose News*, August 18, 1939.

32. Blaine Newnham, "Local Sports Came of Age With a Teen," *Seattle Times*, December 25, 1999; Dan Raley, "From Reds to Ruth to Rainiers," *Seattle Post-Intelligencer*, July 14, 1999.

33. Rich Johnson, "Strike 1 Was For Pay—Early Rainiers Used Sitdown Strategy to Collect Wages From Owner," *Seattle Times*, October 2, 1991.

34. Dan Raley, "A Man Named Sick Made Seattle Well," in *Rain Check: Baseball in the Pacific Northwest*, ed. Mark Armour (Cleveland: Society for American Baseball Research, 2006); Rich Johnson, "Strike 1 Was For Pay—Early Rainiers Used Sitdown Strategy to Collect Wages From Owner," *Seattle Times*, October 2, 1991.

35. Dan Raley, "A Man Named Sick Made Seattle Well," in *Rain Check: Baseball in the Pacific Northwest*, ed. Mark Armour (Cleveland: Society for American Baseball Research, 2006).

36. Blaine Newnham, "Local Sports Came of Age With a Teen," *Seattle Times*, December 25, 1999.

37. Emmett Watson, "In Sunshine or In Shadow," *Sports Illustrated*, August 26, 1957; Personal interview with Patsy Hutchinson, May 11, 2009.

38. Personal interview with Patsy Hutchinson, May 11, 2009.

39. Leigh Montville, *Ted Williams: The Biography of an American Hero* (New York: Doubleday, 2004), 30.

40. "How it was by Hollywood Stars Great Chuck Stevens," www.minorleaguebaseball. com; Leigh Montville, *Ted Williams: The Biography of an American Hero* (New York: Doubleday, 2004), 29–34.

41. Rick Johnson, "Hutch's 19th Birthday Party," *Seattle Times*, August 11, 1996.

42. Ibid.

43. *Spokesman-Review* (Spokane), November 13, 1964.

44. Rick Johnson, "Remember Pennant Fever?—50 Years Ago Rainiers Had Seattle Basking in Glory, Pennant Fever," *Seattle Times*, October 1, 1991.

45. Rick Johnson, "Hutch's 19th Birthday Party," *Seattle Times*, August 11, 1996.

46. Dick Rockne, "Seattle's Top 10 Greatest Moments," *Seattle Times*, December 26, 1999.

47. Emmett Watson, "In Sunshine or In Shadow," *Sports Illustrated*, August 26, 1957.

48. Associated Press, *Gettysburg Times*, May 28, 1938.

49. Associated Press, *The Day* (New London, Conn.), August 18, 1938.

50. *Seattle Times*, September 12, 1938.

51. *Pittsburgh Press*, December 13, 1938.

52. Richard Ben Cramer, *Joe DiMaggio: The Hero's Life* (New York: Simon & Schuster, 2000), 69.

53. Blaine Newnham, "Local Sports Came of Age With a Teen," *Seattle Times*, December 25, 1999; Rich Johnson, "Strike 1 Was For Pay—Early Rainiers Used Sitdown Strategy to Collect Wages From Owner," *Seattle Times*, October 2, 1991.

Chapter 3

1. "Fred Hutchinson Returns to Minors," Associate Press, *Ludington Daily News* (Mich.), May 4, 1939.

2. Ibid.

3. "Hutchinson, 1939 Flop, Set to Get Going This Year," United Press International, *Pittsburgh Post-Gazette*, February 15, 1940.

4. Jack Cuddy, "New Players Show Major League Class," *Miami Daily*, May 16, 1939.

5. Emmett Watson, "In Sunshine or In Shadow," *Sports Illustrated*, August 26, 1957.

6. "Hutchinson, 1939 Flop, Set to Get Going This Year," United Press International, *Pittsburgh Post-Gazette*, February 15, 1940.

7. Ibid.

8. Personal interview with Patsy Hutchinson, May 11, 2009.

9. Birdie Tebbetts with James Morrison, *Confessions of a Baseball Nomad* (Chicago: Triumph Books, 2002), 41–43.

10. "Hutchinson Succeeds as Navy Instructor," Associated Press, *Herald-Journal*, March 21, 1943.

11. www.bally.fortunecity.com.

12. Personal interview with Patsy Hutchinson, May 11, 2009.

13. Emmett Watson, "In Sunshine or In Shadow," *Sports Illustrated*, August 26, 1957.

14. Ibid.

15. Don Wolfe, "Winners Warm Up Mean," *Baseball Digest*, July 1959.

16. George Kell, in *We Played the Game*, ed. Danny Peary (New York: Black Dog, 1994), 47.

17. Arthur Daley, *New York Times*, May 8, 1964.

18. Leigh Montville, *Ted Williams: The Biography of an American Hero* (New York: Doubleday, 2004), 123.

19. Clay Eals, "The Thought of Losing was Just Abhorrent," in *Rain Check: Baseball in the Pacific Northwest*, ed. Mark Armour (Cleveland: Society for American Baseball Research, 2006); Bill Koch, "Hutch–Reds Manager Feared, Loved," *Cincinnati Post*, August 30, 1996.

20. Milton Richman, "What They Say on the Bench," *Baseball Digest*, January 1951.

21. Emmett Watson, "In Sunshine or In Shadow," *Sports Illustrated*, August 26, 1957; Personal interview with Patsy Hutchinson, May 11, 2009; Al Hirshberg, "Baseball's Angriest Man," *Climax*, September 1962.

22. Personal interview with Patsy Hutchinson, May 11, 2009.

Chapter 4

1. Jerry Green, "Red Rolfe ... A True Yankee," *Baseball Digest*, February 1970.

2. United Press International, *The Sunday Star*, July 6, 1952.

3. Associated Press, *Ottawa Citizen*, July 7, 1952.

4. Ibid.

5. Associated Press, *Milwaukee Journal*, August 28, 1953.

6. Fred Hatfield, in *We Played the Game*, ed. Danny Peary (New York: Black Dog, 1994), 237.

7. Jim Sargent, "Jim Delsing," SABR Bioproject, http://bioproject.SABR.org.

8. Clay Eals, "The Thought of Losing was Just Abhorrent," in *Rain Check: Baseball in the Pacific Northwest*, ed. Mark Armour (Cleveland: Society for American Baseball Research, 2006).

9. Al Hirshberg, "Baseball's Angriest Man," *Climax*, September 1962.

10. *Sarasota Journal*, November 12, 1964.

11. Al Hirshberg, "Baseball's Angriest Man," *Climax*, September 1962.

12. Ibid.

13. Ibid.

14. William Arnold, "New Video History of Rainiers Touches All the Bases of Magical Ballclub," *Seattle Post-Intelligencer*, August 23, 1999.

15. William Arnold, "A Fan Remembers the Summer of '55," *Seattle Post-Intelligencer*, August 23, 1999.

16. Emmett Watson, "In Sunshine or in Shadow," *Sports Illustrated*, August 26, 1957.

17. Al Hirshberg, "Baseball's Angriest Man," *Climax*, September 1962.

18. William Arnold, "New Video History of Rainiers Touches All the Bases of Magical Ballclub," *Seattle Post-Intelligencer*, August 23, 1999.

19. Emmett Watson, "In Sunshine or in Shadow," *Sports Illustrated*, August 26, 1957.

20. *Milwaukee Journal*, October 11, 1955; *St. Petersburg Times*, October 13, 1955.

21. Robert Burnes, "Why Lane Picked Hutchinson," *Baseball Digest*, November 1955.

22. Robert Creamer, "Brilliant Enigma," *Sports Illustrated*, September 3, 1956.

23. Hank Sauer, in *We Played the Game*, ed. Danny Peary (New York: Black Dog, 1994), 321–22.

24. Dick Schofield, in *We Played the Game*, ed. Danny Peary (New York: Black Dog, 1994), 354.

25. Emmett Watson, "In Sunshine or in Shadow," *Sports Illustrated*, August 26, 1957.

26. Ibid.

27. Roy Terrell, "Don't Let Hutch Get Mad," *Sports Illustrated*, September 21, 1959.

28. Jim Brosnan, *Pennant Race* (New York: Penguin Books, 1983), 127.

29. Emmett Watson, "In Sunshine or in Shadow," *Sports Illustrated*, August 26, 1957.

30. Personal interview with Al Dark, June 2, 2009.

31. Emmett Watson, "In Sunshine or in Shadow," *Sports Illustrated*, August 26, 1957.

32. Ibid.

33. Ibid; Al Hirshberg, "Baseball's Angriest Man," *Climax*, September 1962.

34. Emmett Watson, "In Sunshine or in Shadow," *Sports Illustrated*, August 26, 1957.

35. Roy Terrell, "Up-and-Down Cubbies and Cards," *Sports Illustrated*, May 19, 1958.

36. Ibid.

37. *Spokesman-Review* (Spokane), November 13, 1964.

38. David Halberstam, *October 1964* (New York: Random House, 1994), 252–53.

39. Associated Press, *Sarasota Herald-Tribune*, September 17, 1958.

40. Personal interview with Patsy Hutchinson, May 11, 2009.

Chapter 5

1. www.Crosley-field.com; John Erardi, "Palace of the Fans," *Cincinnati Enquirer*, April 1, 1996.

2. Robert Boyle, "Cincinnati's Brain-Picker," *Sports Illustrated*, June 13, 1966.

3. *Cincinnati Enquirer*, January 10, 2000.

4. Johnny Klippstein, in *We Played the Game*, ed. Danny Peary (New York: Black Dog, 1994), 366.

5. Frank Robinson with Berry Stainback, *Extra Innings*, (New York: McGraw-Hill, 1988), 38.

6. Jim Brosnan, in *We Played the Game*, ed. Danny Peary (New York: Black Dog, 1994), 437.

7. Jim O'Toole, in *We Played the Game*, ed. Danny Peary (New York: Black Dog, 1994), 435.

8. Roy Terrell, "Don't Let Hutch Get Mad," *Sports Illustrated*, September 21, 1959.

9. Jim Brosnan, *The Long Season* (New York: Harper, 1960), 199–200.

10. Roy Terrell, "Don't Let Hutch Get Mad," *Sports Illustrated*, September 21, 1959.

11. Personal interview with Jim O'Toole, May 15, 2009.

12. Al Hirshberg, "Baseball's Angriest Man," *Climax*, September 1962.

13. Dale Shaw, "Fred Hutchinson: The Manager Down the Stretch," *Sport*, November 1963.

14. Ibid.

Chapter 6

1. Herman Weiskopf, "Baseball's Week," *Sports Illustrated*, August 27, 1962.

2. Robert Boyle, "Cincinnati's Brain-Picker," *Sports Illustrated*, June 13, 1966.

3. Walter Bingham, "Arms and the Men for Cincy," Sports Illustrated, October 9, 1961.

4. Ibid.

5. *Cincinnati Enquirer*, December 6, 2007.

6. Murray Olderman, "Reds Wipe That Scowl Off Hutch's Face," *The Sporting News*, August 2, 1961.

7. Walter Bingham, "The Reds Is Dead," *Sports Illustrated*, March 19, 1962.

8. Earl Lawson, *Cincinnati Seasons: My 34 Years with the Reds* (South Bend, IN: Diamond, 1987), 82.

9. Murray Olderman, "Reds Wipe That Scowl Off Hutch's Face," *The Sporting News*, August 2, 1961.

10. *St. Petersburg Times*, September 30, 1961.

11. Personal interview with Jim O'Toole, May 15, 2009.

12. Earl Lawson, *Cincinnati Seasons: My 34 Years with the Reds* (South Bend, IN: Diamond, 1987), 81.

13. Al Hirshberg, "Baseball's Angriest Man," *Climax*, September 1962.

14. Personal interview with Jim O'Toole, May 15, 2009.

15. Earl Lawson, *Cincinnati Seasons: My 34 Years with the Reds* (South Bend, IN: Diamond, 1987), 79.

16. Personal interview with Jim O'Toole, May 15, 2009.

17. Personal interview with Eddie Kasko, April 14, 2009.

18. Personal interview with Jim O'Toole, May 15, 2009.

19. Personal interview with Eddie Kasko, April 14, 2009.

20. *Cincinnati Enquirer*, April 5, 2009.

21. Jim O'Toole, in *We Played the Game*, ed. Danny Peary (New York: Black Dog, 1994), 510.

22. Frank Robinson with Al Silverman, *My Life Is Baseball* (New York: Doubleday, 1968), 126–27.

23. Personal interview with Jim O'Toole, May 15, 2009.

24. Jim Brosnan, *Pennant Race* (New York: Penguin Books, 1983), 127.

25. Earl Lawson, *Cincinnati Seasons: My 34 Years with the Reds* (South Bend, IN: Diamond, 1987), 85.

26. Personal interview with Jim O'Toole, May 15, 2009.

27. *Cincinnati Enquirer*, April 5, 2009.

28. *New York Times*, August 29, 1961.

29. Personal interview with Jim O'Toole, May 15, 2009.

30. Jim Brosnan, *Pennant Race* (New York: Penguin Books, 1983), 249.

31. Personal interview with Jim O'Toole, May 15, 2009.

32. Personal interview with Patsy Hutchinson, May 11, 2009.

33. Murray Olderman, "Reds Wipe That Scowl Off Hutch's Face," *The Sporting News*, August 2, 1961.

34. *New York Times*, September 28, 1961.

35. *New York Times*, October 6, 1961.

36. Al Hirshberg, "Baseball's Angriest Man," *Climax*, September 1962.

37. *New York Times*, October 10, 1961.

38. *Cincinnati Enquirer*, April 5, 2009.

39. Frank Robinson with Al Silverman, *My Life Is Baseball* (New York: Doubleday, 1968), 131.

40. Personal correspondence with Jerry Lynch, June 2009.

41. Personal interview with Jim Brosnan, May 5, 2009.

42. Personal interview with Jim O'Toole, May 15, 2009.

43. Al Hirshberg, "Baseball's Angriest Man," *Climax*, September 1962.

44. *St. Petersburg Times*, September 30, 1961.

Chapter 7

1. Michael Sokolove, *Hustle: The Myth, Life, and Lies of Pete Rose* (New York: Simon & Schuster, 1990), 45.

2. Ibid., 46.

3. Personal interview with Jack Hutchinson, May 27, 2009.

4. Michael Sokolove, *Hustle: The Myth, Life, and Lies of Pete Rose* (New York: Simon & Schuster, 1990), 51.

5. *Cincinnati Seasons: My 34 Years with the Reds* (South Bend, IN: Diamond, 1987), 183.

6. Jim O'Toole, in *We Played the Game*, ed. Danny Peary (New York: Black Dog, 1994), 575.

7. Personal interview with Jim Brosnan, May 5, 2009.

8. Jim O'Toole, in *We Played the Game*, ed. Danny Peary (New York: Black Dog, 1994), 575.

9. *The Sporting News*, May 11, 2009.

10. Personal interview with Eddie Kasko, April 14, 2009.

11. Frank Robinson with Berry Stainback, *Extra Innings* (New York: McGraw-Hill, 1988), 55.

12. Michael Sokolove, *Hustle: The Myth, Life, and Lies of Pete Rose* (New York: Simon & Schuster, 1990), 57.

13. Pete Rose and Roger Kahn, *Pete Rose: My Story* (New York: McMillan, 1989), 108–09; Michael Sokolove, *Hustle: The Myth, Life, and Lies of Pete Rose* (New York: Simon & Schuster, 1990), 58–59; William A. Cook, *Pete Rose: Baseball's All-Time Hit King* (Jefferson, NC: McFarland, 2004), 22–23.

14. Michael Sokolove, *Hustle: The Myth, Life, and Lies of Pete Rose* (New York: Simon & Schuster, 1990), 194–195.

15. Si Burick, "Winning Attitude Helps Harper Move from Post to Post," *Baseball Digest*, May 1964.

Chapter 8

1. Earl Lawson, *Cincinnati Seasons: My 34 Years with the Reds* (South Bend, IN: Diamond, 1987), 76.

2. Al Hirshberg, "Baseball's Angriest Man," *Climax*, September 1962.

3. Dale Shaw, "Fred Hutchinson: The Manager Down the Stretch," *Sport*, November 1963.

4. Ibid.

5. Ibid.

6. Ibid.

7. Personal interview with Eddie Kasko, April 14, 2009.

8. Johnny Klippstein, in *We Played the Game*, ed. Danny Peary (New York: Black Dog, 1994), 546.

9. Personal interview with Sam Ellis, April 7, 2009.

10. Walter Bingham, "The Reds is Dead," *Sports Illustrated*, March 19, 1962.

11. Personal interview with Johnny Edwards, April 7, 2009.

12. Al Hirshberg, "Baseball's Angriest Man," *Climax*, September 1962.

13. *Cincinnati Post*, April 8, 1991.

14. Murray Olderman, "Reds Wipe That Scowl Off Hutch's Face," *The Sporting News*, August 2, 1961.

15. Personal interview with Rick Hutchinson, May 10, 2009.

16. Personal interview with Jim O'Toole, May 15, 2009.

17. Personal interview with Johnny Edwards, April 7, 2009.

18. Personal interview with Jim O'Toole, May 15, 2009.

19. Earl Lawson, *Cincinnati Seasons: My 34 Years with the Reds* (South Bend, IN: Diamond, 1987), 84.

20. Personal interview with Jim O'Toole, May 15, 2009; Personal interview with Eddie Kasko, April 14, 2009; Personal interview with Johnny Edwards, April 7, 2009.

21. Personal interview with Jim O'Toole, May 15, 2009.

22. Personal interview with Johnny Edwards, April 7, 2009.

23. Personal interview with Eddie Kasko, April 14, 2009.

24. Earl Lawson, *Cincinnati Seasons: My 34 Years with the Reds* (South Bend, IN: Diamond, 1987), 77.

25. Johnny Klippstein, in *We Played the Game*, ed. Danny Peary (New York: Black Dog, 1994), 546.

26. Personal interview with Jim O'Toole, May 15, 2009.

27. Personal interview with Patsy Hutchinson, May 11, 2009.

28. Personal interview with Johnny Edwards, April 7, 2009.

29. Personal interview with Jay Hook, April 27, 2009.

30. Personal interview with Mel Queen, April 15, 2009.

31. Personal interview with Jay Hook, April 27, 2009.

32. Dale Shaw, "Fred Hutchinson: The Manager Down the Stretch," *Sport*, November 1963.

33. Ibid.

34. Al Hirshberg, "Baseball's Angriest Man," *Climax*, September 1962.

35. Ibid.

36. Ibid.

37. Dale Shaw, "Fred Hutchinson, The Manager Down the Stretch," *Sport*, November 1963; Al Hirshberg, "Baseball's Angriest Man," *Climax*, September 1962.

38. Al Hirshberg, "Baseball's Angriest Man," *Climax*, September, 1962. A similar version of this story, in Fred's own words, appears in *Baseball Digest*, August 1961.

39. John Carmichael, "Hutch is Trained for Big Battles," *Seattle Times*, January 10, 1964; Al Hirshberg, "Baseball's Angriest Man," *Climax*, September 1962.

40. *Baseball Digest*, October 1964.

41. Al Hirshberg, "Baseball's Angriest Man," *Climax*, September 1962.

42. Dave Anderson, *New York Times*, July 23, 1987.

Chapter 9

1. Personal interview with Patsy Hutchinson, May 11, 2009.

2. Hal McCoy, *Dayton Daily News*, September 2, 1996.

3. Personal interview with Patsy Hutchinson, May 11, 2009.

4. Ibid.

5. Personal interview with Rick Hutchinson, May 10, 2009.

6. Personal interview with Jack Hutchinson, May 27, 2009.

7. Personal interview with Patsy Hutchinson, May 11, 2009.

8. Lisa Neff, "Child's Play," *The Islander* (Anna Maria, FL), March 5, 2008.

9. Personal interview with Rick Hutchinson, May 10, 2009.

10. Lisa Neff, "Lasting Legacy: A Ballplayer's Record, a Family, a Research Center," *The Islander* (Anna Maria, FL), March 5, 2008.

11. Ibid.

12. Personal interview with Jack Hutchinson, May 27, 2009.

13. Personal interview with Rick Hutchinson, May 10, 2009.

14. Personal interview with Patsy Hutchinson, May 11, 2009.

15. Ibid.

16. Ibid.

17. Ibid.

18. Rick Pezdirtz, "Hutchinson's Sons Star in Legion Ball," *Miami News*, August 7, 1962.

19. Milton Richman, United Press International, in *The Times-News*, March 15, 1965.

20. Personal interview with Rick Hutchinson, May 10, 2009.

21. Personal interview with Jack Hutchinson, May 27, 2009.

22. Personal interview with Rick Hutchinson, May 10, 2009.

Chapter 10

1. Personal interview with Charlotte Hutchinson Reed, December 7, 2009.

2. Personal interview with Patsy Hutchinson, May 11, 2009.

3. Personal interview with Rick Hutchinson, May 10, 2009.

4. Warren King, "William Hutchinson Dies — Doctor Founded Research Center in Seattle, Named it After Brother," *Seattle Times*, October 28, 1997.

5. Personal interview with Charlotte Hutchinson Reed, December 7, 2009.

6. Ibid.

7. Fred Hutchinson with Al Hirshberg, "How I Live with Cancer," *True*, August 1964.

8. Dr. William Hutchinson, Jr. in "Two Brothers — Fred and Bill Hutchinson," video, www.fhcrc.org/about/history/fred/html.

9. Personal interview with Charlotte Hutchinson Reed, December 7, 2009.

10. Charlotte Hutchinson Reed, in ""Two Brothers — Fred and Bill Hutchinson," video, www.fhcrc.org/about/history/fred/html.

11. Personal interview with Charlotte Hutchinson Reed, December 7, 2009.

12. Personal interview with Patsy Hutchinson, May 11, 2009.

13. Personal interview with Charlotte Hutchinson Reed, December 7, 2009.

14. Ibid.

15. Scott Merkin, "Hutch Award Finalists Announced" (October 28, 2006), www.mlb.com.

16. Personal interview with Charlotte Hutchinson Reed, December 7, 2009.

17. Louis Fiset, "Dr. William B. Hutchinson" (December 20, 2004), www.historylink.org.

18. Personal interview with Charlotte Hutchinson Reed, December 7, 2009.

19. Fred Hutchinson with Al Hirshberg, "How I Live with Cancer," *True*, August 1964.

20. Jimmy Mann, "Cancer is Overmatched," *St. Petersburg Times*, January 6, 1964.

21. Fred Hutchinson with Al Hirshberg, "How I Live with Cancer," *True*, August 1964.

22. Ibid.

23. Personal interview with Rick Hutchinson, May 10, 2009.

24. Personal interview with Patsy Hutchinson, May 11, 2009.

25. Fred Hutchinson with Al Hirshberg, "How I Live with Cancer," *True*, August 1964.

26. Ibid.

27. Ibid.

Chapter 11

1. *Cincinnati Post*, January 3, 1964.

2. Ibid.

3. Associated Press, "Redleg Manager Has Malignancy," *TriCity Herald* (Kennewick, WA), January 3, 1964.

4. Georg Meyers, "'It's Cancer'—You Don't Know What to Think," *Seattle Times*, January 4, 1964.

5. Arthur Daley, *New York Times*, January 3, 1964.

6. Georg Meyers, "'It's Cancer'—You Don't Know What to Think," *Seattle Times*, January 4, 1964.

7. Ibid.

8. Ibid.

9. Arthur Daley, *New York Times*, January 3, 1964.

10. Red Smith, "Tribute to Big Bear, He Wins Respect With Inner Power," *Seattle Times*, January 5, 1964.

11. John Carmichael, "Hutch is Trained For Big Battles," *Seattle Times*, January 10, 1964.

12. Mickey Mantle and Robert Creamer, "Honest Hutch," in *The Quality of Courage* (Lincoln: University of Nebraska Press, Reprint edition, 1999).

13. Fred Hutchinson with Al Hirshberg, "How I Live with Cancer," *True*, August 1964.

14. Personal interview with Jack Hutchinson, May 27, 2009.

15. Personal interview with Rick Hutchinson, May 10, 2009.

16. Personal interview with Charlotte Hutchinson Reed, December 7, 2009.

17. Jimmy Mann, "Cancer is Overmatched," *St. Petersburg Times,* January 6, 1964.

18. Personal interview with Rick Hutchinson, May 10, 2009.

19. Personal interview with Patsy Hutchinson, May 11, 2009.

20. Ibid.

21. Personal interview with Charlotte Hutchinson Reed, December 7, 2009.

22. Ibid.

23. Ibid.

24. Richard Ben Cramer, *Joe DiMaggio: The Hero's Life* (New York: Simon & Schuster, 2000).

25. Personal interview with Rick Hutchinson, May 10, 2009.

26. Earl Ubell, "Cigaret Smoke Smells Of Death, Says Report," *New York Herald Tribune News Service*, printed in *Seattle Times*, January 12, 1964.

27. Gil Lyons, "Hutch Expects to Manage Many More Years," *Seattle Times*, January 9, 1964.

28. Ibid.

29. Fred Hutchinson with Al Hirshberg, "How I Live with Cancer," *True*, August 1964.

30. Personal interview with Patsy Hutchinson, May 11, 2009.

31. Fred Hutchinson with Al Hirshberg, "How I Live with Cancer," *True*, August 1964.

32. Ibid.

33. Ibid.

34. Associated Press, *St. Petersburg Times*, February 5, 1964.

35. Personal interview with Charlotte Hutchinson Reed, December 7, 2009.

36. Fred Hutchinson with Al Hirshberg, "How I Live with Cancer," *True*, August 1964.

37. Earl Lawson, *Cincinnati Seasons: My 34 Years with the Reds* (South Bend, IN: Diamond, 1987), 77.

Chapter 12

1. *New York Times*, March 3, 1964.

2. Ibid.

3. Jimmy Mann, "A Promise is Kept," *St. Petersburg Times*, February 24, 1964.

4. *New York Times*, March 3, 1964.

5. "Hutch Keeps Promise—On Hand For Training," *Dayton Journal-Herald*, March 2, 1964.

6. Jim O'Toole, in *We Played the Game* (New York: Black Dog, 1994), 545.

7. Michael Sokolove, *Hustle: The Myth, Life, and Lies of Pete Rose* (New York: Simon & Schuster, 1990), 49.

8. Earl Lawson, *Cincinnati Post*, March 17, 1964.

9. Earl Lawson, "McCool, 19, Likely to Pitch for 1964 Reds," *Cincinnati Post*, March 4, 1964.

10. Ibid.

11. *Cincinnati Post*, March 14, 1964.

12. *Cincinnati Post*, March 2, 1964.

13. Earl Lawson, "Joey Jay Says He Took $5000 Slash," *Cincinnati Post,* March 5, 1964.

14. Ritter Collett, *Dayton Journal-Herald*, March 10, 1964.

15. Personal interview with Bill McCool, March 27, 2009.

16. Si Burick, "Cool Billy," *Baseball Digest*, May 1965.

17. Personal interview with Sammy Ellis, April 7, 2009.

18. Earl Lawson, "Neville Realizing Dream," *Cincinnati Post*, March 3, 1964; Personal interview with Dan Neville, March 31, 2009.

19. Personal interview with Dan Neville, March 31, 2009.

20. *Cincinnati Post*, March 2, 1964.

21. Lou Smith, *Cincinnati Enquirer*, March 6, 1964.

22. Personal interview with Dave Bristol, April 2, 2009.

23. Personal interview with Bobby Klaus, April 3, 2009.

24. Personal interview with Al Worthington, March 27, 2009.

25. Personal interview with Jim O'Toole, May 15, 2009.

26. Personal interview with Sammy Ellis, April 7, 2009.

27. Personal interview with Mel Queen, April 15, 2009.

28. Personal interview with Dan Neville, March 31, 2009.

29. *Cincinnati Post*, March 16, 1964.

30. Walter Bingham, "The Reds is Dead," *Sports Illustrated*, March 19, 1962.

31. Pete Rose and Roger Kahn, *Pete Rose: My Story* (New York: McMillan, 1989).

32. Earl Lawson, *Cincinnati Post*, March 10, 1964.

33. Lou Smith, *Cincinnati Enquirer*, March 22, 1964.

34. Ibid.

35. Lou Smith, "Pete Wins Popularity Poll," *Cincinnati Enquirer*, March 19, 1964.

36. Lou Smith, *Cincinnati Enquirer*, March 14, 1964.

37. Earl Lawson, *Cincinnati Post*, March 17, 1964.

38. Ritter Collett, *Dayton Journal-Herald*, March 4, 1964.

39. "Cincinnati Reds," *Sports Illustrated*, April 9, 1962.

40. *Sports Illustrated*, April 19, 1965.

41. Jim O'Toole, in *We Played the Game* (New York: Black Dog, 1994), 605.

42. Personal interview with Sammy Ellis, April 7, 2009.

43. Personal interview with Mel Queen, April 15, 2009.

44. Personal interview with Bobby Klaus, April 3, 2009.

45. Ritter Collett, *Dayton Journal-Herald*, March 6, 1964.

46. Lou Smith, *Cincinnati Enquirer*, March 10, 1964; Ritter Collett, "Reluctant Reliever," *Dayton Journal-Herald*, March 13, 1964.

47. Lou Smith, *Cincinnati Enquirer*, March 10, 1964.

48. Ritter Collett, "Reluctant Reliever," *Dayton Journal-Herald*, March 13, 1964.

49. *Cincinnati Post*, March 19, 1964.

50. Milton Richman, United Press International, *Times-News*, March 15, 1965.

51. Personal interview with Jack Hutchinson, May 27, 2009.

52. Lou Smith, *Cincinnati Enquirer*, March 3, 1964.

53. Jim Selman, "Just Glad to be Around Says Redlegs' Hutchinson," Associated Press, *Tuscaloosa News*, February 26, 1964.

54. Joe Reichler, "Reds Want to Win For Hutch," *The Day*, April 1, 1964.

55. Jimmy Mann, "Hutchinson Doing What Doctor Ordered," *St. Petersburg Times*, March 20, 1964.

56. Pat Harmon, "This is Hutch Today," *Cincinnati Post*, April 1, 1964.

57. *Cincinnati Post*, April 2, 1964.

58. *Cincinnati Post*, April 3, 1964.

59. Joe Reichler, "Reds Want to Win For Hutch," *The Day*, April 1, 1964.

60. *Cincinnati Post,* April 6, 1964; Personal interview with Sammy Ellis, April 7, 2009.

61. Personal interviews with Patsy Hutchinson, May 11, 2009; Rick Hutchinson, May 10, 2009; Jack Hutchinson, May 27, 2009.

Chapter 13

1. Personal interview with Jim O'Toole, May 15, 2009.

2. *Cincinnati Enquirer*, April 2, 2007.

3. *Cincinnati Enquirer,* April 4, 2005.

4. *Cincinnati Post*, April 14, 1964.

5. Personal interview with Mike Holzinger, March 31, 2009.

6. www.crosley-field.com.

7. *Cincinnati Post*, April 6, 1990.

8. *Cincinnati Enquirer*, March 31, 2002.

9. Dale Shaw, "Fred Hutchinson: The Manager Down the Stretch," *Sport*, November 1963.

10. *Cincinnati Post*, April 14, 1964.

11. *Cincinnati Post*, April 15, 1964.

12. David Halberstam, *October 1964* (New York: Villard Books, 1994).

13. Personal interview with Sammy Ellis, April 7, 2009.

14. Personal interview with Bernie Stowe, April 18, 2009.

15. Jim O'Toole, in *We Played the Game* (New York: Black Dog, 1994), 575.

16. Personal interview with Mike Holzinger, March 31, 2009.

17. Personal interview with John Edwards, April 7, 2009.

18. Personal interview with Rick Hutchinson, May 10, 2009.

19. Personal interview with Billy McCool, March 27, 2009.

20. Personal interview with Sam Ellis, April 7, 2009.

21. Si Burick, "Cool Billy," *Baseball Digest*, May 1965.

22. Personal interview with John Edwards, April 7, 2009.

23. Jim Brosnan, *Pennant Race* (New York: Harper, 1962), 124.

Chapter 14

1. Arthur Daley, *New York Times*, May 8, 1964.

2. Personal interview with Ryne Duren, April 5, 2009.

3. Ibid.

4. Personal interview with John Edwards, April 7, 2009.

5. Ibid.

6. Personal interview with Ryne Duren, April 5, 2009.

7. Personal interview with John Edwards, April 7, 2009.

8. Personal interviews with John Edwards, Jim O'Toole, Ryne Duren and Billy McCool.

9. Personal interview with Ryne Duren, April 5, 2009.

10. Earl Lawson, *Cincinnati Seasons: My 34 Years with the Reds* (South Bend, IN: Diamond, 1987), 39.

11. Personal interview with Ryne Duren, April 5, 2009.

12. Personal interview with Mike Holzinger, March 31, 2009.

13. Personal interview with Ryne Duren, April 5, 2009.

14. Ibid.

15. *Cincinnati Post*, July 23, 1964.

16. Ron Fimrite, "Hell-Raisers in Halos," *Sports Illustrated*, July 19, 1993.

17. Earl Lawson, *Cincinnati Seasons: My 34 Years with the Reds* (South Bend, IN: Diamond, 1987), 89.

18. *Cincinnati Enquirer*, April 2, 2007.

19. Personal interview with Jay Hook, April 27, 2009.

20. *Cincinnati Enquirer*, April 2, 2007.

21. Personal interview with Mike Holzinger, March 31, 2009.

22. *Cincinnati Post*, March 20, 1964; Earl Lawson, *Cincinnati Seasons: My 34 Years with the Reds* (South Bend, IN: Diamond, 1987), 83–85.

23. *Cincinnati Post*, March 20, 1964; Earl Lawson, *Cincinnati Seasons: My 34 Years with the Reds* (South Bend, IN: Diamond, 1987), 83–85.

24. *Cincinnati Post*, March 20, 1964.

25. Earl Lawson, *Cincinnati Seasons: My 34 Years with the Reds* (South Bend, IN: Diamond, 1987), 85.

26. Personal interview with John Edwards, April 7, 2009.

27. Personal interview with Eddie Kasko, April 14, 2009.

28. Personal interview with Dan Neville, March 31, 2009.

29. Personal interview with Sammy Ellis, April 7, 2009.

30. *Cincinnati Post*, November 16, 2007.

31. Personal interview with Billy McCool, March 27, 2009.

32. *Cincinnati Enquirer*, November 17, 2008.

33. Earl Lawson, *Cincinnati Post*, April 10, 1964.

34. Personal interview with Eddie Kasko, April 14, 2009.

35. Personal interview with Billy McCool, March 27, 2009.

36. Lou Smith, Cincinnati Enquirer, April 11, 1964.

37. Ron Smith, "Big Brother to All the Latins," *Baseball Digest*, August 1963.

38. Frank Robinson with Al Silverman, *My Life Is Baseball* (New York: Doubleday, 1968), 155.

39. David Halberstam, *October 1964* (New York: Villard Books, 1994), 113–14.

40. Personal interview with Ryne Duren, April 5, 2009.

41. Personal interview with Jim O'Toole, May 15, 2009.

42. Ibid.

43. Bill Ford, *Cincinnati Enquirer*, November 12, 1964.

44. Earl Lawson, *Cincinnati Post*, March 7, 1964.

45. Ritter Collett, *Dayton Journal-Herald*, March 11, 1964.

46. Personal interview with Sammy Ellis, April 7, 2009.

47. Personal interview with Mel Queen, April 15, 2009.

48. Gary Ronberg, "The Bottom Part of the Lineup," *Sports Illustrated*, August 25, 1969.

49. Personal interview with Mel Queen, April 15, 2009.

50. Earl Lawson, *Cincinnati Seasons: My 34 Years with the Reds* (South Bend, IN: Diamond, 1987, 34.

51. Gary Ronberg, "The Bottom Part of the Lineup," *Sports Illustrated*, August 25, 1969.

52. Earl Lawson, *Cincinnati Post*, March 7, 1964.

53. Ibid.

Chapter 15

1. *Cincinnati Post*. June 3, 1964.

2. Ibid.

3. Ibid.

4. *Cincinnati Post*, June 8, 1964.

5. Ibid.

6. Ritter Collett, *The Cincinnati Reds: A Pictorial History of Professional Baseball's Oldest Team* (Virginia Beach: Jordan-Powers, 1976), 140.

7. *Cincinnati Post*, June 9, 1964.

8. *Cincinnati Post*, June 2, 1964.

9. Morton Sharnik, "The Moody Tiger of the Reds," *Sports Illustrated*, June 17, 1963.

10. Earl Lawson, *Cincinnati Seasons: My 34 Years with the Reds* (South Bend, IN: Diamond, 1987), 157.

11. Frank Robinson with Al Silverman, *My Life Is Baseball* (New York: Doubleday, 1968), 75–76.

12. Morton Sharnik, "The Moody Tiger of the Reds," *Sports Illustrated*, June 17, 1963.

13. Frank Robinson with Al Silverman, *My Life Is Baseball* (New York: Doubleday, 1968), 96.

14. Ritter Collett, *Dayton Daily News*, October 24, 1995.

15. Ralph Moses, "Vada Pinson," SABR Baseball Biography Project, http://bioproj.SABR.org.

16. Harry Grayson, "Reds Vada Pinson Has Become an 'Oh-and-Ah' Ballplayer," NEA printed in *Ocala Star-Banner*, March 13, 1960.

17. Jim O'Toole, in *We Played the Game* (New York: Black Dog, 1994), 436.

18. Personal interview with Mel Queen, April 15, 2009.

19. Morton Sharnik, "The Moody Tiger of the Reds," *Sports Illustrated*, June 17, 1963.

20. Ibid.

21. Ibid.

22. Personal interview with Eddie Kasko, April 14, 2009.

23. Personal interview with Ryne Duren, April 5, 2009.

24. Personal interview with Eddie Kasko, April 14, 2009.

25. Frank Robinson with Al Silverman, *My Life Is Baseball* (New York: Doubleday, 1968), 92–93.

26. Ibid., 99.

27. Earl Lawson, *Cincinnati Seasons: My 34 Years with the Reds* (South Bend, IN: Diamond, 1987), 155.

28. Personal interview with Jim O'Toole, May 15, 2009.

29. Frank Robinson with Al Silverman, *My Life Is Baseball* (New York: Doubleday, 1968), 148–149.

30. Ibid., 115.

31. Al Hirshberg, "Baseball's Angriest Man," *Climax*, September 1962.

32. Frank Robinson with Al Silverman, *My Life Is Baseball* (New York: Doubleday, 1968), 115.

33. Morton Sharnik, "The Moody Tiger of the Reds," *Sports Illustrated*, June 17, 1963.

34. Frank Robinson with Al Silverman, *My Life Is Baseball* (New York: Doubleday, 1968), 124.

35. Personal interview with Rick Hutchinson, May 10, 2009.

36. Personal interview with Patsy Hutchinson, May 11, 2009.

37. Personal interview with Jim Brosnan, May 5, 2009.

38. Jim Brosnan, in *We Played the Game*, ed. Danny Peary (New York: Black Dog, 1994), 576.

39. Earl Lawson, *Cincinnati Seasons: My 34 Years with the Reds* (South Bend, IN: Diamond, 1987), 116–130.

40. Ibid.

41. Ibid.

42. Pete Rose and Roger Kahn, *Pete Rose: My Story* (New York: McMillan, 1989), 107–108; Pete Rose with Bob Hertzel, *Charlie Hustle* (Englewood Cliffs, NJ: Prentice-Hall, 1975), 42–43.

43. Personal interview with Dan Neville, March 31, 2009.

44. Personal interview with Mike Holzinger, March 31, 2009.

45. Personal interview with Eddie Kasko, April 14, 2009.

46. Personal interview with Mel Queen, April 15, 2009.

47. Frank Robinson with Al Silverman, *My Life Is Baseball* (New York: Doubleday, 1968), 51.

48. Ritter Collett, *Dayton Daily News*, October 24, 1995.

49. Personal interview with Patsy Hutchinson, May 11, 2009.

50. William A. Cook, *Pete Rose: Baseball's All-Time Hit King* (Jefferson, NC: McFarland, 2004), 10.

51. Morton Sharnik, "The Moody Tiger of the Reds," *Sports Illustrated*, June 17, 1963.

52. Personal interview.

53. Frank Robinson and Berry Stainback, *Extra Innings* (New York: McGraw-Hill, 1988), 57.

54. Frank Robinson with Al Silverman, *My*

Life Is Baseball (New York: Doubleday, 1968), 104.

55. Ibid., 156.

56. Frank Robinson, in *We Would Have Played for Nothing*, ed. Fay Vincent (New York: Simon & Schuster, 2008), 274–75.

57. "Cincinnati Reds, " *Sports Illustrated*, April 13, 1964.

58. Mark Kram, "Not Enough Talkative Bats in Cincy," *Sports Illustrated*, August 24, 1964.

59. Dave Anderson, *1964 Major League Baseball Handbook* (New York: J. Lowell Pratt, 1964), 46.

60. Frank Robinson with Al Silverman, *My Life Is Baseball* (New York: Doubleday, 1968), 150–51.

61. Dave Anderson, *1964 Major League Baseball Handbook* (New York: J. Lowell Pratt, 1964), 46.

62. Personal interview with Sam Ellis, April 7, 2009.

63. Personal interview with Billy McCool, March 27, 2009.

64. Personal interview with Dan Neville, March 31, 2009.

65. *Cincinnati Post*, July 2, 1964.

66. Personal interview with Rick Hutchinson, May 10, 2009.

67. Lester Biederman, "Pennant Expected," *Pittsburgh Press*, April 7, 1965.

Chapter 16

1. Personal interview with Mel Queen, April 15, 2009.

2. Jack Hand, "How Can You Beat a Man Like Hutch," Associated Press, *Tuscaloosa News*, March 22, 1964.

3. Mickey Mantle and Robert Creamer, "Honest Hutch," in *The Quality of Courage* (Lincoln: University of Nebraska Press, Reprint edition, 1999).

4. Arthur Daley, *New York Times*, November 13, 1964.

5. Associated Press, "Cincinnati Chief Not Resigning," *Sarasota Herald-Tribune*, July 8, 1964.

6. Ibid.

7. Ibid.

8. Personal interview with Mel Queen, April 15, 2009.

9. *Cincinnati Post*, July 15, 1964.

10. Ibid.

11. Ibid.

12. Mark Kram, "Not Enough Talkative

Bats in Cincy," *Sports Illustrated*, August 24, 1964.

13. *Cincinnati Post*, June 11, 1964.

14. *New York Times*, January 13, 2000.

15. Personal interview with Mel Queen, April 15, 2009.

16. Personal interview with Dave Bristol, April 2, 2009.

17. Associated Press, "Hutch Moving Slower, But: 'I Think I'm Doing All Right,'" *Eugene Register-Guard*, July 21, 1964.

18. Personal interview with Ryne Duren, April 5, 2009.

19. Personal interview with Mike Holzinger, March 31, 2009.

20. Personal interview with Billy McCool, March 27, 2009.

21. Personal interview with Ryne Duren, April 5, 2009.

22. Personal interview with John Edwards, April 7, 2009.

23. Personal interview with Don Pavletich, March 12, 2009.

24. Arthur Daley, *New York Times*, November 13, 1964.

25. Personal interview with Rick Hutchinson, May 10, 2009.

26. Pete Rose and Roger Kahn, *Pete Rose: My Story* (New York: McMillan, 1989).

27. Personal interview with Eddie Kasko, April 14, 2009.

28. Associated Press, "Hutch Moving Slower, But: 'I Think I'm Doing All Right,'" *Eugene Register-Guard*, July 21, 1964.

29. Personal interview with Rick Hutchinson, May 10, 2009.

30. *Cincinnati Post*, July 28, 1964.

31. *Cincinnati Post*, July 29, 1964.

32. Personal interview with Bobby Klaus, April 3, 2009.

Chapter 17

1. *Cincinnati Post*, August 4, 1964.

2. Personal interview with Bernie Stowe, April 18, 2009.

3. Fred Hutchinson with Al Hirshberg, "How I Live with Cancer," *True*, August 1964.

4. Ibid.

5. Ritter Collett, *Dayton Daily News*, August 13, 1991.

6. Mark Kram, "Not Enough Talkative Bats in Cincy," *Sports Illustrated*, August 24, 1964.

7. Frank Robinson, with Al Silverman, *My*

Life Is Baseball (New York: Doubleday, 1968), 157.

8. *Cincinnati Post*, September 16, 1994.

9. Personal interview with Rick Hutchinson, May 10, 2009.

10. Personal interview with Patsy Hutchinson, May 11, 2009.

11. Mark Kram, "Not Enough Talkative Bats in Cincy," *Sports Illustrated*, August 24, 1964.

12. Personal interview with Charlotte Hutchinson Reed, December 7, 2009.

13. Personal interview with Jack Hutchinson, May 27, 2009.

14. Personal interview with Jim O'Toole, May 15, 2009.

15. *Cincinnati Post*, August 13, 1964.

16. Bill Ford, *Cincinnati Enquirer*, November 12, 1964.

17. *Cincinnati Post*, August 13, 1964.

18. Ibid.

19. Ibid.

20. *New York Times* August 14, 1964.

21. Mark Kram, "Not Enough Talkative Bats in Cincy," *Sports Illustrated*, August 24, 1964.

22. William A. Cook, *The Summer of '64: A Pennant Lost* (Jefferson, NC: McFarland, 2002), 189–90; Earl Lawson, *Cincinnati Seasons: My 34 Years with the Reds* (South Bend, IN: Diamond, 1987), 66.

23. Earl Lawson, *Cincinnati Seasons: My 34 Years with the Reds* (South Bend, IN: Diamond, 1987), 64–65.

24. Billy Moran in *We Played the Game*, ed. Danny Peary (New York: Black Dog, 1994), 575.

25. *Cincinnati Enquirer*, August 30, 1964.

26. Earl Lawson, *Cincinnati Seasons: My 34 Years with the Reds* (South Bend, IN: Diamond, 1987), 66.

27. William Leggett, "The Big Red Surge," *Sports Illustrated*, October 5, 1964.

Chapter 18

1. *Cincinnati Post*, September 28, 1964.

2. William Leggett, "The Big Red Surge," *Sports Illustrated*, October 5, 1964.

3. *Spokesman-Review (Spokane)*, November 13, 1964.

4. Personal interview with Ryne Duren, April 5, 2009.

5. Personal interview with Mike Holzinger, March 31, 2009.

6. Personal interview with Sammy Ellis, April 7, 2009.

7. Personal interview with Ryne Duren, April 5, 2009.

8. *Baseball Digest*, December 2005.

9. Ibid.

10. Jim Brosnan, *Pennant Race* (New York: Harper, 1962), 35.

11. David Halberstam, *October 1964* (New York: Villard Books, 1994), 302–303.

12. www.baseball-almanac.com.

13. Earl Lawson, *Cincinnati Post*, March 24, 1964.

14. Franz Lidz, "Whatever Happened to ... Dick Allen," *Sports Illustrated*, July 19, 1993.

15. *Sports Illustrated*, August 10, 1964.

16. Personal interview with Rick Hutchinson, May 10, 2009.

17. *Cincinnati Post*, September 22, 1964.

18. William Leggett, "The Rise and Fall of the Fabulous Phillies," *Sports Illustrated*, March 1, 1965.

19. Personal interview with Billy McCool, March 27, 2009.

20. Personal interview with Sammy Ellis, April 7, 2009.

21. Pete Rose with Bob Hertzel, *Charlie Hustle* (Englewood Cliffs, NJ: Prentice-Hall, 1975), 151.

22. *Cincinnati Post*, September 22, 1964.

23. Ibid.

24. Ibid.

25. David Halberstam, *October 1964* (New York: Villard Books, 1994), 305.

26. *Cincinnati Post*, September 23, 1964.

27. Ibid.

28. Ibid.

29. *Philadelphia Inquirer*, September 24, 1964.

30. Ibid.

31. Personal interview with Sam Ellis, April 7, 2009.

32. William Leggett, "The Rise and Fall of the Fabulous Phillies," *Sports Illustrated*, March 1, 1965.

33. Earl Lawson, Cincinnati Post, September 23, 1964.

34. Ibid.

35. William Leggett, "The Rise and Fall of the Fabulous Phillies," *Sports Illustrated*, March 1, 1965.

36. Earl Lawson, *Cincinnati Post*, September 26, 1964.

37. Ibid.

38. Personal interview with Jim O'Toole, May 15, 2009.

39. William Leggett, "The Big Red Surge," *Sports Illustrated*, October 5, 1964.

40. United Press International, *Cincinnati Post*, September 28, 1964.

Chapter 19

1. *Cincinnati Post*, September 16, 1994.

2. Personal interview with Jim O'Toole, May 15, 2009.

3. *New York Times*, October 2, 1964.

4. Personal interview with Jim O'Toole, May 15, 2009.

5. Personal interview with Ryne Duren, April 5, 2009.

6. Personal interview with Sam Ellis, April 7, 2009.

7. Personal interview with Bill McCool, March 27, 2009.

8. Personal interview with Ryne Duren, April 5, 2009.

9. Jimmy Cannon, *New York Journal*, October 1, 1964.

10. Personal interview with Jim O'Toole, May 15, 2009.

11. Personal interview with Dan Neville, March 31, 2009.

12. William Leggett, "The Big Red Surge," *Sports Illustrated*, October 5, 1964.

13. *New York Times*, September 24, 1964.

14. Bill Conlin, *Philadelphia Daily News*, September 28, 2009.

15. *Philadelphia Inquirer*, September 28, 1964.

16. Frank Lidz, "The Beautiful Losers: An Oral History of the Philadelphia Phillies," *Sports Illustrated*, July 2, 2007.

17. Personal interview with Billy McCool, March 27, 2009.

18. The events of the last part of this game and its aftermath are taken from the following combined accounts: David Halberstam, *October 1964* (New York: Villard Books, 1994), 302–03; Frank Robinson with Al Silverman, *My Life Is Baseball* (New York: Doubleday, 1968), 159–60; Ritter Collett, *The Cincinnati Reds: A Pictorial History of Professional Baseball's Oldest Team* (Virginia Beach: Jordan-Powers, 1976), 140–42; Earl Lawson, *Cincinnati Seasons: My 34 Years with the Reds* (South Bend, IN: Diamond, 1987), 91–92; William A. Cook, *The Summer of '64: A Pennant Lost* (Jefferson, NC: McFarland, 2002); Larry Merchant, "Now What Really Happened in Reds' Dressing Room?" *Baseball Digest*, December 1965; Frank Deford,

"Debacle in Cincinnati," *Sports Illustrated*, October 12, 1964; Jim O'Toole and Ryne Duren, in *We Played the Game*, ed. Danny Peary (New York: Black Dog, 1994), 605–06; Personal interviews with Jim O'Toole, Sammy Ellis, Bill McCool, Dan Neville, John Edwards, Ryne Duren, Mike Holzinger and Mel Queen; *Cincinnati Enquirer*, October 5, 1964.

19. Personal interview with Jim O'Toole, May 15, 2009.

20. Personal interview with Ryne Duren, April 5, 2009.

21. Ibid.

22. Personal interview with Jim O'Toole, May 15, 2009.

23. Personal interview with Dan Neville, March 31, 2009.

24. Personal interview with Ryne Duren, April 5, 2009.

25. Personal interview with Jim O'Toole, May 15, 2009.

26. Personal interview.

27. Personal interview.

28. Earl Lawson, *Cincinnati Seasons: My 34 Years with the Reds* (South Bend, IN: Diamond, 1987), 92.

29. Ritter Collett, *The Cincinnati Reds: A Pictorial History of Professional Baseball's Oldest Team* (Virginia Beach: Jordan-Powers, 1976), 140.

30. Frank Robinson with Al Silverman, *My Life Is Baseball* (New York: Doubleday, 1968), 159.

31. *Cincinnati Enquirer*, October 3, 1964.

32. Personal interview with Jim O'Toole, May 15, 2009.

33. Ibid.

34. Ibid.

35. Frank Robinson with Al Silverman, *My Life Is Baseball* (New York: Doubleday, 1968), 160.

36. Jim O'Toole, in *We Played the Game*, ed. Danny Peary (New York: Black Dog, 1994), 606.

37. Earl Lawson, *Cincinnati Seasons: My 34 Years with the Reds* (South Bend, IN: Diamond, 1987), 92.

38. Personal interview with Jim O'Toole, May 15, 2009.

39. *Cincinnati Post*, September 16, 1994.

40. Personal interview with Sam Ellis, April 7, 2009.

41. Bill Ford, *Cincinnati Enquirer*, October 3, 1964.

42. Larry Merchant, "Now What Really

Happened in Reds' Dressing Room?" *Baseball Digest*, December 1965.

43. United Press International, *St. Louis Post-Dispatch*, October 3, 1964.

44. Frank Robinson with Al Silverman, *My Life Is Baseball* (New York: Doubleday, 1968), 160.

45. Frank Deford, "Debacle in Cincinnati," *Sports Illustrated*, October 12, 1964.

46. Bill Ford, *Cincinnati Enquirer*, October 4, 1964.

47. Bob Elliott, *Toronto Sun*, August 10, 2005.

48. *Cincinnati Enquirer*, October 5, 1964.

49. Earl Lawson, *Cincinnati Post*, October 5, 1964.

50. *Cincinnati Post*, October 5, 1964.

51. Frank Robinson with Al Silverman, *My Life Is Baseball* (New York: Doubleday, 1968), 160.

52. *Philadelphia Inquirer*, October 5, 1964.

53. *Cincinnati Post*, October 5, 1964.

54. Personal interview with Billy McCool, March 27, 2009.

55. Personal interview with Sam Ellis, April 7, 2009.

56. *Cincinnati Enquirer*, October 5, 1964; *Cincinnati Post*, October 5, 1964.

57. Personal interview with Jim O'Toole, May 15, 2009.

58. Personal interview with Sam Ellis, April 7, 2009.

59. Personal interview with Billy McCool, March 27, 2009.

60. Bill Ford, *Cincinnati Enquirer*, October 5, 1964.

Epilogue

1. Cincinnati Enquirer, October 12, 1964.

2. Jim Haynes, "350 Pay Last Respects," *Sarasota Herald-Tribune*, November 15, 1964.

3. *Cincinnati Enquirer*, November 13, 1964.

4. *Sport*, January 1965.

5. *Seattle Times*, April 17, 1988.

6. Pete Rose with Bob Hertzel, *Charlie Hustle* (Englewood Cliffs, NJ: Prentice-Hall, 1975), 216.

7. Ralph Moses, "Vada Pinson," SABR Baseball Biography Project, http://www.bio proj.SABR.org.

8. Personal interview with Sammy Ellis, April 7, 2009.

9. Personal interview with Billy McCool, March 27, 2009.

10. Ritter Collett, *Dayton Daily News*, August 13, 1991.

11. Personal interview with Dan Neville, March 31, 2009.

12. Personal interview with Jim O'Toole, May 15, 2009.

13. *Cincinnati Post*, March 28, 1998.

14. Personal interview with Ryne Duren, April 5, 2009.

15. Lisa Neff, "Lasting Legacy: A Ballplayer's Record, A Family, A Research Center," *The Islander* (Anna Maria, FL), March 5, 2008.

16. Personal interview with Charlotte Hutchinson Reed, December 7, 2009.

17. Personal correspondence with Christi Ball Loso, Media Relations Manager, Fred Hutchinson Cancer Research Center, February 8, 2010.

18. Personal interview with Jim O'Toole, May 15, 2009.

19. *Seattle Times*, October 28, 1997.

20. Emmett Watson, "Hutch: His Days Were Full of Deeds," *Seattle Times*, November 4, 1997.

21. Personal Interview with Charlotte Hutchinson Reed, December 7, 2009.

22. Dan Raley, "Athletes of the Century," *Seattle Post-Intelligencer*, December 24, 1999.

23. Linda Keene, "A Glowing Opening Night — Mariners Fans Lift Emotions to the Sky," *Seattle Times*, July 16, 1999; Dan Raley, "Hutchinson — Seattle Institution," *Seattle Post-Intelligencer*, July 16, 1999.

24. Ritter Collett, *Dayton Daily News*, May 6, 1994; Earl Lawson, *Cincinnati Seasons: My 34 Years with the Reds* (South Bend, IN: Diamond, 1987), 75.

Bibliography

Primary Sources

Bingham, Walter. "Arms and the Men for Cincy." *Sports Illustrated*, October 9, 1961.

_____. "The Reds Is Dead." *Sports Illustrated*, March 19, 1962.

Boyle, Robert. "Cincinnati's Brain-Picker." *Sports Illustrated*, June 13, 1966.

_____. "The Private World of the Negro Ballplayer." *Sports Illustrated*, March 21, 1960.

Brosnan, Jim. *The Long Season*. New York: Harper and Brothers, 1960.

_____. *Pennant Race*. New York: Penguin Books, 1983.

Burick, Si. "Cool Billy." *Baseball Digest*, May 1965.

Burnes, Robert. "Why Lane Picked Hutchinson." *Baseball Digest*, November 1955.

Collett, Ritter. *The Cincinnati Reds: A Pictorial History of Professional Baseball's Oldest Team*. Virginia Beach: Jordan-Powers Corporation, 1976.

Cook, William A. *Pete Rose: Baseball's All-Time Hit King*. Jefferson, NC: McFarland, 2004.

_____. *The Summer of '64: A Pennant Lost*. Jefferson, NC: McFarland, 2002.

Creamer, Robert. "Brilliant Enigma." *Sports Illustrated*, September 3, 1956.

Deford, Frank. "Debacle in Cincinnati." *Sports Illustrated*, October 12, 1964.

Eals, Clay. "The Thought of Losing Was Just Abhorent." In *Rain Check: Baseball in the Pacific Northwest*, edited by Mark

Armour. Cleveland: Society for American Baseball Research, 2006.

Halberstam, David. *October 1964*. New York: Random House, 1994.

Hirshberg, Al. "Baseball's Angriest Man." *Climax*, September 1962.

Hutchinson, Fred, with Al Hirshberg. "How I Live with Cancer." *True*, August 1964.

Kram, Mark. "Not Enough Talkative Bats in Cincy." *Sports Illustrated*, August 24, 1964.

Lawson, Earl. *All My Cincinnati Seasons: My 34 Years with the Reds*. South Bend, IN: Diamond, 1987.

Leggett, William. "The Big Red Surge." *Sports Illustrated*, October 5, 1964.

_____. "The Rise and Fall of the Fabulous Phillies." *Sports Illustrated*, March 1, 1965.

Maxwell, James A. "Crazy Day at Crosley Field." *Sports Illustrated*, April 4, 1960.

Merchant, Larry. "Now What Really Happened in Reds' Dressing Room?" *Baseball Digest*, December 1965.

Montville, Leigh. *Ted Williams: The Biography of an American Hero*. New York: Doubleday, 2004.

Olderman, Murray. "Reds Wipe That Scowl off Hutch's Face." *The Sporting News*, August 2, 1961.

Peary, Danny. *We Played the Game: Memories of Baseball's Greatest Era*. New York: Black Dog and Leventhal, 1994.

Rhodes, Greg. *Cincinnati Reds Hall of Fame Highlights*. Cincinnati: Clerisy Press, 2007.

Robinson, Frank, with Al Silverman. *My*

Life Is Baseball. New York: Doubleday, 1968.

_____, with Berry Stainback. *Extra Innings.* New York: McGraw-Hill, 1988.

Rose, Pete, with Bob Hertzel. *Charlie Hustle.* Englewood Cliffs, NJ: Prentice-Hall, 1975.

Rose, Pete, and Roger Kahn. *Pete Rose: My Story.* New York: McMillan, 1989.

Shamik, Morton. "The Moody Tiger of the Reds." *Sports Illustrated,* June 17, 1963.

Shaw, Dale. "Fred Hutchinson: The Manager Down the Stretch." *Sport,* November 1963.

Smith, Ron. "Big Brother to All the Latins." *Baseball Digest,* August 1963.

Sokolove, Michael. *Hustle: The Myth, Life, and Lies of Pete Rose.* New York: Simon & Schuster, 1990.

Stallard, Mark. *Echoes of Cincinnati Reds Baseball: The Greatest Stories Ever Told.* Chicago: Triumph Books, 2007.

Tebbetts, Birdie, with James Morrison. *Confessions of a Baseball Nomad.* Chicago: Triumph Books, 2002.

Terrell, Roy. "Don't Let Hutch Get Mad." *Sports Illustrated,* September 21, 1959.

_____. "Up-and-down Cubbies and Cards." *Sports Illustrated,* May 19, 1958.

Walker, Robert Harris. *Cincinnati and the Big Red Machine.* Bloomington: Indiana University Press, 1988.

Watson, Emmett. "In Sunshine or in Shadow." *Sports Illustrated,* August 26, 1957.

Wendel, Tim: *The New Face of Baseball.* New York: Harper Collins, 2003.

Web sites

Baseball Almanac, www.baseball-almanac.com.

The Baseball Cube [Statistics], www.thebaseballcube.com.

Crosley Field, www.crosley-field.com.

History Link, www.historylink.org.

Index

Numbers in *bold italics* indicate pages with photographs.